Condition Red

POETS ON POETRY
Marilyn Hacker and Kazim Ali, Series Editors
Donald Hall, Founding Editor

New titles

Kazim Ali, *Resident Alien*
Bruce Bond, *Immanent Distance*
Marianne Boruch, *The Little Death of Self*
Yusef Komunyakaa, *Condition Red*
Khaled Mattawa, *How Long Have You Been with Us?*
Aaron Shurin, *The Skin of Meaning*
David Wojahn, *From the Valley of Making*

Recently published

Kazim Ali, *Orange Alert*
David Baker, *Show Me Your Environment*
Annie Finch, *The Body of Poetry*
Marilyn Hacker, *Unauthorized Voices*
Joyelle McSweeney, *The Necropastoral*
Natasha Sajé, *Windows and Doors*

Also available, collections by

Elizabeth Alexander, Meena Alexander, A. R. Ammons, John Ashbery,
Robert Bly, Philip Booth, Marianne Boruch, Hayden Carruth,
Amy Clampitt, Alfred Corn, Douglas Crase, Robert Creeley, Donald Davie,
Thomas M. Disch, Ed Dorn, Martín Espada, Tess Gallagher, Sandra M.
Gilbert, Dana Gioia, Linda Gregerson, Allen Grossman, Thom Gunn,
Rachel Hadas, John Haines, Donald Hall, Joy Harjo, Robert Hayden,
Edward Hirsch, Daniel Hoffman, Jonathan Holden, John Hollander,
Paul Hoover, Andrew Hudgins, T. R. Hummer, Laura (Riding) Jackson,
Josephine Jacobsen, Mark Jarman, Lawrence Joseph, Galway Kinnell,
Kenneth Koch, John Koethe, Yusef Komunyakaa, Marilyn Krysl, Maxine
Kumin, Martin Lammon (editor), Philip Larkin, David Lehman, Philip
Levine, Larry Levis, John Logan, William Logan, David Mason, William
Matthews, William Meredith, Jane Miller, David Mura, Carol Muske,
Alice Notley, Geoffrey O'Brien, Gregory Orr, Alicia Suskin Ostriker, Ron
Padgett, Marge Piercy, Grace Schulman, Anne Sexton, Karl Shapiro,
Reginald Shepherd, Charles Simic, William Stafford, Anne Stevenson,
Cole Swenson, May Swenson, James Tate, Richard Tillinghast,
C. K. Williams, Alan Williamson, Charles Wright, James Wright,
John Yau, and Stephen Yenser

Yusef Komunyakaa

Condition Red

ESSAYS, INTERVIEWS,
AND COMMENTARIES

Edited by Radiclani Clytus

UNIVERSITY OF MICHIGAN PRESS

Ann Arbor

Published in the United States of America by the
University of Michigan Press
Manufactured in the United States of America
⊛ Printed on acid-free paper

2020   2019   2018   2017   4   3   2   1

A CIP catalog record for this book is available from the British Library.

Library of Congress Cataloging-in-Publication Data

Names: Komunyakaa, Yusef, author. | Clytus, Radiclani, editor.
Title: Condition red : essays, interviews, and commentaries / Yusef
    Komunyakaa ; edited by Radiclani Clytus.
Description: xk14 : University of Michigan Press, [2017] | Series: Poets on
    poetry | Includes bibliographical references.
Identifiers: LCCN 2016046277 | ISBN 9780472053445 (paperback : acid-free
    paper) | ISBN 9780472073443 (hardcover : acid-free paper) |
    ISBN 9780472122745 (e-book)
Subjects: LCSH: Komunyakaa, Yusef—Interviews. | Poets, American—20th
    century—Interviews. | Poetry—Authorship. | Poetics. | BISAC: LITERARY
    CRITICISM / American / African American. | POETRY / American /
    African American.
Classification: LCC PS3561.O455 A6 2017 | DDC 811/.54 [B]—dc23
LC record available at https://lccn.loc.gov/2016046277

Contents

Language in Our Blood   vii
Radiclani Clytus

I. Essays

Red   3

Erasure   4

An Ode to Raccoon   16

Sorrow Songs and Flying Away:
Religious Influence on Black Poetry   19

A Needful Thing   29

Crossroads   32

A Supreme Signifier: Etheridge Knight   34

The Devil's Secretary   37

The Blue Machinery of Summer   52

The Blood Work of Language   61

Son of Pop: Floyd D. Tunson's Neo-blues   65

Conundrum   72

Clarence Major's Cosmopolitan Vision   79

Dark Waters   83

The Method of Ai   96

II. *Interviews*

Collaboration and the Wishbone   107

Three Shades of Past   126

Excursions   138

Getting a Shape   148

*The Wolf/*Interview   157

Celebration and Confrontation: Walt Whitman   164

III. *Commentaries*

Notes from a Lost Notebook   179

You Made Me   190

More Than a State of Mind   193

Eros, Words   195

A Letter to *Poetry*   196

Small Illuminations   199

How Poetry Helps People to Live Their Lives   212

Picking a Lock to the Mind-Jail in the City of Asylum   214

A Note from *The Best American Erotic Poems*   219

The Mission of American Poets
and Writers Visiting the 2008 Kolkata Book Fair   220

Rewriting Dante   221

Language in Our Blood

Radiclani Clytus

Of the hues that make up the chromatic spectrum, the color red is perhaps unrivaled in its metaphorical range and symbolic resonance. In many of our sacred myths, it either implies the presence of life or augurs a certain death. Throughout the Abrahamic faiths, it colors the etymological roots of Adam as a ruddy progenitor, but it is also the complexion of war and apocalypse. For billions, it represents good fortune and prosperity and yet from Caravaggio to Hawthorne, its vividness exclaims lust, shame, and even sin. No other color lends itself to such an assortment of cultural tropes or appears to be as intrinsically woven into the very fabric of our psyche. So it is not surprising that Yusef Komunuyakaa has chosen *Condition Red* as the title for his second installment of essays, interviews, and commentaries. His corpus of published works, which spans nearly four decades, reveals a writer who is fascinated by dualisms and contradictions, and denotes a mind that is keen to interrogate those aspects of our humanity that are evocative of red's paradoxical status.

When considering "Bloodpictures," for example, one of Komunyakaa's earliest uncollected poems, we find him scrutinizing humankind's capacity for violence through crimson-toned motifs that illumine his already graphically charged language:

> Orders from the top
> filter down through the ranks
> to the lowest peon.
> "Private First Class,
> if it moves kill it!
> Fill it with so much goddamn lead

it can't walk away
under its own soft strength."

Rice paddies & thatch huts
go up in smoke—
shattered rice bowls
tremble on dirt floors.
A young Marine from the Southside
of Chicago gets hit;
he rocks his machine gun
in his arms
like a girlfriend.
Bodycount computers mutter
red, white & blue ticker tape.

The villagers stare ahead
at nothing, at the setting sun.
The hierarchical brain
passes out drunk on death.[1]

Given the associative meanings that result from the poem's
phantasmagoric title and red's figurative and literal recurrence
in each of the irregularly lined stanzas, one gains the impression
that carnal will (and not geopolitics) serves as the root cause of
societal discord. Such a reading may seem like an overstatement
since "Bloodpictures" is singularly concerned with the death
toll that occasioned the Vietnam War. But unlike most anti-war
poems, "Bloodpictures" ascribes its understanding of martial
conflict to our primordial apprehension of the world through
language. Besides parodying the almost comic hyperviscerality
of military commands, the poem's opening stanza arguably de-
livers a bold critique of our baser instincts, insofar as the blood-
lust for violence that is implicit in the soldier's orders is all that
is necessary to convince him of his lethal obligation. In other
words, what Komunyakaa appears to be suggesting here is that
humankind exists in a state of inherent culpability. If the impas-
sioned language of carnal excess finds its motivation from both
without and within, there can be no innocents among the living;
rather, we are all potential victims of ourselves as well as others.
    Such subtle thinking animates much of the logic behind *Con-*

dition Red and suggests that our current social and political realities warrant that we exercise deliberative care when taking stock of where we now find ourselves, some two decades after the publication of *Blue Notes* (2000). For there is an urgency in this latest prose compilation that surpasses the former collection's focus on aesthetic influence as its organizing principle. Whereas *Blue Notes* explicitly reveals the integral relationship between Komunyakaa's creative practice and the black expressive cultures of blues and jazz music, the materials here demand that we consider why art matters and why it should continue to remain so profoundly relevant to the human condition.

But it also stands to reason that *Condition Red's* color-coded title speaks to our nation's continuous investment in armed conflict as a means to resolve matters that would best be served by acts of diplomacy. In Komunyakaa's lifetime, there hasn't been a single decade in which the United States hasn't engaged in major military operations abroad or hasn't facilitated countless casualties (civilian or otherwise) through the practice of clandestine warfare. That this troublesome fact is an issue for American poetry is laid bare in his 2004 open letter to *Poetry* magazine, wherein Komunyakaa critiques both Laura Bush's 2003 cancellation of a White House symposium on poetry, owing to her fear that invited poets might use the occasion to protest American military action in Iraq, and the National Endowment for the Art's 2004 report "Reading At Risk," which determined that fewer citizens participate in literary reading as a leisure activity. By opening his analysis with a cautionary epigraph taken from Lord Byron's *Don Juan* ("This is the patent age of new inventions / For killing bodies, and for saving souls, / All propagated with the best intentions")[2] and providing cursory readings of Homer's *The Iliad* and Barry Sadler's "The Ballad of the Green Beret," it is clear that Komunyakaa perceives poetry to be as much a moral calling as it is a reflection of an artist's pursuit of "honest language."[3] This is not to suggest that Komunyakaa understands poetry's literary ambition as a critical commitment to social and political inquiry or transparent retrospection. Although he states that "we writers (artists) cannot forget that we are responsible for what we conjure and embrace through language, whether in essays, novels, plays, poems, or songs," he also asserts that "poetry cannot serve as an emotional bandage for the blood and guts of warfare; such an industry is doomed to dishonor the dead as well as the living."[4] Rather, for his own part, Komunyakaa defines poetry as "a kind of distilled insinuation [. . .] a way of expanding and talking around an idea or a question."[5]

It is rather fitting then that much of the material in this collection is concerned with qualifying poetry's ethical imperatives. There is scarcely an occasion in which Komunyakaa doesn't take the opportunity to stress that the origin of "early poetry seems to have developed as a way of glancing into mystery, of gaining a semblance of control over the unknown and the unknowable" in order that we might face up to the terror of life's "immense existential void."[6] Most especially because Komunyakaa considers each poem to be "a composite of images that keeps us connected to the real world," his statements on poetry's raison d'etre reflect his conviction that there must be a "synthesis" between content and form that allows for the experience of readerly recognition.[7] As precious as such value-laden ideals may seem, especially in a world where Facebook and reality television now lay claim to the concepts of "friendship" and "actuality," Komunyakaa's idealism is never far removed from his organic concern for what he thinks poetry is supposed to achieve on the printed page. This matter is well delineated by several rhetorical questions that open his introductory essay to *The Best American Poetry 2003*:

> Are some American poets writing from a privileged position— especially after the fiery 1960s and '70s—from a place that reflects the illusions of class through language and aesthetics, and is the "new" avant-garde an old aspect of the high-brow and low-brow divide within the national psyche? And there's also this terrifying thought: Are there poets who have purposefully set out to create work that (doesn't matter) only matters to the anointed, those who might view themselves as privileged above content?[8]

Although these queries are intended to frame Komunyakaa's critique of contemporary poetry's tendency towards "over experimentation" without cause or merit, they also confirm that motive is just as essential to his notion of the creative process. If poetry, as Komunyakaa writes, "encourages us to have dialogue through the observed, the felt, and the imaginary, in this world and beyond," it follows that the experiential life of poets constitutes the wellspring of their creative vitality and will undoubtedly inform the nature of their intention. When Komunyakaa declares that poets should know the names of things, know the world that they come from, is he not also challenging poets—and readers—to look more deeply into their social locations and experiences, so as to be more *meaningful*, even if they can't explain the realities in which they reside? After all, language, as he states in a 2008 interview, "is an attempt to recapture that first moment when humans began to measure themselves against the immensity of things" for the purposes of being and belonging.[9]

This elemental urge is depicted in Komunyakaa's 2006 stage adaptation of the *Epic of Gilgamesh*, a poem that is largely regarded as a literary first given its modern assessment of human mortality. But while this matter of existence is central to Komunyakaa's theatrical rendition, it is important to note how he extends Gilgamesh's overarching metaphysical concerns to the uncivilized forest dweller Enkidu. At the pivotal moment in which The Woman of Red Sashes (Shamat) transforms Enkidu into a rank-and-file member of humanity, it is the simple act of her typifying him and not their coupling that carries the weight of symbolic value in Komunyakaa's verse:

THE WOMAN OF RED SASHES

Do you own a name?

Was your name
lost and betrayed
the same as mine,
and now you cannot remember
if you ever had a name?

A name would cast you away,
from the other animals,
from the wolves and jackals,
from the lions and deer,
from the rat and serpent

You are—
you are a meteor.
A smoldering star.
I call you Enkidu.
You are a man.[10]

Through this dramatization of our human propensity to engage in ritual acts of naming, it seems that Komunyakaa is not just content to measure himself against the "immensity of things" but that he is simultaneously contemplating the extensive history of mythos and logos that precedes him.[11] By having The Woman of Red Sashes declare to Enkidu that "God is language, / and all the ohs and ahs / weave man to woman," Komunyakaa demonstrates that the idea of the poet is both inherently propagative and rooted in an archetypal myth-making psyche.

There is also a great deal that Komunyakaa says here about the state of modern verse culture and the motely assemblage of arrivistes that former National Endowments for the Arts chairman Dana Gioia deems responsible for a "new popular poetry."[12] According to Gioia, many of these "Spoken Word artists, slam poets, cowboy poets and rappers" are skilled formalists in their own right, create from the margins of academia, and manage careers that are not overdetermined by literary poetry's institutional imperatives.[13] What is more, Gioia also argues that the emergence of these would-be interlopers is perhaps necessary at a time when typography is losing its foothold as the primary vehicle for the transmission of poetic language. But if Gioia regards this new poetry as a boon for the genre, it is evident that Komunyakaa prefers a qualitative boundary between literary poetry and its flagrant counterparts. As readers will discern from this volume, Komunyakaa is a rather unforgiving critic of rap and hip-hop. In a 2006 *Callaloo* interview by poet Kyle Dargan, he is not only apprehensive of the persistence of misogyny in these two art forms but also ambivalent about what might be described as the inessential character of rap music: "I think built into hip-hop, having listened to some of it, not very much, is limitation," asserts Komunyakaa. "The musician who's very efficient on an instrument, such as the saxophone or trumpet, though there are limitations there, there's also this need to reach for the blue note—the impossible note, which is pure challenge, and I just don't think that basic concept inhabits hip-hop or rap, this need to transcend."[14] Although Dargan and Gioia might agree that the affective immediacy of hip-hop is of some benefit to consumers of this new poetic culture, Komunyakaa, on the other hand, is at best skeptical of treating accessibility as manifestly advantageous. And yet the dialogue between Dargan and Komunyakaa is a must for those cultural enthusiasts who are interested in a spirited exchange on whether rap should be conflated with the definitional qualities of literary poetry or regarded on its own accord. Even if the two poets are unable to find common ground, there are moments in *Condition Red* that suggest that Komunyakaa shares a modicum of affinity for rap and hip-hop's linguistic priorities, particularly since he contends in "Eros, Words" that "language equals conscious life, or an almost-conscious knowing. Feeling. Meaning. Rhythm."[15] Beyond the representational politics of rap's metrical speech, the question of what lies below or within hip-hop's ontological cadence requires a more measured engagement with the importance of repetitive syncopation in black music's extolment of the groove.

Of the commentaries gathered here, there are two exemplary introductory essays for posthumous collections by Ai and Etheridge Knight. Considering Komunyakaa was a contemporary and confidant of sorts to each of these acclaimed poets, readers will appreciate the personal inflections that occasionally contextualize his analysis of why Ai and Knight should have such a lasting impact on American poetry. In addition to demystifying some of the biographical lore that often misrepresents these larger-than-life wordsmiths, Komunyakaa's sensitive treatment of Ai's and Knight's craft arguably provides as much insight into his own sense of creative risk as it assuredly addresses their poetic capabilities. The following commentary on Ai's first book of poetry *Cruelty* (1973) conjures up what is indeed salient about Komunyakaa's own eagerness to explore the spaces in between art and reality, myth and oblivion, outlaw and citizen:

But Ai knows—like any great actor—that language and pace are also crucial. Sometimes a poem may seem like personalized folklore, a feeling culled from the imagination. The characters hurt each other out of a fear of being hurt, and often they are doubly hurt. Do we believe her characters because they seem to evolve from some unchartered place beyond us but also inside us? They are of the soil, as if they've always been here; but they also reside on borders—spiritually, psychologically, existentially, and emotionally—as if only half-initiated into the muscular terror of ordinary lives. All the contradictions of so-called democracy live in her speakers. Most of the characters in Ai's poetry are distinctly rural, charged in mind and belly with folkloric signification, always one step or one trope from homespun violence and blasphemy.[16]

Although Komunyakaa's explication is both probing and elliptical, the effect is poetically precise. So much so that we could very well reach for this same language to ascertain the stakes involved in the concluding stanzas of his "Three Figures at the Base of a Crucifixion," a poem in which an ostensibly romantic couple is left bereft of solace after attending a Francis Bacon exhibition:

It was always here, hiding behind
gauze, myth, doubt, blood, & spit.
After the exhibit on New Bond Street
they walked blocks around a garden
of April roses, tiger lilies, duckweed,
& trillium, shaking their heads.
The burning of mad silence left
powder rooms & tea parlors smoky.

Brushstrokes formed a blade to cut
the hues. A slipped disk
grew into a counterweight,
& the muse kept saying,
Learn to be kind to yourself.
A twisted globe of flesh
is held together by what
it pushes against.[17]

What "Three Figures" tries to come to terms with—what "was always here, hiding behind / gauze, myth, doubt, blood, & spit"—is nothing more than our ultimate certainty: that we are only equal in our inconsequential mortality. This sentiment is prevalent throughout much of Komunyakaa's more recent war-related poems, which are thematically prominent in collections such as *Talking Dirty to the Gods* (2001), *Warhorses* (2008), and *The Chameleon Couch* (2011). Where an earlier war poem, such as "Facing It," enables a surreal but generative moment of empathic connection during a veteran's encounter with Maya Lin's memorial wall, the concluding stanza of "Poppies" (from *The Chameleon Couch*) is rather unequivocal in its awareness that there is no safe harbor for the living:

> I am a black man, a poet, a bohemian,
> & there isn't a road my mind doesn't travel.
> I also have my cheap, one-way ticket
> to Auschwitz & know of no street or footpath
> death hasn't taken. The poppies rush ahead,
> up to a cardinal singing on barbed wire.[18]

Condition Red does not oversentimentalize the power attributed to poetry's ineffable essence. In response to the query, "Can poetry save nations?" in the *American Poetry Review*'s 2008 forum "How Poetry Helps People to Live Their Lives" (in this volume) Komunyakaa's reply ultimately errs on the side of caution: "Even with hundreds of roses tossed on García Lorca's burial ground, with the image of Víctor Jara's hands cut off in a Santiago stadium, and other countless attempts to suppress voices of inquiry, poetry possesses the deep power to summon truths. And, I would at this moment ask what has happened to the poets in Kosovo. The answers to this question outwit us."[19]

It would be wise to read *Condition Red* in conjunction with any of Komunyakaa's collections since the millennial publication of *Blue Notes*. The prose pieces that he makes available here evolve out of his persistent regard for what is possible through the craft of poetry as it is practiced and debated.[20] To this end, Komunyakaa makes no excuses for his belief in a poetry that is commensurate with the aestheticization of how our sacred ideals measure up to the grim reality of our compromises. Instead, his conception of poetry corroborates the interminable mess that we continually find ourselves confronting. *Condition Red* is therefore much more than a critical warning of the dire times that surely lie ahead; it is also a trenchant reminder that our innate capacity for language is and always has been that which defines us.

Notes

1. Yusef Komunyakaa, "Bloodpictures," in *Hoo-Doo* (Houston: Earth Energy Communication, 1978), 30.

2. Byron qtd. in Komunyakaa, "A Letter to Poetry," *Poetry* (Nov. 2004): 144.

3. Komunyakaa, "A Letter to Poetry," *Poetry* (Nov. 2004): 145.

4. *Ibid*, 146.

5. Komunyakaa qtd in "Notations in Blue: Interview with Radiclani Clytus," in *Blue Notes: Essays, Interviews and Commentaries*, ed. Radiclani Clytus (Ann Arbor: U Michigan P, 2000).

6. Komunyakaa, "Small Illuminations," published here for the first time.

7. Komunyakaa, "Erasure," *The Best American Poetry 2003* (New York: Scribner, 2003), 11.

8. Komunyakaa, "Erasure," *The Best American Poetry 2003* (New York: Scribner, 2003), 11.

9. "Getting a Shape," in this volume.

10. Komunyakaa, *Gilgamesh* (Middletown, CT: Wesleyan UP, 2006), 16.

11. Komunyakaa, "Getting a Shape."

12. Dana Gioia, *Disappearing Ink: Poetry at the End of Print Culture* (Saint Paul: Graywolf P, 2004), 7.

13. *Disappearing Ink*, 29.

14. Komunyakaa, qtd. in "'Excursions': A Conversation with Yusef Komunyakaa," *Callaloo* 29.3 (Summer 2006): 747.

15. Komunyakaa, "Eros Words," published here for the first time.

16. Komunyakaa, "Introduction," *The Collected Poems of Ai*, by Ai, (New York: W. W. Norton, 2013), 12.

17. Komunyakaa, "Three Figures at the Base of a Crucifixion," in *The Chameleon Couch* (New York: Farrar, Straus and Giroux, 2011), 47.

18. Komunyakaa, "Poppies," in *The Chameleon Couch*, 43.

19. Komunyakaa, "How Poetry Helps People to Live Their Lives" (Part 2). By Robert Hass, et al. *American Poetry Review* 37, no. 4 (2008): 32.

20. For this second installment to the Poets on Poetry Series, I am especially indebted to the generous advice and support provided by Ian Duncan Brown, LeAnn Fields, Laren McClung, and Erica Sklar.

I
Essays

Red

The insides of something. An answer inside a question. An unholy thing turned inside out, left quivering in the last hour of Saturnalia. The juicy, blood-red heart of a watermelon placed on the altar for the dead. This I know because Uncle Jesse took out his pearl-handled pocketknife, cut into the green rind, and plucked out a square of red meat to show me. Red is always its own proof. Rage feels red because it is the first definition of Shango. Something wounded or something healing. Fruit of the Second Coming—mayhaw or raspberry—trampled on a battlefield. We all know what blood is. Even if it's a friend's or stranger's, a woman's or man's, a pig's or a bird's, we all know. Can we believe in a god's ichor? What kind of evidence do we need? Red on a Chinese New Year names the dragon: wild joy, uncontrollable lust, pomegranate juice on a virgin's tongue. The color of warning. A siren drunk on moonlight. A scream at 2 a.m. A resounding silence. A dress twirling on a dance floor. The first thread of a myth about to open its mouth. The hue of ideology. A bird's eye inside an egg. Carmine. Cinnabar. A lunatic rose. I don't care what you say, I'm going back to Baton Rouge, she said.

From *Dossier* 4 (2009).

Erasure

In John Hawkes's novel *Travesty*, the narrator speaks to his daughter's lover as he drives the three of them toward death:

> Murder, Henri? Well, that is precisely the trouble with you poets. In your pessimism you ape the articulation you achieve in written words, you are able to recite your poems as an actor his lines, you consider yourselves quite exempt from all those rules of behavior that constrict us lesser-privileged men in feet, hands, loins, mouths. Yet in the last extremity you cry moral wolf.

With an almost incantatory irony, "lesser-privileged" ricochets in the brain; it echoes a question that has dogged me for years: Are some American poets writing from a privileged position— especially after the fiery 1960s and '70s—from a place that reflects the illusions of class through language and aesthetics, and is the "new" avant-garde an old aspect of the high-brow and low-brow divide within the national psyche? And there's also this terrifying thought: Are there poets who have purposefully set out to create work that (doesn't matter) only matters to the anointed, those who might view themselves as privileged above content? I know such questions were on my mind as I read numerous periodicals, searching for poems that touched me through content and aesthetics. It has been rewarding to work with David Lehman on *The Best American Poetry 2003*. For those who have hammered nails into poetry's coffin again and again, as if afflicted with wishful thinking, I was delighted to be reminded that

From *The Best American Poetry 2003*, ed. Yusef Komunyakaa (New York: Scribner Poetry, 2003).

American poetry is in steady hands. Though this anthology is limited to seventy-five poems, I still wish all the deserving voices could have been included.

Also, while reading the healthy heap of literary magazines, I was reminded that there exists a poetry that borders on cultivated solecism and begs theorists to decipher it. But it isn't for me to say if this so-called exploratory movement verges on a literary deception, though it does follow an era that praised content and the empirical.

Yes, sometimes our artists and intellectuals let us down through silence and erasure. This was provocatively driven home to me in Lewis M. Dabney's introduction to Edmund Wilson's *The Sixties*:

> The public world is here only a backdrop for Wilson's account of his own experience. The assassination of Kennedy receives a single biting paragraph. Wilson supports Johnson till the escalation of the Vietnam War, which occasions an argument with a summer friend in Talcottville that—characteristic of the times—almost comes to blows. He is pleased, in 1966, when Robert Kennedy is reported to be reading one of his books while waiting at the polls in New York. The next year [Robert] Lowell tells him of the protest march on the Pentagon, but by now his energies are given to the expanded Dead Sea Scrolls. He notes a fraying in the American social fabric, from upstate to the changing appearance of New York City. In 1968, however, the journal leaves unmentioned Johnson's decision not to run for reelection, the assassination of Robert Kennedy and Martin Luther King, Jr., the uproar at the Democratic convention.

We know that many of our artists and intellectuals didn't suffer such amnesia; however, some did. Can we risk a deficit in memory, in the erasure of recent history? Where Wilson's head seems to have been momentarily filled with a certain kind of forgetting, his friend Robert Lowell writes one of his most poignant poems during the 1960s that cannot be dismissed or easily forgotten, as is shown in these first six stanzas of "For the Union Dead":

The old South Boston Aquarium stands
in a Sahara of snow now. Its broken windows are boarded.
The bronze weathervane cod has lost half its scales.
The airy tanks are dry.

Once my nose crawled like a snail on the glass;
my hand tingled
to burst the bubbles
drifting from the noses of the cowed, compliant fish.

My hand draws back. I often sigh still
for the dark downward and vegetating kingdom
of the fish and reptile. One morning last March,
I pressed against the new barbed and galvanized

fence on the Boston Common. Behind their cage,
yellow dinosaur steam shovels were grunting
as they cropped up tons of mush and grass
to gouge their underworld garage.

Parking lots luxuriate like civic
sand piles in the heart of Boston.
A girdle of orange, Puritan-pumpkin-colored girders
braces the tingling Statehouse, shaking

over the excavations, as it faces Colonel Shaw
and his bell-cheeked Negro infantry
on St. Gaudens' shaking Civil War relief,
propped by a plank splint against the garage's earthquake.

With lines drawn in the dirt—intellectual and moral, social and
aesthetic, cultural and political—a poem such as "For the Union
Dead" could waylay friendships and allegiances. Robert Lowell
wrote his poem in the middle of the Civil Rights Movement. Of
course, he wasn't the only American poet to respond to "the six-
ties" with verve and fervor, as Carolyn Forché's important 1993
anthology, *Against Forgetting: Twentieth-Century Poetry of Witness*,
attests to with astounding examples. I cannot forget that some
critics and poets spoke disparagingly about *Against Forgetting*. In
fact, the title underlines what many Americans were trying to do,
especially in regard to the 1960s and '70s; they were lamenting

the fall of the good old days with good old boys at the moral helm, and were talking about the newly frayed fabric of American society. The reverberation of Allen Ginsberg's *Howl* was still in the sacred air of possibility. Some artists seem to desire a reinvestment in silence; the phrase "silent majority" echoed. The 1950s were peering around the corner again. Apathy again had us in a stranglehold; reverse discrimination became a mantra. And some poets began to pen their own unique silence through a language that deliberately confuses and blurs meaning. Poems began to sound like coded messages to the void, maps to nowhere, as if language shouldn't *mean*—an antipoetry. In his book *Consilience*, Edward O. Wilson says:

> The defining quality of the arts is the expression of the human condition by mood and feeling, calling into play all the senses, evoking both order and disorder.

In some of the exploratory texts, those of over experimentation, disorder becomes the norm—a blurred design that is supposed to depict wit, opacity, and difficulty as virtue. And Wilson continues, saying:

> Artistic inspiration common to everyone in varying degree rises from the artesian wells of human nature. Its creations are meant to be delivered directly to the sensibilities of the beholder without analytic explanation. Creativity is therefore humanistic in the fullest sense. Works of enduring value are those truest to these origins. It follows that even the greatest works of art might be understood fundamentally with knowledge of the biologically evolved epigenetic rules that guided them.

Content over aesthetics is problematic also; there has to exist a synthesis, one informing the other. In the middle of the Civil Rights Movement, in 1966, at the Black Writers' Conference at Fisk University, four years after Robert Hayden published *A Ballad of Remembrance* in which poems such as "Homage to the Empress of the Blues," "Middle Passage," "Runagate Runagate," appeared, he was chastised because of the attention he'd given to the aesthetic character of his poetry. One has only to hear the language of the first stanza in the title poem, "A Ballad of Remembrance," to see where his critics went wrong:

Quadroon mermaids, Afro angels, black saints
balanced upon the switchblades of that air
and sang. Tight streets unfolding to the eye
like fans of corrosion and elegiac lace
crackled with their singing: Shadow of time. Shadow of
    blood.

Of course, this is a cogent example of form shaped by content. Poetry encourages us to have dialogue through the observed, the felt, and the imaginary, in this world and beyond, and few seem to have known this better than Robert Hayden, W. H. Auden's faithful student. His acknowledgment to craft and voice is clearly illustrated in the poem's penultimate stanza:

Then you arrived, meditative, ironic,
richly human; and your presence was shore where I rested
released from the hoodoo of that dance, where I spoke
with my true voice again.

Gwendolyn Brooks was also "dissed" at the Fisk conference. But where she gave in, Hayden stood his ground—troubled within.

Oftentimes, the poetry of erasure presents a false dazzle that lays on white space—indifferent—and seems to emulate an epicurean netherworld that's contrary to Edward O. Wilson's thoughts on the artist. Indeed, this need to belittle and mistrust content, at times, seems like a kind of high-brow slapstick that takes us away from the body, making us even more indebted to insignificance and abstraction. This makes one think of William Carlos Williams's observations about language:

There are plenty who use the language well, fully as well as Pound, but for trivial purposes, either journalism, fiction or even verse. I mean the usual stroking of the material with-out penetration where anything of momentous significance is instinctively avoided. There are on the other hand poets of considerable seriousness who simply do not know what language is and unconsciously load their compositions with minute anachronisms as many as dead hairs on a mangy dog.

I believe content is a part of process, which is essential to technique and form. There isn't any topic that's taboo; however, there have to exist refined principles of aesthetics. This folly by the so-called new avant-garde, those exploratory poets, seems like an attempt to undermine the importance of recent history, to introduce tonal and linguistic flux as the center of the poem—anything goes because the poet or the poem's speaker doesn't exist. It's death in language. At times, it seems that this movement embraces our obsession with technology. The scrambled, amorphous texture of most exploratory poetry also parallels what happened in modern jazz after John Coltrane died in 1967, whenever a musician attempted to get away from the blues, from melody. David G. Such says in *Avant-Garde Jazz Musicians*:

> Most of the criticisms leveled against out jazz generally focus on features in the music that are "cacophonous" and too difficult for average listeners to comprehend. Out jazz, with its rapidly played flurries of tones, squeaks and squawks, collective improvisation, variable rhythms, and so forth, aggressively challenges most listeners' expectations and can burden them with too many complex bits of information.

I believe it was Miles Davis who said, "The reason I stopped playing ballads is because I love them so much." Afraid of tonal narrative, the story the music could tell? Afraid of being uncool and growing old, or duped by the sexual bluster of rock and roll? Plus, some jazz musicians were still jamming in after-hour sets for a few drinks on the house and sheer joy of playing together, hardly making ends meet. But how could Miles have recorded *Sketches of Spain* and *The Birth of the Cool*, and then betray himself playing on fusion pieces? Likewise, for the poet who has always embraced content as form, any experimentation not in service of meaning is antipoetry. After the movement era—as well as during—there's an effort to diminish the importance of the 1960s and '70s, to roll back the clocks. It is interesting to consider this: when voices that were based on experience began to rise from the fringes of our society, the new avant-garde, armored with critical theory, began to make "preemptive strikes" at those who saw content as a reflection of their lives and visions. The witness became suspect—seen as passé, old-timey, unevolved, and not part of a progressive outlook. Afraid of any accusation of sentimentality, for some poets distance and detachment developed. Often, if the poet gives the speaker in a poem feelings, he or she risks being called retrograde and boring.

One question that dogs the poet is this: Where is poetry going? Isn't it our duty to keep it exciting? Recently, we have invested a lot of energy in the spoken word movement. *Def Poetry Jam on Broadway* is playing at the moment, and some people are walking away, saying, "Very little of it works on the page." Poetry and music? Well, the idea of the lyre takes us to the lyric poem, doesn't it? When there's mutual respect between musician and poet, some provocative collaborations can take place— sometimes without the poet's say-so. Here's what I found on my CD shelves, some examples not that recent: Genny Lim / Francis Wong's *Devotee*, with Glenn Horiuchi and Elliot Humberto Kavee; Yevgeny Yevtushenko / Dmitri Shostakovich's *Babi Yar*, with Men of the New York Choral Artists and the New York Philharmonic; Philip Glass / Allen Ginsberg's *Hydrogen Jukebox*; Elliot Goldenthal's *Fire Water Paper: A Vietnam Oratorio*, with Yo-Yo Ma, Ann Panagulias, James Maddalena, Ngan-Khoi Vietnamese Children's Chorus, and Pacific Symphony Orchestra conducted by Carl St. Clair; Langston Hughes / Charles Mingus's *Weary Blues*, with Leonard Feather. I couldn't find Marion Brown's recording of Jean Toomer's prose poem *Karintha*. However, I did find Branford Marsalis's *Scenes in the City*, with narrator Wendell Pierce speaking a rendition of this Mingus piece (not really poetry, though Mingus says he was influenced as an artist by a "streetcorner poet in LA"). What really caught my attention are a couple sentences in A. B. Spellman's notes: "We are in an eclectic age, when there aren't a lot of brilliant new ideas around. The avant-garde of the 1960s left a lot of innovation to be resolved, and that's what a mainstream does." Indeed, maybe that's the problem with some of the exploratory poets, where the text of a poem may seem muddled through over experimentation: In this quest for a few brilliant new ideas, with the Ego riding shotgun, to what extent can language be distorted before it loses meaning, before it erases itself?

Keeping the idea of erasure in the foreground, one of my favorite spoken-word compositions is *Sing Me a Song of Songmy*, cut in 1971. I think that this tantalizing LP was clearly ahead of its time; and it's like a well-kept secret. *Sing Me a Song of Songmy*, subtitled *A Fantasy for Electromagnetic Tape*, features Freddie Hubbard and his quintet, with reciters, chorus, string orchestra, Hammond organ, synthesized and processed sounds, composed and realized by Ilhan Mimaroglu. Here's an example of the poetry: Nha-Khe's "Lullaby for a Child in War"; Fazil Husnu Daglarca's "Poverty," "Colored Soldier," and "Before the Bombs Struck the Dark Breasts." And there are also haunting quotations from Søren Kierkegaard's essay "The Individual." The entire CD emphasizes content as well as form and structure—if content forces one to think about all wars, not merely the war in Vietnam. I think of Muriel Rukeyser's statement in "The Life of Poetry":

> We are a people tending toward democracy at the level of hope; on another level, the economy of the nation, the empire of business within the republic, both include in their basic premise the concept of perpetual warfare. It is the history of the idea of war that is beneath our other histories.

With September 11 still resounding, we sought poetry that embodies content.

Why poetry? Well, it seems the natural direction, a way to calm our fears and anger. Whether attempting to see into the mystery of things or the human soul, poetry has long been the instrument and the path. Some of our most sacred texts are composed in "poetic" language, and this is Edward O. Wilson's point when he says:

> Recognize that when introits and invocations prickle the skin we are in the presence of poetry, and the soul of the tribe, something that will outlive the particularities of sectarian belief and perhaps belief in God itself.

Wilson is speaking of a people's tongue and the power of language—perhaps even prior to our naming of things—a "poetry" that helps us to see into the flux, spiritually and psychologically, because it assists us in facing the immensity of primordial mystery. I'm not suggesting here that our first utterance was a prayer. In thinking about September 11 and poetry, it is important to underline the poems we sought, to think about why we embraced them. Why W. H. Auden's "September 1, 1939" or Marianne Moore's "What Are Years?"; why Edwin Arlington Robinson, Carlos Drummond de Andrade, Czeslaw Milosz, and the other voices? Maybe it has almost everything to do with content and aesthetics, with language as communication.

And now (February 2003) there's war talk. We have a long roster of voices that have spoken against human violence: even those poems that are directly about war, made of blood and guts, are in fact antiwar—from translations of Homer to the poetry on Desert Storm, Bosnia, and Somalia. But few have erasure at their nexus. So, in this light, it is more than interesting to consider the following invitation: *Laura Bush requests the pleasure of your company at a reception and White House Symposium on "Poetry and the American Voice" on Wednesday, February 12, 2003, at one o'clock East Entrance The White House Salute to America's Authors Series.* Let me say this from the onset: I do think that Ms. Bush's gesture is right, but the timing completely wrong. There's hawkish talk about war in the White House, and this is contrary to the numerous American poets who patterned their hearts and visions on Walt Whitman: "I rose from the chill ground and folded my soldier well in his blanket, / And buried him where he fell." Of course, as you probably already know by now, the White House event was canceled after Sam Hamill sent out his invitation:

War looms on the horizon. I live in a navy town and worked for the navy for nearly 40 years, but I believe that this is the wrong war at the wrong time. I don't expect anyone else to agree with me, but if you do, send a poem for peace to Sam.

Almost overnight, Sam received over five thousand poems. And on February 17 at Lincoln Center's Avery Fisher Hall, The Not in Our Name Statement of Conscience presented *Poems Not Fit for the White House.* I don't think that a single poet from the exploratory movement read that night to a packed hall of people who trudged through snow to hear poetry.

Recently, I lost two very dear people in my life. Both loved wearing fantastic hats made of beads and satin, felt and feathers, some almost somber and others bright as a peacock at daybreak.

My paternal grandmother, Mrs. Elsie Magee Otis, was a churchgoing woman, born in 1906 and raised in a small black village, and she was known to say, "Honey, you can't believe the changes I seen in my lifetime." Outside of Hackley, Louisiana, in Franklinton, *Magee* is stenciled across public buildings. But these are the white Magees; lately, however, the older white ones have been saying to the black ones: "Damnit, we are family." Yes, indeed, my grandmother saw changes. She spent the last few years of her long life at the Rest Haven Nursing Home in Bogalusa, Louisiana. Sometimes, she'd just start singing her favorite spiritual, "You Got to Move," and doctors, nurses, the staff, and visitors, everyone would crowd around her. The language in the song, what W. E. B. DuBois called "sorrow songs," seemed to momentarily empower her. The song was always strong, but her voice grew feeble whenever she'd stop singing. At her funeral in a small country church, one of her close friends, Mrs. Verlean Bickham (the Bickhams are also kin to the Magees) sang "You Got to Move":

You may be rich
You may be poor
But when the Lord calls
You got to move

You may be high
You may be low
But when the Lord calls
You got to move

The song continues for a few more verses. But there's something about this piece that possesses the power and presence of folk poetry. It has content.

For the past five years, Zoe Anglesey was my close friend and confidante. Usually, she knew where and how to contact me, whether in Florence, New Orleans, or only God knows where. By contrast, her memorial service was held at the Lafayette Avenue Presbyterian Church, 85 South Oxford Street, in Brooklyn, the same block she'd lived on for years. This is the church where Frederick Douglass once spoke. The historic stained-glass windows rise and loom—thirteen of which were created by Louis Tiffany himself. There's also the "Miracle of Creation" window in the Lecture Room, a part of three panels, one of which is on display at the Metropolitan Museum of Art. And we can't forget that Marianne Moore's poem "The Steeple Jack" describes the removal of the church's steeple. These days the church is also home to the arts: The Audre Lorde Project, BAM 651 Arts, The InterSchool Orchestras of New York, Uptown String Quartet, and so forth. It was the perfect place to remember an activist poet and intellectual who cared about content in the arts. One of the most telling moments came when the poet Carl Hancock Rux read a letter that Zoe e-mailed to him on March 15, 2001. Here's an excerpt from Zoe's letter:

> Languages are disappearing along with the peoples who speak them, and they represent the ancient sources of our cultures. The movements to preserve and conserve the green of the earth—we are already buying water. Rich folks have the beautiful spots of the earth bought up and the remaining forests will soon be deserts. What future do we have for our young ones? Many people in Africa and South America are facing deserts that once were green and productive when war, exploitation and over-population set forces in motion to speed up the whole process of the extinction of the people on the land and the land going to desert. Movement? We just saw a coup. Our right to vote was scorned by the highest court in the land. Two governors conspired to rob the election. What is the penalty?
>
> There is no movement to prevent this. Instead sex scandals wag in the faces of those who were articulate on behalf of a passive population. Movement? When many of my college students admit to watching t.v. 3 to 7 hours a day—that's a half day's or whole day's work. We NEED a movement to empower people with the spirit of life and that spirit depends on working for one's life, family and community. Work gives us the

connections to others and provides the ligaments to strong group action when it is required. Our values are at stake. The major poets live and die. Poets are the ones, as Neruda knew, who can articulate what ordinary people cannot or are too timid to articulate. This is part but not all of the poet's calling. As you mentioned, Carl, craft, letting the art develop, learning the craft, and letting the art exist for itself too—the freedom to create art—even that is under threat with this NYC Mayor and U.S. President. It's up to us, just like a day's work, to keep on keepin' on—on all fronts, on all issues.

These two women whom I lost from my life had more than hats in common: both were seers, too. One was unlettered, and the other was just downright gifted and caring as a poet and a citizen. The two of them would have known exactly what Martin Luther King Jr., meant in his "I Have a Dream" speech when he says, "I have a dream my four little children will one day live in a nation where they will not be judged by the color of their skin but by the *content* [my italics] of their character."

Not that we strive or wish to become Borges's infamous character who cannot forget a single sensation, who's imprisoned in his skin and brain, unable to venture toward the future. But as poets, as artists, we do want meaning to remain in our words, and not have the essence of our lives and visions become like that moment when Robert Rauschenberg erases the de Kooning drawing and says that the erasure is his work of art.

An Ode to Raccoon

In early May 1981, I returned to Bogalusa, Louisiana, embarrassed by my lack of "meaningful employment," living on next to nothing, and again depending on the love and kindness of my maternal grandmother, Mama Mary. I had served in the U.S. Army in Vietnam, attended colleges in Colorado and California, spent seven months as a fellow at the Fine Arts Work Center in Provincetown, and also had written a handful of poems I couldn't yet discard. But here I was back in my hometown, the place I'd declared was a good place to be at least one thousand country miles away from.

I wanted to earn my keep. So I decided that I would prepare Mama Mary's meals. That was the least I could do. Plus, it was a sly way to assure she'd eat healthier, to take a few steps back from that traditional Southern cooking, which was often both a curse and a blessing. Immediately, I realized I'd taken on a very difficult job. Whenever I declined to put salt and ham hocks into the butter beans and collard greens, or skipped putting globs of butter into the grits and gravy, Mama Mary would say, "Boy, I do believe the Devil sent you home to starve me to death."

Sometimes I'd stand my ground. Sometimes I'd acquiesce. I'd sit there, remembering when I was eight or nine years old, how my grandmother would dig into her apron pocket, pull out a white handkerchief that contained three or four dollar bills, unknot it, and then give me a greenback. Half lost in reverie and the ruckus of crows, I wondered if this was the price of inspiration, and if I'd ever live up to her rituals of sacrifice.

Time slowed down for me. I was writing poems that would later work their way into *Copacetic* and *Magic City*. Summer eased

From *Oxford American* 49 (Spring 2005).

16

away. Fall stumbled through the pines. So many mornings with a nip of dew in the air. So many afternoons with the metallic weight of the sky reflecting down. So many birds still singing at dusk. So many half-drunken midnights in the middle of nowhere.

One morning, I took another of my many four-mile walks to an off-lying area of Bogalusa called Mitch, which was slightly more rural, to visit Mama Elsie, my paternal grandmother. I walked straight down the railroad tracks as I'd done as a boy. Mitch was clustered with pear trees; the place seemed like the edge of a plantation.

While we drank oversweetened coffee and munched on molasses teacakes, Mama Elsie said, "I wish my father had sent me to school, 'cause I was smart as a whip." Then she began her roll call of the dead, the demise of dreams and dreamers. My body and mind remembered the taste of the teacakes, back when my own dreams were simple and the idea of the futures was manageable. The thick aroma of pines seasoned the afternoon air.

After I strolled those four miles back to Mama Mary's, recalling faces I hadn't summoned for years, dragging up images from the past, I was yanked out of my daydream when I saw a white hunter climb back into his green Ford truck, and Mama Mary standing on the back porch holding a raccoon that had been skinned and dressed.

She was smiling at me.

The truck pulled off.

"I bet you don't know how to cook this."

"I bet I do," I countered.

"He's still got his head on. I wouldn't buy a coon from a white man if it didn't have its head," she said.

"I see."

"I believe the musk glands have already been cut out. That should save you a little trouble." She handed the raccoon to me, and I walked into the kitchen, washed my hands, and went to work.

When I was young, I would watch both my grandmothers closely; I still remembered their moves. Both are part of me. Their words and inflections had everything to do with me falling in love with language. Also, I'd watched them cook teacakes, pound cakes, lemon pies, sweet-potato pies, chicken and dumplings, gumbo, coon, and dozens of other dishes.

Mama Mary sat at the kitchen table, watching my moves.

I washed the raccoon. I gazed at it, as if I could detect its state of being. And it felt strange to think of this creature's ritual of washing everything it ate.

"Now, you know you have to half-boil the wildness out of him, don't you?"

"I remember."

After placing the raccoon into a large pot, I added pinches of salt and black pepper, and then turned the flame on.

I washed six or seven good-sized sweet potatoes, and then rubbed butter over their reddish-brown skins.

Mama Mary wanted to know about the newspaper clipping I had taped on the dresser mirror in my bedroom.

"That's James Van Der Zee," I said.

"Well, that old man looks like *somebody*."

"He's a great photographer."

"He definitely looks like *somebody*. I can see it in his face."

"He recently died."

"I'm sorry about that."

I wondered what she could see in my face. What did my future look like?

When I thought the wildness had been half boiled-out, I drained off the water, placed the raccoon into a large roasting pan, and then arranged the sweet potatoes around it. I sprinkled dried red pepper over the contents and slid the pan into the preheated oven—around 350 degrees.

"You always was a good learner," she said.

The late November dusk leapt through the screen door. My grandmother was in her world. I was almost back inside my skin. And I knew that the sweet, peppery, wild taste of this delicacy of the poor would bring me the full distance. In that moment, I believed there was a basic truth in this taste. Nothing creamy and fancy, it was down-to-earth, almost sinful in its goodness.

Sorrow Songs and Flying Away

Religious Influence on Black Poetry

When blacks first encountered Europeans and their religion, a strange and complex bond was forged. Newly encased in the manacles of slavery, they had their first taste of Christianity. Usually, there was a chapel at the center of each holding pen. It was a symbol of conquest and power. In my recent visit to Ghana's Cape Coast Castle, the presence of the chapel hit me harder than the small cells for slaves, harder than that stone path that slanted down to where the ships would have been anchored, waiting in the deep night of no return. The priests were there to baptize each shackled captive, giving him or her a Christian name before the merciless, endless journey began on the salty winds of the sea.

True, from the outset, Christianity was at least a double bind for persons of African descent. It marked the loss of their gods and their freedom, but it also offered a refuge. It became both a state of being and a state of mind where a covenant could be enacted and exacted. The old traditional gods had been diminished, defeated, silenced. And if they existed at all, they could now only linger in disguise.

Although African slaves were at first unwilling converts, after they survived months in the bellies of ships on the rough seas and lived under the constant threat of cat-o'-nine-tails, some of them embraced Christianity. In the new world, they would build their churches on that infamous rock—on hope, possibility, and imagination. The idea of God protected them. And because of this covenant, a spiritual being would fight their earthly battles.

From *Crosscurrents* 57, no. 2 (2007).

Through obedience—momentarily on the other side of fear—
they delivered themselves to God.

Even so, there were questions hiding inside these doubly
bowed heads. This precarious uncertainty is evoked in the fol-
lowing excerpt from the verse at the end of the *Narrative of the
Life of Frederick Douglass, an American Slave*:

> They loudly talk of Christ's reward,
> And bind his image with a cord,
> And scold, and swing the lash abhorred,
> And sell their brother in the Lord
> To handcuffed heavenly union.

The binding of image and cord echoes the binding double-
ness of this two-sided covenant. The new black Christians were
bound both for good and for ill. The misery of their captivity
was balanced against the promise of a fairer world beyond this
one. Inevitably, this covenant found expression in spirituals, folk
songs, and poetry. It was a literature that responded directly to
the many sorrows of slavery, the desire for rescue and flight, and
did so within the empowering framework of Christian faith.

Do the Sorrow Songs Sing True?

The African American church has long been a paradigm of un-
broken rituals, a place of refuge, a safe haven, a psychological
space where a protracted performance of confrontation and
release could exist, and it has also been a temple—whether
converts were assembled under branches of a gigantic oak or
beneath a heavy, blue sky—where sacred allegiances are creat-
ed through sermons, testimonies, and songs. Of course, these
songs are what W. E. B. DuBois (1868–1963) called "sorrow
songs," lyrics that plunge us back into the spirit and flesh of oral
expression. In *The Souls of Black Folk*, he poses some fundamental
questions:

> Through all the sorrow of the Sorrow Songs there breathes
> a hope—a faith in the ultimate justice of things. The minor

cadences of despair change often to triumph and calm confidence. Sometimes it is faith in life, sometimes a faith in death, sometimes assurance of boundless justice in some fair world beyond. But whichever it is, the meaning is always clear: that sometimes, somewhere, men will judge men by their souls and not by their skins. Is such a hope justified? Do the Sorrow Songs sing true?"

The sentiments of the believer in the old song "When My Blood Runs Chilly and Cold" allow us to hear "the minor cadences of despair" changing to "calm confidence" and the hope of triumph:

> I'm so glad I got religion in time,
> I'm so glad I got religion in time,
> I'm so glad I got religion in time,
> Oh mah Lawd, Oh mah Lawd, what shall ah do to be saved?

But DuBois was also cognizant of the fact that the sorrow songs are not always merely passive anthems expressing that "assurance of boundless justice in some fair world beyond." Rather, they might also at another time embody moments of protuberant insinuation. Although sacred, the lyrics of these sorrow songs are nonetheless political, coded with an astute awareness of the temporal struggle for survival, the need for protest, and the expectation of injustice redressed. Listen to the middle verses of "Mary, Don You Weep":

> Mary, don you weep an Marthie don you moan,
> Mary, don you weep an Marthie don you moan;
> Pharaoh's army got drown-ded,
> Oh Mary don you weep.

> I think every day an I wish I could,
> Stan on de rock whar Moses stood,
> Oh Pharaoh's army got drown-ded,
> Oh Mary don you weep.

Of course, when we realize that an anguished insinuation pulses at the heart of the sorrow song of protest it doesn't take much effort in decoding what "Pharaoh" actually meant to the slaves. This questioning of the covenant exacted in the transaction of slavery resonates even more dramatically in the sixth and seventh stanzas of Paul Laurence Dunbar's (1872–1906) "An Ante-Bellum Sermon":

> But I tell you, fellah christuns,
>> Things'll happen mighty strange;
> Now, de Lawd done dis fu' Isrul,
>> An' his ways don't nevah change,
> An' de love he showed to Isrul
>> Was n't all on Isrul spent;
> Now don't run an' tell yo' mastahs
>> Dat I's preachin' discontent.
> 'Cause I is n't; I'se a-judgin'
>> Bible people by deir ac's;
> I'se a-givin' you de Scriptuah,
>> I'se a-handin' you de fac's.
> Cose ole Pher'oh b'lieved in slav'ry,
>> But de Lawd he let him see
> Dat de people he put bref in,
>> Evah mothah's son was free.

Dunbar's antebellum preacher is revolutionary. Not only is he personally questioning the slavocracy of the South, but he is also planting seeds of unrest and rebellion. ("Oh, yeah, so you think you have the power to hold me in chains? Well, me and my God will show you who's boss!") He doesn't believe that the meek are destined to inherit the earth. Dunbar's preacher hears the message of emancipation in the gospel and proclaims to his fellow Christians the validity it should have here on earth. In this sense, the sorrow songs do indeed sing true because they express faith in a God of fairness and constancy who has and will free all of his people. The covenant exacted in their captivity is reforged in the foundry of the Christian slave's imagination to enact something "mighty strange," to turn power on its head.

The sorrow songs tell us that the African American church has always been a mecca for metaphor and double entendres. This music gives elastic voice to the desire for emancipation either in this world or the next. In this way, the sorrow songs influenced the blues, their secular stepchild. Both underline how the language of black men and women uses double meaning to veil the expression of dangerous truths and desires.

The Flight Motif

Unquestionably, where the narrator of Dunbar's poem is committed to the pursuit of freedom and justice in this life, many other songs and poems rooted in the tenets of early African American Christianity are defined by the impulse to fly away. This desire for flight takes many forms. The impulse to throw off the bonds of slavery by fleeing from one's worldly master is sometimes overshadowed by a fascination with transcendence, with psychological and spiritual leave-taking that constitutes a second uprooting and is transformed into the hope for ascension to heaven.

Because of the depth of belief and the vagaries associated with historical circumstance, it appears that many of the earlier black believers embraced a flight motif that attempted to defy physics and logic, and that the reality of this belief could be viewed as a desperate covenant with the unknowable and indefinable. Numerous references to such physical transcendence are embedded in the sacred songs, as in the final verse of "I Thank God I'm Free at Las'":

Some o' dese mornin's bright and fair,
I thank God I'm free at las',
Gwineter meet my Jesus in de middle of de air,
I thank God I'm free at las'.

Other poets cast the flight motif in a different context. For Jupiter Hammon (1711–1806), deeply influenced by the Bible and author of the first poem published by an African American man, abduction from Africa and enslavement in the new world was a journey toward "God's tender mercy." His poem "An Address to Miss Phillis Wheatley, Ethiopian Poetess" (1778) sketches the silver lining of slavery through which his people emerged from the darkness of Africa into the light of Christianity. (Wheatley,

[1753?–1784], who was born in Senegal and brought to America as a slave at the age of eight, published the first volume of African American poetry in 1773.)

1.
O, come, you pious youth! adore
   The wisdom of thy God,
In bringing thee from distant shore,
   To learn His holy word,

2.
Thou mightst been left behind,
   Amidst a dark abode;
God's tender mercy still combined,
   Thou hast the holy word.

Hammon's tribute poem closes with the following lines:

19.
The humble soul shall fly to God,
   And leave the things of time,
Start forth as 'twere at the first word,
   To taste things more divine.

20.
Behold! the soul shall waft away,
   Whene'er we come to die,
And leave its cottage made of clay,
   In twinkling of an eye.

21.
Now glory be to the Most High,
   United praises given.
By all on earth, incessantly,
   And all the host of heaven.

Did the old ones literally believe in acts of mercy on their behalf whereby the laws of gravity would be suspended? After all, didn't faith move mountains and hadn't Joshua fought the battle of Jericho? At the very least, such metaphors became a psychological weapon, language used in the service of enacting the covenant.

Indebted to Christian Belief

From the outset, as illustrated by Hammon's poem, African American poetry has been indebted to Christian belief. One sees this trend in the works of such voices as George Moses Norton, Daniel A. Payne, Ann Plato, James M. Whitfield, Frances Ellen Watkins Harper, Henrietta Cordelia Ray, Joseph Seamon Cotter Sr., and James David Corrothers.

But nowhere in American poetry, white or black, is religion so intrinsically interwoven into a poet's work as that of James Weldon Johnson's (1871–1938). This is apparent in the volume *God's Trombones*, published in 1927, with such a poem as "The Creation." Listen to the last two stanzas:

Up from the bed of the river
God scooped the clay;
And by the bank of the river
He kneeled him down;
And there the great God Almighty
Who lit the sun and fixed it in the sky,
Who flung the stars to the most far corner of the night,
Who rounded the earth in the middle of his hand;
Like a mammy bending over her baby,
Kneeled down in the dust
Toiling over a lump of clay
Till he shaped it in his own image;

Then into it he blew the breath of life,
And man became a living soul.
Amen. Amen.

"The Creation" was one of the first two poems I learned by heart as a child. And, in retrospect, I believe that the image of God as a slave woman "toiling over a lump of clay" is what compelled me to memorize it. A certain irresistible audacity resides in this image, which brings forward DuBois's characterizations of the sorrow songs expressing a faith in life, in justice, and a hope that men and women will be judged "by their souls and not by their skins."

Indeed, the sorrow songs are at the center of almost everything Johnson wrote. And he pays tribute to the voices who before him were "singing in the wilderness" by highlighting the importance of their gift to the long history of black creative expression. Here are the two first stanzas of "*O* Black and Unknown Bards":

> *O* black and unknown bards of long ago,
> How came your lips to touch the sacred fire?
> How, in your darkness, did you come to know
> The power and beauty of the minstrel's lyre?
> Who first from midst his bonds lifted his eyes?
> Who first from out the still watch, lone and long,
> Feeling the ancient faith of prophets rise
> Within his dark-kept soul, burst into song?
>
> Heart of what slave poured out such melody
> As "Steal Away to Jesus"? On its strains
> His spirit must have nightly floated free,
> Though still about his hands he felt his chains.
> Who heard great "Jordan roll"? Whose starward eye
> Saw chariot "swing low"? And who was he
> That breathed that comforting, melodic sigh,
> "Nobody Knows de Trouble I See"?

And the last stanza:

> You sang not deeds of heroes or of kings;
> No chant of bloody war, no exulting paean
> Of arms-won triumphs; but your humble strings
> You touched in chord with music empyrean.
> You sang far better than you knew; the songs
> That for your listeners' hungry hearts sufficed
> Still live—but more than this to you belongs:
> You sang a race from wood and stone to Christ.

Johnson fills his paean with clear references to the sorrow songs and the flight motif that undergirded and sustained the generations during and since slavery. Johnson's is a conscious voice, not ideological, but highly political in its time, at the apex of the struggle for black self-definition.

• • •

After the Harlem Renaissance (roughly 1920–1940), for the most part, religion isn't overtly expressed in African American poetry. Though the spirituals and gospel music remain the cornerstone of the black church, the new black poetry is more direct in its critique of America. However, one can always find the exception. One example that owes its content and cadence to the old sorrow songs and flight motif is Robert Hayden's (1913–1980) "*O* Daedalus, Fly Away Home":

   (For Maia and Julie)
Drifting night in the Georgia pines,
coonskin drum and jubilee banjo.
   Pretty Malinda, dance with me.

Night is juba, night is congo.
   Pretty Malinda, dance with me.

Night is an African juju man
weaving a wish and weariness together
   to make two wings.

   O fly away home fly away

Do you remember Africa?

   O cleave the air fly away home

My gran, he flew back to Africa,
just spread his arms and
   flew away home.

Drifting night in the windy pines;
night is a laughing, night is a longing.
   Pretty Malinda, come to me.

Night is a mourning juju man
weaving a wish and a weariness together
    to make two wings.

    O fly away home fly away

Most of Hayden's poetry forms a covenant with the past. In this poem, the references to religion are indirect; they exist mainly through the italicized lines that connect us to the sorrow songs. However, the poet's Icarus of the imagination is more than a flight of fantasy: it relates to psychological survival and an abiding faith in the human spirit. "*O* Daedalus, Fly Away Home" honors and reflects what DuBois refers to "as the most beautiful expression of human experience born this side the seas."

A Needful Thing

I have been greatly influenced by Robert Hayden, the man and his poetry, but recently I argued with myself for days, wondering if I have been perhaps more profoundly influenced by Frederick Douglass. I arm-wrestled myself, going back and forth, and, of course, Douglass finally overpowered Hayden. When I return to the pages Douglass amassed, his spirit prevails. Here is a man born a slave; his mother dies when he is only seven; he confronts the slave-owner and the slave-breaker, educates himself, and demands to be heard. He was not only a great observer but an acute listener—and most likely this is why there's a pristine tonality in his language: a language of unearthing, not obfuscation.

As a poet, I read everything aloud as I write; after thinking about the music pulsing in Douglass's prose, I believe he also read his work aloud as he traversed the deep night of the soul. One doesn't have to tick off this man's attributes to realize he invented himself through a superb imagination.

Douglass portrays himself through vivid imagery. We find ourselves facing a man anointed by violence, touched by an urgency embedded in language, moved by a dignified music. What he says is momentous, but how he says it is momentous also, with reverence for beauty and concision. The timbre of his voice doesn't convey a hint of sentimentality. His call is rendered through the shape of a merciless question beckoning in the double darkness of a personal history that still tinctures our presence. His voice is a struck bell left quivering in the metallic air lit by "a cowskin and a heavy cudgel." Ironically, I have returned repeatedly to Hayden's "Frederick Douglass" to grasp his presence again:

From *PEN America* 13 (2010).

When it is finally ours, this freedom, this liberty, this
    beautiful and terrible
thing, needful to man as air,
usable as earth; when it belongs at last to all,
when it is truly instinct, brain matter, diastole, systole,
reflex action; when it is finally won; when it is more
than the gaudy mumbo jumbo of politicians:
this man, this Douglass, this former slave, this Negro
beaten to his knees, exiled, visioning a world
where none is lonely, none hunted, alien,
this man, superb in love and logic, this man
shall be remembered. Oh, not with statues' rhetoric,
not with legends and poems and wreaths of bronze alone,
but with the lives grown out of his life, the lives
fleshing his dream of the beautiful, needful thing.

Hayden's Douglass, "this man" shaped by a heroic reasoning, is for many of us a signpost. To be a true citizen is to honor what he stands for. This becomes apparent especially in "What to the Slave Is the Fourth of July? An Address Delivered in Rochester, New York, on 5 July 1852." Returning to this piece after many years, I was surprised by the poetry in Douglass's prose— which has been measured and honed—as well as the inclusion of quotations from Longfellow's "A Psalm of Life," Garrison's "The Triumph of Freedom," Shakespeare's *Julius Caesar*, and, of course, numerous poetic biblical references throughout. The echo of poetry guides Douglass to moments such as this: "From the round top of your ship of state, dark and threatening clouds may be seen. Heavy billows, like mountains in the distance, disclose to the leeward huge forms of flinty rocks! That bolt drawn, that chain broken, and all is lost. Cling to this day—cling to it, and to its principles, with the grasp of a storm-tossed mariner to a spar at midnight."

Nowhere in the text does his inclination toward poetry resonate more poignantly than here: "When the dogs in your streets, when the fowls of the air, when the cattle on your hills, when the fish of the sea, and the reptiles that crawl, shall be unable to distinguish the slave from a brute, then will I argue with you that the slave is a man!" One hears in the orator a rhetoric of urgent necessity informed by cadences that seem natural. The passion is bare to the bone.

It was Paul Laurence Dunbar's "Douglass" that first brought me to this man. I came to his work when I was twelve, before Walt Whitman and James Baldwin, a decade or so before engaging the works of Gwendolyn Brooks, Robert Hayden, Elizabeth Bishop, Pablo Neruda, and James Wright. Douglass's voice refracts all the other voices I have deeply embraced through the years, and still his spirit and language reconstitute themselves in my psyche and call up my own need to reimagine the world and confront it.

Crossroads

The crossroads is a real place between imaginary places—points of departure and arrival. It is also a place where negotiations and deals are made with higher powers. In the West African and Haitian traditions of Legba, it is a sanctified place of reflection (mirrors are used in symbolic travel). The crossroads is a junction between the individual and the world.

When I was asked to edit this issue of *Ploughshares*, I did not have a thematic trope in mind. But halfway into the editing, after the wonderful stories and poems had begun to accumulate, a shaped presence began to jell within the collection. As if from some unknown station, the characters and narrators began to wander across varied psychological and emotional territories, and the shape of the crossroads imprinted itself on this issue of *Ploughshares*.

Maybe this overall feeling also arose from the energy of *The Sky Is Crying: The History of Elmore James* pouring from the Sony speakers. James's "Standing at the Crossroads" conjured up Robert Johnson. Momentarily, as I sat in my Park Plaza apartment in St. Louis, reading and rereading the stories and poems, I glimpsed that legendary figure standing somewhere in the Mississippi Delta night, clutching his guitar, ready to make a Faustian deal with the Devil. But, of course, it wasn't long before the delta night became a countryside road somewhere in Haiti.

From the cult of Legba, my mind turned to the essence of the cross. Since creative artists are indebted to the industry of symbolism and numinosity (concerned with how the object is a map for the internal terrain), at this juncture it became illuminating to embrace C. G. Jung: "The imagination liberates itself from the

From *Ploughshares* (Spring 1997).

concretism of the object and attempts to sketch the image of the invisible as something which stands behind the phenomenon. I am thinking here of the simplest basic form of the mandala, the circle, the quadrant or, as the case may be, the cross." As with most myths and legends, each is a composite of contradictions and oppositions. Example: Constantine's dream of the cross was probably prompted by how the streets of Rome were patterned; Robert Johnson's deal with the Devil probably occurred beneath a full moon somewhere in San Antonio, Texas.

In this sense, many of the stories and poems in this issue seem to exist in two or more places simultaneously, and a narrator or speaker is forced to negotiate multiple worlds. There is an accrued bravery here. It is this cultural dualism, this ability to be two places at once, to be a shape-changer, that strengthens the creative quest. Thus, this collection has a fractured design. There's a jagged persistence that documents and duplicates the awkward reality of our contemporary lives and imaginations.

Many of us are still reeling from the death of Larry Levis. And since this issue of *Ploughshares* encompasses numerous paths and diversions, it seems natural to dedicate it to the memory of this American poet who created bridges through his poetry. Throughout his several books Larry was not afraid to invite voices from all communities into his vision. His was a poetry of inclusion: he was not afraid of being in two or more places at once. We can be grateful that his poetry keeps a part of him here with us.

About the colorful, poignant cover: The joined hands of the "Three Great Freedom Fighters" seem to form a symbolic crossroads, a true image of the indivisible. This trinity—John Brown, Harriet Tubman, and Frederick Douglass—creates a point of departure and arrival. Of course, the artist, William H. Johnson, seems to have been born at the crossroads in Florence, South Carolina. Here is a black man raised in the heart of Dixie, who ventures to New York City, to Provincetown, and then to Europe. He paints impressionistic pieces of Florence and Denmark, and then decides on portraying black Americans through a "semiprimitive" mode. The colors seem to convey a visual jazz that springs out of the 1920s into our lives today.

A Supreme Signifier
Etheridge Knight

Etheridge Knight is hard to pin down, but Jean Anaporte-Easton's lucid, revealing introduction captures the elusive toastmaster—the man, the poet. What she knows rises out of the personal—because she knew the poet—and softly collides within her scholarship to reveal to us, the readers, Etheridge in all of his complexity. Her criticism honors the man and his work. But Etheridge would have been the first among us to have stood up to say, "I'm not perfect." And at that moment the mask would have shifted slightly askance. Then, almost smiling, he would have said, "I wish I were a blues singer. Matter of fact, tonight I'm gonna sing for you 'Willow Weep for Me.'" And he would've left tears in our eyes.

Etheridge Knight possessed a genius for surviving the harsh realities of America. Having read his poetry carefully during the 1970s, I thought I knew an aspect of the man before I met him. He could've hailed from my hometown, Bogalusa, Louisiana. He could've come from my family near Columbia, Mississippi. I'd written him in the early 1980s from New Orleans to request poems for *The Jazz Poetry Anthology* I was editing. I received a handwritten letter from him that began with the endearment "Bro." And years later, Kenneth May, then a student of mine, told me that he was taking a poetry workshop with Etheridge at the Slippery Noodle Inn (a historical building that had been a stop along the Underground Railroad) in Indianapolis.

While some may see Etheridge as a trickster straight out of

Foreword to a forthcoming volume of prose writings by Etheridge Knight.

African American folklore or out of central casting, decked out in his blue denim overalls, we could also rightfully say that he was an intellectual survivalist who knew the sharp turns of urban America. The man left a legend of stories behind him. Some takes were contradictory, but they were always intriguing, always filled with vim and vigor, with emotional sleight of hand, always disguised by a shim of innocence. It seems that sometimes he wanted to appear in contradiction, not wrestling with but embracing a duality: unlettered and wise, rural and urban, good and bad, or tough and sweet, cool and uncool. I remember once suggesting that someone should follow Etheridge's trail and collect all the contradictory stories about him into a postmodern biography. In fact, I've heard many such tales of Etheridge. Legend has it that he once sold an old car to someone and then left town driving in it.

It seems that I'm one of the few people that Etheridge didn't try to pull a game on. I wonder what he was reading in me that curtailed him. When we first met he thought I had been in prison; perhaps it was my shyness, my body language, that place where one carries the unsaid. He was surprised that I had never done time, and he seemed to have respected that fact, especially since he knew I had grown up in Bogalusa. And as two black men writing poetry with an awareness of the worlds we'd come from and what we'd survived with a certain grace, in us lived a mutual respect and, for me, deep admiration.

In many ways, this compilation of letters, interviews, essays, and musings deepens our understanding of Etheridge and shows him to us intimately, and in his own words, and what inherently emerges is a fuller portrait, the full thrust of his intellect and wit. I have heard some of the spoken word poets portray Etheridge as the unlettered runagate badass, someone to emulate and imitate. I've been inclined to reprimand such portrayals while acknowledging within myself that any attempt at prettying-up his image would betray him.

Etheridge loved reading books. I think books made him feel more complete, and maybe this is another thing he had in common with Malcolm X. I do know that he also at times attempted to disguise his love of intellectual pursuits. And in this sense, like Miles Davis, he seemed afraid that his intellectual currency would undermine his credit on the block. For the poet who's in the business of vamping on what he sees and feels, on what he or she knows, to ride roughshod on the brain can be a self-deceptive affair, and it is hard to believe that Etheridge wouldn't have known this in his gut.

In the late eighties, Kenneth took me to Indy to meet one of my favorite poets. We visited Etheridge at his humble apartment. He seemed filled with energy: he was a natural-born storyteller, a poet who knew numerous poems by heart, and also a jailhouse toastmaster. I remember Sonny Bates holding on to Etheridge's every word. I remember a great reading he gave at Butler University; that evening he sang "Willow Weep for Me" and closed with Melissa Orion's poem "Where Is the Poet?" I remember him saying that he wished he had written the poem. I remember an entourage of his sitting in a small art gallery owned by Francis and Steve Stroller, and the place was on fire with Etheridge's signifying.

A year or two later Etheridge was on his deathbed. Many poets and friends came from across the country to Indy to say their good-byes. When Etheridge died I broke a pact with myself. At ten or eleven years old, after my great-grandmother passed, I promised myself that I wouldn't attend another funeral, but I found myself that March day in 1991 at Crown Hill Cemetery trying to say good-bye to a poet whose work had touched me deeply.

And it seems that poets are still saying their hellos and good-byes. One disciple of the toastmaster is John Murillo, a poet who fully understands the scope of Etheridge's gift to us, which is self-evident as he pays homage walking Crown Hill in his long poem "Flowers for Etheridge" that begins with these lines: "I'm spending half this afternoon apologizing to ghosts, / Stepping over gravestones, the poet's *Belly Song* / In one hand, a ten dollar bouquet in the other." Now, as I talk to many young poets drawn to the core-music of Etheridge's down-to-earth life and art, to see them fully engaged and moved, as his voice insinuates beyond ordinary boundaries of time and place, I realize that this poet, this man, is still "poeting" for the twenty-first century.

The Devil's Secretary

A year ago, someone broke into my apartment. He left greasy handprints on the door and its metal frames; great effort and violence had been used, which left the frame bent—a template of desperation.

Mentioning the incident to three people, each asked in their own way, "Don't you feel violated?"

"Yes," I said.

The thief had emptied out a small inlaid box that held cuff links I'd collected through the years; a pocket watch, silver buttons, old coins. He also took my laptop: a research tool I'd purchased so my friends, fellow researchers Radiclani Clytus and Louise Bernard, could enter data on Marcus Christian, a Louisiana writer, archivist, poet, and historian—we were attempting to bring his literary contributions to life.

The thief also appropriated my leather jacket. I could see him wrapping the laptop in the jacket, emerging from the building, and walking out onto the streets—the stage where he was soon to be a different man by appearances, wearing my jacket made in Australia and laying down bucks from the sale of the laptop. He had effectively raided my private goods to effect his persona out there in public.

Don't you feel violated? ran inside my head. Papers and books lay scattered across the apartment. He had taken everything that shines. The door had stood open. Was he drug-crazed, hurting for a fix? Was that it? What had driven him to risk his life? The Devil had been busy.

I was out of town. The residents in the building had noticed

From *The Private I: Privacy in a Public World*, ed. Molly Peacock (Saint Paul: Graywolf, 2001).

the open door and notified the manager and police department. A friend had been called, and she informed me that the police spent hours in my apartment, dusting the place for fingerprints, trying to discern a modus operandi, or were they going through my personal effects?

Violated?

The thief had spent a few minutes there, probably running out of his skin as he ravaged the two small rooms.

Violated? Violence. Violent. In America, at times it seems that violence against property gets more attention than violence against a person.

As the cops sifted through my notes, letters, snapshots, bills, files, résumés, and revised poems, notes in the margins of books, everything in disarray, as they attempted to create some logic to the clutter, who is now violating whom?

I grew up in a place where one's privacy was almost sacred— so much so it was taken for granted.

With four brothers and one sister, in a three-bedroom home, we grew up with a sense of privacy—lines that we couldn't cross: "Always a knock on the door before turning the knob." "Never touch anything that isn't yours, without an okay first." "Don't eavesdrop." "Don't be nosy." "Curiosity killed the cat."

To know is to be responsible: "Boy, you knew and didn't tell me. I'm not going to beat him for what he did, but I am going to wear your hide out for not telling me. You knew."

In retrospect, this issue about privacy seems like a mixed message, or confused.

The busybody or nosy person didn't survive in our neighborhood: "Cora Mae never could mind her own business. There she is kneeling on the floor as if she's at a prayer meeting, peeking through the keyhole of the front door, spying on two jokers arguing in the street. Now the Lord don't like ugly, but the Devil loves it."

"She's on her knees. One of the jokers pulls out a Colt .45 and fires it at the other and misses. But he shoots Cora Mae dead in the right eye. And she's on the floor dead as a doornail."

Many houses are built like stages. The picture window seems more like a transparent screen. Or a display case. Mainly, things are envied when seen in the erasure of privacy through display.

Private property defines us; it tells the world who we are. It gives us power. I remember hearing the following statement: "If you shoot a thief outside your door, you better pull him into your house." So, private property can mean the difference between protection and murder. If it possesses such power, logic says that we dream to display it, flaunting its illusion of power. "Do you think she would be wearing that dress if the rest of us couldn't see it?" "Do you think he'd own that house or car if we were blind?"

What is privacy's value? Is it something we humans crave initially: Do children desire privacy when they become conscious of their space as separate human beings, does it define them? Or is the concept of privacy taught? Are they acculturated into attitudes about privacy?

The scientist reveals. The artist reveals. The prophet reveals. Creativity seems to always involve some form of revelation—a kind of disrobing, a facing up to, and seeing into. Writers reveal. And sometimes those such as family, friends, lovers, fellow workers, and so forth, may feel skittish. They don't want their lives to drive the plot. But nothing's ironclad: there are people who will attempt to insinuate themselves into a painting, a photograph, the block of granite a sculptor works on, the novel, the film, or the poem. Their privacy becomes a commodity: sold for money, the idea of money, or notoriety (which sometimes also translates into dollar signs). No shame.

If privacy didn't exist as a concept, and/or principle, would it still have value? Some go to great limits to protect their privacy. We have heard about Thomas Pynchon and J. D. Salinger. And it seems to mention their names is to invade their privacy. We have terms such as *hermit* and *recluse*. Of course, in Western society, both are weird or negative. Yet solitude seems positive when it is associated with something spiritual in Western society. In this sense many of us are in awe of the east.

The impingement on privacy pulsates throughout Shakespeare as an act of violence against nature. But we only have to return to his "Dark Lady" sonnet series to see how complicated this is. Consider the mere speculation surrounding the woman's identity (or a young man's). It is like a soap-operaish roll call:

Some dark-skinned woman in a Clerkenwell brothel; the Moor discussed by Gobbo in *The Merchant of Venice*; "Lucy Negro," "Abbess de Clerkenwell": at Gray's Inn on Christmas in 1594; Mary Fitton, or Mall, the pale Maid of Honor to the Queen; or is the Dark Lady an emotional composite, a courtesan of the psyche? In this sense, can literature violate one's privacy through conjecture and guesswork on the part of readers?

In literature (or for its creators), rumors of lust and flesh have long been grist for the mill. And, in some cases, as is true of Alexander Pushkin, rumors have ushered in an author's demise. Like a character in his novel in verse *Eugene Onegin*, he was shot in a duel. Before, as Henri Troyot writes in the biography *Pushkin*, "Pushkin received an anonymous letter informing him that his wife had met d'Anthes alone in the home of a friend and that he was now, technically and irrefutably, a cuckold. Pushkin immediately asked Natalya where she had been, and Natalya, panic-stricken and in despair, told him all and wept copiously on his shoulder." Of course, we know Pushkin's challenge of a duel (not the first) ended his life—an elongated soap opera that snowy day on January 27, 1837, at Chernaya Rechka.

There are people who consciously and unconsciously attempt to align themselves with celebrity, often purposefully divulging real and imaged affairs, dreamt-up collisions, or soft torture. Such revelations are, in fact, exhibitionism: all have witnessed the tossing of underwear onto the stage where Elvis Presley and Muddy Waters performed.

When I wrote the poem "1984" (Orwell wanted to call his novel *1948*), I kept erasing the words and putting them back. They sounded weird, though I had heard that the monument to J. Edgar Hoover is one endless system of computer terminals and whatnot. Back then, these lines which began this poem frightened me:

> The year burns an icon
> into the blood. Birdlime
> discolors the glass domes
> & roof beams grow shaky as old men
> in the lobby of Heartbreak Hotel.

Purple oxide gas lamps light
the way out of this paradise.
We laugh behind masks and lip-sync Cobol.
We're transmitters for pigeons
with microphones in their heads.

I knew about psyops, how this group of military men believe the United States could win a war without rockets, M16s, planes, or throwaway grenade launchers. The media. Technology. Subliminal messages as maps of the future. I was afraid of sounding paranoid, a worshiper of conspiracy theories.

Onel de Guzman was seventeen years old in 1984, and could hardly have been daydreaming of writing a program that would "steal and retrieve Internet accounts of the victim's computer." The Internet didn't seem to exist in the minds of everyday citizens. "E-mail Password Sender Trojan" would have sounded like a line from a language poem back in the Pleistocene mid-1980s. De Guzman's blueprint for the Love Bug Virus may have caused over $15 billion in damages around the world. These college-generated cells of Love Bugs commit electronic vandalism against the industrialized world, creating cyber cops who make the lingo of J. Edgar Hoover' era sound like baby talk. Loss of control over money and space is generating some nationalistic tough talk that has little to do with the concept of privacy. This has more to do with the trading of commodities and capital. So, these hackers from the Philippines, China, Serbia, Pakistan, or God only knows where, trying to rise to the middle class and its illusions through "hacktwist," seem not aware that cyber horseplay can turn ugly and murderous. The various names are thinly disguised codes for discontent: "Love Bug," "The Pakistan Hacking Club," "Dr. Nuke," "Kosovo in Serbia," "Hello Kitty," et cetera.

When people define themselves by proximity to others, they sometimes reveal intimate details in order to psychologically legitimize their status, and the more intimate the details, the closer they feel to celebrity, "the real thing." Elaborating with sordid details allows one to construct a kind of moral superiority, to outdo the other by increasing his or her own currency—

elevated through the reduction of the other. In this sense, the ego is a monster, a chimera that cannot be trusted.

Nietzsche says in "On the Uses and Disadvantages of History for Life" (1874) that "no one dares to appear as he is, but masks himself as a cultivated man, as a scholar, as a poet, as a politician. . . . Individuality has withdrawn within: from without it has become invisible."[1]

After a man attempted to break into my Lower East Side apartment for the third time within a year, the security person talked me into giving her copies of my keys, stating that she wished to enter my apartment in my absence to install a camera, aimed through a peephole in the door to video the intruder-to-be, since he was likely to return. She insisted that he was an amateur, because she, on the other hand, knew how to jimmy in a matter of minutes any lock known to man or woman. She assured me the person who had attempted to break in was no expert, and that the camera and video gear she bought at an electronics outlet would prove her point.

From this experience, I'd venture to say we don't possess a foolproof means of attaining safety or privacy. Since the eyes in back of our heads really don't protect us, such solutions as security cameras present a whole set of questions centered on the purpose of surveillance and how many use the information that it yields.

Some people would have us believe that they know things about others that they couldn't prove to save their lives. Of course, this is especially true when it comes to ordinary people attracted to celebrities. There are a number of people so out of touch with their own private lives that they delve into the public intimacies of celebrities, and then to the extreme, become obsessed even to the point of stalking the stars. Most people, fortunately, express awe for actors, entertainers, and sports figures in a modest sort of way. If, however, their lives are deemed insignificant compared to celebrities, these individuals may deploy their puny lives to the sidelines to involve themselves vicariously inside the boob tube or on the big screen as if it were life itself.

In such pursuits, who can deny that some horrific crimes have been committed with the objective of gaining instant celebrity, even if it ends up defamatory. This extreme behavior manifests the desire to sacrifice one's privacy for the public spotlight. A life becomes an open book for three minutes on the news, which then feeds the insatiable appetites of a certain kind of audience for private or grotesque details. The quality that immunizes people against becoming involved in these complex behaviors is the ability to feel comfortable with one's own achievements.

When Eastman invented the Brownie Kodak camera, many instant photographers began to plague the beaches. Some bathers felt that they didn't want to have their pictures taken with wet cloth clinging to every curve (today it is the opposite). Roland Barthes writes in *Camera Lucida*: "The age of photography corresponds precisely to the irruption of the private into the public, or rather, to the creation of a new social value, which is the publicity of the public: the private is consumed as such, publicly (the incessant aggressions of the press against the privacy of stars and the growing difficulties of legislation to govern them testify to this movement)."[2]

I remember all these dream gadgets and trinkets for eavesdropping and spying in the back of *Dick Tracy*, *Flash Gordon*, and *Spider-Man* comics. They usually cost ninety-nine cents or one dollar, postage included. They never worked as well as our imagination; we usually felt tricked.

But now if one walks into a Spy Store, he or she expects for the Dan Drew gadget to work. And it does. It is scary business. How do these spy tricks come about? Who did the research? Has some secret war been going on in front of our eyes? There are cameras that can fit into the eyes of a crystal bird. There are listening devices that use the windowpane as a transmitter. Workers are complaining about video cameras in the restrooms of the workplace. Customers are being spied on in the elevators. Parents are videotaping the babysitter. Orwell's *1984* and Huxley's *Brave New World* are as out of step with the glut of electronic thingamajigs as Dick Tracy. If the government has satellites spying from outer space, why not have bosses checking up on the new secretaries? (Eastman of Kodak positioned his office close to the women's restroom so he could see how many treks they took.)

Remember the book called the *Cult of Counterintelligence*? For those of us conscious of the potential incursions of technology in our world and craving privacy, we cannot be the only ones playing the devil's advocate because everyone's privacy is being invaded. In this sense, technology takes us back to the cave, to prehistoric times when a stone could be a tool or a weapon. So much depends on the individual holding it—the state of mind, knowing right from wrong.

The privacy issue is very complex, especially since we live in a society where so many of us are hurting for attention, for acknowledgment. This may have been influenced by the touchy-feely syndrome of the 1960s, the feel-good decade for what has been called the "me" generation. When we began to love our bodies more, to pull away from anything puritanic, did we divest ourselves of a sense of privacy? Is there anywhere left to hide from commerce and the wide gaze of the picture window?

Maybe the gossip machine was invented in small towns or suburbia, but it seems to have been put in motion in our cities. Small towns still exist in the psyches of people strutting around. Products of this phenomenon are the many music videos featuring half-dressed names who grab their crotches as if they were on back roads deep in the backwoods with nobody watching. Just as it is carefully calculated, everybody who is tuned to that channel is looking. The city is the place where people believe they can reveal anything. Of course, there is the fractured psyche talking to reflections in a shop window, half-lost among shadows and images of blow-up life-size dolls and posters of Ricky Martin. In countless bars, after 5:00 p.m., men in three-piece business suits spill the beans to the Norma Jeane look-likes about an unfortunate love life, even about business partners.

So many of us seem as if we're on some perpetual talk show. This is now our church, the place to testify, to show off our new wardrobe. When the camera is aimed, the brain seems to close down and the tongue overloads. There must be hundreds who tell their most intimate secrets for payment.

"It startled us no more than a blue vase or a red rug." I have been intrigued by the poetry and rage in this phrase from Richard Wright's *Black Boy*. So simple and complex, the words say so much about the idea of privacy and racism in America. The words relate to a white prostitute and her john in Memphis, how the bellhops are summoned to serve them drinks in bed, while the two lie there naked. It is an act centered on reducing the bellhop's humanity: he doesn't own the eyes in his head—to see or not see. The bellhop is invisible to them. A naked man or woman will not pull up a cover when a dog or cat passes by an open bedroom door. Wright's couple belittles the bellhop by the bold display of themselves. Decadent exhibitionism diminishes the servant bellhop. If this is the psychology underlying this fictive situation, does it seem to have reversed itself? Now persons of power reveal themselves to equals and cover themselves when servants enter the room (not only in the Deep South). Display is now lure as courtship, or the definition of freedom. But some in this dumb show play blind and are reminded of their status: "What the fuck are you looking at?"

After bloody World War I, with the decline of Victorianism and the flourishing of Freudian psychoanalysis, people began to openly express their sexuality, especially artists and so-called free thinkers. Communities of like-minded souls began to spring up in New York City and Paris (as well as in small enclaves of other cities). Ann Douglas's *Terrible Honesty* delves into one scene:

> In Greenwich Village, Manhattan below Fourteenth Street where the avant-garde made its headquarters after the war, the adventurous red-haired Edna St. Vincent Millay of "I Burn My Candle at Both Ends" fame was "It"; her lovers, male and female, were so numerous, "Vincent," or so she liked to be called, generously let two men make love to her at the same time; Edmund Wilson was assigned to the top half of her body, John Peale Bishop the lower. Louise Brooks, the "secret bride" of New York, early acquired the nickname of "hellcat," and she referred to herself as "a startling little barbarian." Some thought her full name should read "Louise Brooks No Restraint," for she pursued with avidity what she dubbed "the truth, the full sexual truth." "I like to drink and fuck," she announced, and drink and fuck she did, usually in public places.[3]

Such actions often seem to have been advertisements for the ego. At least with the blues and its sexual innuendo, its bold insinuation, names aren't mentioned (but sometimes first names such as Frankie and Johnny).

In our modern society it seems that many have great difficulty enduring silence, in the same way that some are so easily bored or cannot risk anonymity. Their skins seem not to contain them: the whole content and motion of their lives are on the exterior. Consumer marketing depends on a good number of people buying into playing dress-up for pass and review. Some individuals do not acknowledge their own existence until others validate it. Some people crave that their privacy be violated; they awake to an energy from eyes beholding what was once unseen.

Across the Atlantic, in the Parisian neighborhood of Montparnasse lived Man Ray's photogenic model Kiki (born Alice Ernestine Prin—a "love baby"), an artist and writer. Writing *Kiki's Paris: Artists and Lovers 1900–1930*, Billy Klüver and Julie Martin divulge,

> Kiki celebrated lovemaking and would announce over morning coffee at the Dôme, "I have been well-laid." She took many lovers and once chastised Julian Levy, who didn't want to sleep with her, "vous n'etes pas un home, mais un hommelette" [You're not a man, but a manlette]: Kiki didn't hesitate to use her sexuality to help friends in need. She would collect money on the spur of the moment by showing her breasts or lifting her skirts in a bar or restaurant, telling the delighted patrons, "That will cost you a franc or two."[4]

Man Ray almost wore out his camera on Kiki, since it appears that she loved the black box as much as it loved her. Of course, at twenty-eight she wrote a book entitled *Kiki's Memoirs*, making her a forerunner of the present-day memoir industry. It seems that many take risks and create antics to have something to write about. There seems to be a need to testify, people hurting to confess; some are talking to lampposts or to reflections in shop windows and others are wearing out the keys on the computer. Louis Armstrong sings, "I got a memory in Chicago. I got a memory in New Orleans. And I got a memory in St. Louis, too." But here the memories remain unnamed; they are a bluesy mystery that seek a basic universality. His personal pronouns become less self-centered or egotistical.

In times of flourishing soap operas and talk shows, privacy has lost its sacredness. Ritual as public unmasking often requires new masks. And sometimes, we doubt if we can trust the masking. Of course this touches art as well. Much negative criticism has been written about the so-called confessional poets. An unholy aping of the confessional sentiment has taken hold over the last five decades.

A friend of mine who taught a poetry-writing workshop related the following story:

> I had a high-school student in my workshop—a good writer who shocked the other members of the class with such compellingly vivid details about rape, incest, and sexual abuse. I didn't know what I'd say to her during our conference. We sat facing each other. I said, "The autobiographical details in your poems are very vivid." She replied, "Autobiographical?" I said, "Your life has been harsh." She said, "Isn't this what poetry is supposed to be about?"

The problem with an example of false witness is that we grow callous and doubtful about real abuses happening around us. We cannot think of them as fictional; our lives cannot accommodate more theater on the latest talk show aiming for bloated ratings.

We live in a time of theater—life as theater. It is like tugging on a bit of thread and the whole garment unravels till we are naked in public. Many of these antics seem to have been a desperate push at the last walls of Victorianism or as antiestablishment acts, whereby privacy becomes secondary. The mores of the 1920s and '30s with a diminished sense of privacy transfused the literature of the Beat movement even if the other side of the coin offered more freedom to the public. The boldness of such figures as Millay, Brooks, and Kiki permeates the social litany dominant during the 1950s. The contradictions between what is private and privacy compared to public freedom really didn't square off. Instead, the personal pronoun "I" fueled the engine of outpourings. This uncensored telling appears in the beginning of Allen Ginsberg's *Howl*: "I saw the best minds of my generation destroyed by madness, starving hysterical naked, / dragging themselves through the negro streets at dawn looking for an angry fix" and continues with "angelheaded hipsters . . . who were expelled from the academies for crazy and publishing obscene odes on the windows of the skull." The trails to the private are not disguised. The insinuation and innuendo are thinly veiled, and we can peer through and see the real characters at play. We know who the "angelheaded hipsters" are, that Ginsberg was suspended from Columbia University for writing a derogatory phrase about Jews on a dirty classroom window with his forefinger. We know all the bad actors in this boy's club: Kerouac, Neil Cassady, Burroughs, Orlovsky, Corso, et cetera. We know that Corso spent time in Dannemora, that he boasted he never combed his hair: "although I guess I'd get the bugs out of it if I did."

Publicity translates into currency, and, as the passage of time has revealed, many of the Beats were keenly aware of the benefits that flow from publicity. It was, and still is, a means of producing capital. But sometimes the antics almost misfired, though Ginsberg knew the value of an empirical controversy. At the time, however, he would find himself hemmed in by his own design, as depicted in the exchange between him and Britain's Dame Edith Sitwell: "My you *do* smell bad, don't you?" she said upon their introduction. "What was your name again? Are you one of the action poets?" Ginsberg's nervous fingers produced a cigarette, which only made her dig her nails in deeper. "Is that a narcotic one? Does it contain heroin?" "No," he said, "but I've got some here. Do you want a shot?" "Oh, dear no," said Dame Sitwell. "Dope makes me come out all over in spots."

Of course, this moment of playful banter was instant grist for the publicity mill and it led to Dame Sitwell's rejoinder that appeared in *Life* on February 8, 1960:

Sirs: My attention has been called to a most disgusting report in your paper—one mass of lies from beginning to end—which pretends to describe my meeting with Mr. Allen Ginsberg. . . . There is not one word of truth in a single sentence of it.

Mr. Ginsberg never offered me heroin, and as I have never, in my life, taken heroin, it can scarcely "bring me out in spots." (An affliction from which, incidentally, I do not suffer.)

The English upper class do not use the expression "my!" (We leave that to persons of your correspondent's breeding.) Nor do we tell people who are introduced to us they "smell bad."

This is the most vulgar attack, actuated evidently by an almost insane malice, probably by some person whom I have refused to receive socially, that I have ever seen.

You had better apologize, publicly, both to Mr. Ginsberg and me immediately.

Life replied, "The anecdote . . . had been widely circulated at Oxford. Mr. Ginsberg joins Dame Edith in denying it and *Life* apologizes to both."

In Jack Kerouac's "Belief and Technique for Modern Prose," published in the *Evergreen Review* in 1959, two items underline this issue about privacy:

24. No fears or shame in the dignity of yr experience, language & knowledge
25. Write for the world to read and see yr exact pictures of it

Before the Beats, there have been numerous persons who walked into literary plots and became thinly disguised character; hardly has this been more evident than in Richard Bruce Nugent's short story "Smoke Lilies and Jade" (1926), where the impressionistic landscape is peopled by drugs, androgyny, and homosexuality. Beauty, its Greenwich Village protagonist, is a dual figure, a composite of Rudolph Valentino and the artist Miguel Cavarrubias; Countee Cullen's lover Harold Jackman; and Langston Hughes. Many felt that DuBois's prophecy had come true—if the emphasis on culture is diminished by the artistic: "turn the Negro renaissance into decadence."

But Wallace Thurman's *Infants of the Spring* (1932) dismantles and caricatures the entire Harlem Renaissance. All the major players and philosophers are on the scene. In the novel's last chapter, Paul Armstrong, modeled after Thurman's friend Richard Bruce Nugent, is a suicide discovered in Nigeratti Manor (Thurman's rent-free house at 267 West 136th Street in Harlem) by Raymond, who represents Thurman.

I ride the New Jersey Transit train from New York's Penn Station to Princeton Junction, and am often amazed by the numerous people hollering into their cell phones. These New Age travelers seem to trust their anonymity, talking at decibels to make the conversations anything but private. Everyone within earshot hears intimate love talk to trading on the stock market. There might be an air of keeping up with the Joneses. There's always been the strategy to let others "overhear" the price of their houses and cars. Perhaps the first attempt at name-dropping is when boys and girls drop the names of popular dates.

In Thailand, one can buy cell phones that don't have any guts, just the shell of the thing. Ultimately it suggests that owner of the mock cell phone is not worth the breath they inhale and exhale. While everyone is getting plugged in, ironically, people are disconnecting from each other.

The technology of illusion seems here to say, but this is not without some threat to the species. A few years after J. Edgar Hoover died—he's the one who initiated the bugging industry—it was suggested that an appropriate monument to him would be a complex of computers. Hoover specialized in revealing little "dirty" details about the personal lives of those he wanted to discredit. An expert at concealing counterintelligence, he himself diverted any sort of revelations that would divulge some of his personal pastimes including dressing up in black taffeta and pearls. Personal freedom depends on privacy and everyone is entitled to it.

In early 1995, I spent a day on a nude beach in Queensland, Australia, near Cairns. My two friends took to this easier than me. The two turned backflips and floated atop the sea, gazing up into the hurting light. I cowered, craving at least a fig leaf. Paradise was twenty yards away, among the trees and ferns, where white-plumed honeyeaters and cockatoos flickered through the green and plagued the salty air like winged sentinels. I wanted to pull my clothes back on, to see if I could find and stare down another four-foot, stout cassowary armored in blue feathers. I can see that outlandish character aiming his spyglasses at everyone, strutting around the edge of the water in his birthday suit. Even if this joker hadn't been there, making me mindful of why some rejoice in such a display, I would still have been shy—sinking down into the waves, like some nameless bottom fish nudging coral with its bright nose.

I won't claim at that moment I was thinking of A. D. Hope's "The Double Looking Glass" that portrays an apocryphal moment between Susannah and the Elders. Her garden has sprouted out of the imagination, cut off from the larger world; its centralized peace is destroyed by the elders—this garden where the real and imagined merge as one. This place of meditating, silence, and contemplation is a sanctuary for the human imagination where Susannah's sexuality lives: "A mirror for man's images of love." I believe a lack of privacy deadens the imagination and the world of sexual love.

Feeling half-ashamed, not wanting to look at the nude figures displayed on the beach, a dance not unlike the male peacock's flare of many-colored plumage and blazon sexual fanfare, I felt as if all eyes were on me. Maybe this self-consciousness was linked to my childhood back in Bogalusa where a sense of privacy was almost sacred. The knock on a closed door said that the person on the other side belonged to his or her own skin.

Notes

1. Friedrich Nietzsche, *Untimely Meditations*, trans. R. J. Hollingdale (New York: Cambridge UP, 1983), 84.
2. Roland Barthes, *Camera Lucida* (New York: Hill and Wang, 1981), 98.
3. Ann Douglas, *Terrible Honesty: Mongrel Manhattan in the 1920s* (New York: Farrar, Straus and Giroux, 1995), 48.
4. Billy Klüver and Julie Martin, *Kiki's Paris: Artists and Lovers, 1900–1930* (New York: Abrams, 1989), 154.

The Blue Machinery of Summer

"I feel like I'm part of this damn thing," Frank said. He carried himself like a large man even though he was short. A dead cigarette dangled from his half-grin. "I've worked on this machine for twenty-odd years, and now it's almost me."

It was my first day on a summer job at ITT Cannon in Phoenix in 1979. This factory manufactured parts for electronic systems—units that fit into larger, more complex ones. My job was to operate an air-powered punch press. Depending on each item formed, certain dies or templates were used to cut and shape metal plates into designs the engineers wanted.

"I know all the tricks of the trade, big and small, especially when it comes to these punch presses. It seems like I was born riding this hunk of steel."

Frank had a gift for gab, but when the foreman entered, he grew silent and meditative, bent over the machine, lost in his job. The whole day turned into one big, rambunctious dance of raw metal, hiss of steam, and sparks. Foremen strutted about like banty roosters. Women tucked falling curls back into hairnets, glancing at themselves in anything chrome.

This job reminded me of the one I'd had in 1971 at McGraw Edison, also in Phoenix, a year after I returned from Vietnam. Back then, I had said to myself, this is the right setting for a soap opera. Muscle and sex changed the rhythm of this place. We'd call the show *The Line*.

I'd move up and down the line, shooting screws into metal cabinets of coolers and air conditioners—one hour for Mont-

From *The Best American Essays 2001*, ed. Kathleen Norris (New York: Houghton Mifflin, 2011).

gomery Ward or Sears, and the next two hours for a long line of cabinets stamped *McGraw Edison*. The designs differed only slightly, but made a difference in the selling price later on. The days seemed endless, and it got to where I could do the job with my eyes closed.

In retrospect, I believe I was hyper from the war. I couldn't lay back; I was driven to do twice the work expected—sometimes taking on both sides of the line, giving other workers a hand. I worked overtime two hours before 7:00 a.m. and one hour after 4:00 p.m. I learned everything about coolers and air conditioners, and rectified problem units that didn't pass inspection.

At lunch, rather than sitting among other workers, I chose a secluded spot near the mountain of boxed-up coolers to eat my homemade sandwiches and sip iced tea or lemonade. I always had a paperback book in my back pocket: Richard Wright's *Black Boy*, Albert Camus's *The Fall*, Frantz Fanon's *The Wretched of the Earth*, or C. W. E. Bigsby's *The Black American Writer*. I wrote notes in the margins with a ballpoint. I was falling in love with language and ideas. All my attention went to reading.

When I left the gaze of Arizona's Superstition Mountain and headed for the Colorado Rockies, I wasn't thinking about higher education. Once I was in college, I vowed never to take another job like this, and yet here I was, eight years later, a first-year graduate student at the University of California at Irvine, and working another factory job in Phoenix, hypnotized by the incessant clang of machinery.

Frank schooled me in the tricks of the trade. He took pride in his job and practiced a work ethic similar to the one that had shaped my life early on even though I had wanted to rebel against it. Frank was from Little Rock; in Phoenix, everyone seemed to be from somewhere else except the indigenous Americans and Mexicans.

"If there's one thing I know, it's this damn machine," Frank said. "Sometimes it wants to act like it has a brain of its own, as if it owns me, but I know better."

"Iron can wear any man out," I said.

"Not this hunk of junk. It was new when I came here."

"But it'll still be here when you're long gone."

"Says who?"

"Says iron against flesh."

"They will scrap this big, ugly bastard when I'm gone."

"They'll bring in a new man."

"Are you the new man, whippersnapper? They better hire two of you to replace one of me."

"Men will be men."

"And boys will be boys."

The hard dance held us in its grip.

I spotted Lily Huong the second day in a corner of the wiring department. The women there moved their hands in practiced synchrony, looping and winding color-coded wires with such graceful dexterity and professionalism. Some chewed gum and blew bubbles, other smiled to themselves as if they were reliving the weekend. And a good number talked about the soap operas, naming off the characters as if they were family members or close friends.

Lily was in her own world. Petite, with long black hair grabbed up, stuffed beneath a net and baseball cap, her body was one fluid motion, as if it knew what it was doing and why.

"Yeah, boys will be boys," Frank said.

"What do you mean?"

"You're looking at trouble, my friend."

"Maybe trouble is looking for me. And if it is, I'm not running."

"She is nothing but bona fide trouble."

I wonder if she was thinking of Vietnam while she sat bent over the table, or when she glided across the concrete floor as if she were moving through lush grass. Lily? It made me think of waterlily, lotus—how shoots and blooms were eaten in that faraway land. The lotus grows out of decay, in lagoons dark with sediment and rot.

Mornings arrived with the taste of sweet nighttime still in our mouths, when the factory smelled like the deepest ore, and the syncopation of the great heaving presses fascinated me.

The nylon and leather safety straps fit our hands like fingerless gloves and sometimes seemed as if they'd pull us into the thunderous pneumatic vacuum faster than an eye blink. These beasts pulsed hypnotically; they reminded everyone within earshot of terrifying and sobering accidents. The machinery's dance of smooth heft seemed extraordinary, a masterpiece of give-and-take precision. If a foolhardy novice wrestled with one of these metal contraptions, it would suck up the hapless soul. The trick was to give and pull back with a timing that meant the difference between life and death.

"Always use a safety block, one of these chunks of wood. Don't get careless," Frank said. "Forget the idea you can second-guess this monster. Two months ago we had a guy in here named Leo on that hunk of junk over there, the one that Chico is now riding."

"Yeah, and?"

"I don't believe it. It's crazy. I didn't know Leo was a fool. The machine got stuck, he bent down, looked underneath, and never knew his last breath. That monster flattened his head like a pancake."

One morning, I stood at the checkout counter signing out my tools for the day's work and caught a glimpse of Lily out of the corner of my eye. She stopped. Our eyes locked for a moment, and then she glided on toward her department. Did she know I had been in 'Nam? Had there been a look in my eyes that had given me away?

"You can't be interested in her," Paula said. She pushed her hair away from her face in what seemed like an assured gesture.

"Why not?" I said.

"She's nothing, nothing but trouble."

"Oh?"

"Anyway, you ain't nobody's foreman."

I took my toolbox and walked over to the punch press. The buzzer sounded. The gears kicked in. The day started.

After three weeks, I discovered certain social mechanisms ran the place. The grapevine, long, tangled, and thorny, was merciless. After a month on the job I had been wondering why Frank disappeared at lunchtime but always made it back just minutes before the buzzer.

"I bet Frank tells you why he comes back here with a smile on his mug?" Maria coaxed. She worked as a spot-welder, with most of her day spent behind heavy black goggles as the sparks danced around her.

"No."

"Why don't you ask Paula one of these mornings when you're signing out tools?"

"I don't think so," I said.

"She's the one who puts that grin on his face. They've been tearing up that rooming house over on Sycamore for years."

"Good for them," I said.

"Not if that cop husband of hers come to his senses."

It would have been cruel irony for Frank to work more than twenty years on the monster and lose his life at the hands of a mere mortal.

The grapevine also revealed that Lily had gotten on the payroll because of Rico, who was a foreman on the swing shift. They had been lovers and he had put in a good word for her. Rico was built like a lightweight boxer, his eyes bright and alert, always able to look over the whole room in a single glance. The next news said Lily was sleeping with Steve, the shipping foremen, who wore western shirts, a silver and turquoise bent buckle, and cowboy boots. His red Chevy pickup had a steer's horn on the hood. He was tall and lanky and had been in the marines, stationed at Khe Sanh.

I wondered about Lily. What village or city had she come from—Chu Chi or Da Nang, Saigon or Hue? What was her story? Did she still hear the war during sleepless nights? Maybe she had had an American boyfriend, maybe she was in love with a Vietnamese once, a student, and they had intimate moments besides the Perfume River as boats with green and red lanterns passed at dusk. Or maybe she met him on the edge of a rice paddy, or in some half-lit place in Da Nang a few doors down from the Blue Dahlia.

She looked like so many who tried to outrun past lovers, history. "*She's nothing but trouble . . .*" Had she become a scapegoat? Had she tried to play a game that wasn't hers to play? Didn't anyone notice her black eye one week, the corner of her lip split the next?

I told myself I would speak to her. I didn't know when, but I would.

The women were bowed over their piecework.

As a boy I'd make bets with myself, and as a man I was still making bets, and sometimes they left me in some strange situations.

"In New Guinea those Fuzzy Wuzzies saved our asses," Frank said. "They're the smartest people I've ever seen. One moment almost in the Stone Age, and the next they're zooming around in our jeeps and firing automatic weapons like nobody's business. They gave the Japanese hell. They were so outrageously brave it still hurts to think about it."

I wanted to tell him about Vietnam, a few of the things I'd witnessed, but I couldn't. I could've told him about the South Vietnamese soldiers who were opposites of Frank's heroes.

I gazed over toward Lily.

Holding up one of the doodads—we were stamping out hundreds hourly—I said to Frank, "Do you know what this is used for?"

"No. Never crossed my mind."

"You don't know? How many do you think you've made?"

"God only knows."

"And you don't know what they're used for?"

"No."

"How much does each sell for?"

"Your guess is as good as mine. I make 'em. I don't sell 'em."

He's right, I thought. Knowing wouldn't change these workers' lives. This great symphony of sweat, oil, steel, rhythm, it all made a strange kind of sense.

"These are used in the firing mechanisms of grenade launchers," I said as I scooped up a handful. "And each costs the government almost eighty-five dollars."

The buzzer sounded.

In the cafeteria, most everybody sat in their usual clusters. A few of the women read magazines—*True Romance, Tan, TV Guide, Reader's Digest*—as they nibbled at sandwiches and sipped Cokes. One woman was reading her Bible. I felt like the odd man out as I took my paperback from my lunch pail: a Great Books Foundation volume, with blue-white-black cover and a circle around *GB*. My coworkers probably thought I was reading the same book all summer long, or that it was a religious text. I read Voltaire, Hegel, and Darwin.

Voltaire spoke to me about Equality:

All the poor are not unhappy. The greater number are born in that state, and constant labor presents them from too sensibly feeling their situation; but when they do strongly feel it, then follow wars such as these of the popular party against the Senate at Rome, and those of the peasantry in Germany, England and France. All these wars ended sooner or later in the subjection of the people, because the great have money, and money in a state commands every thing: I say in a state, for the case is different between nation and nation. The nation that makes the best use of iron will always subjugate another that has more gold but less courage.

Maybe I didn't what to deal with those images of 'Nam still in my psyche, ones that Lily had rekindled.

"You catch on real fast, friend," Frank said. "It is hard to teach a man how to make love to a machine. It's almost got to be in your blood. If you don't watch out, you'll be doing twenty in this sweatbox too. Now mark my word."

I wanted to tell him about school. About some of the ideas filling my head. Lily would smile, but she looked as if she were gazing through me.

One morning in early August, a foreman said they needed me to work on a special unit. I was led through the security doors. The room was huge, and the man working on the big, circular-dome object seemed small and insignificant in the voluminous space. Then I was shaking hands with the guy they called Dave the Lathe. Almost everyone has a nickname here, as in the Deep South, where it turned out, many of the workers were from. The nicknames came from the almost instinctual impulse to make language a game of insinuation.

Dave was from Paradise, California. He showed me how to polish each part, every fixture and pin. The work led to painstaking tedium. Had I posed too many questions? Was that why I was working this job?

Here everything was done by hand, with patience and silence. The room was air-conditioned. Now the clang of machines and whine of metal being cut retreated into memory. Behind this door Dave the Lathe was a master at shaping metals, alloyed with secrets, a metal that could be smoothed but wouldn't shine, take friction and heat out of the world. In fact, it looked like a fine piece of sculpture designed aeronautically, that approached perfection. Dave the Lathe had been working on this nose cone for a spacecraft for more than five months.

Dave and I seldom talked. Lily's face receded from my thoughts. Now I stood across from Dave the Lathe, thinking about two women in my class back at the University of California with the same first name. One was from New York. She had two reproductions of French nudes over her bed and was in love with Colette, the writer. The other woman was part Okinawan from Honolulu. If we found ourselves in a room alone, she always managed to disengage herself. We had never had a discussion, but here she was, undressing in my mind. At that moment, standing a few feet from Dave the Lathe, I felt that she and I were made for each other but she didn't know it yet.

I told Dave that within two weeks I'd return to graduate school. He wished me luck in a tone that suggested he knew what I'd planned to say before I said it.

"Hey, college boy!" Maria shouted across the cafeteria. "Are you in college or did you do time like Frank says?" I wanted the impossible, to disappear.

Lily's eyes caught mine. I still hadn't told her I felt I'd left part of myself in her country. Maria sat down beside me. I fished out the ham sandwich, but left Darwin in the lunch box. She said, "You gonna just soft-shoe in here and then disappear, right?"

"No. Not really."

"*Not really*, he says," she mocked.

"Well."

"Like a lousy lover who doesn't tell you everything. Doesn't tell the fine print."

"Well."

"Cat got your tongue, college boy?"

"Are you talking to me or somebody else?"

"Yeah you! Walk into somebody's life and then turn into a ghost. A one-night stand."

"I didn't think anyone needed to know."

"I suppose you're too damn good to tell us the truth."

She stood up, took her lunch over to another table, sat down, and continued to eat. I didn't know what to say. I was still learning.

There's good silence. There's bad silence. Growing up in rural Louisiana, along with four brothers and one sister, I began to cultivate a life of the imagination. I traveled to Mexico, Africa, and the Far East. When I was in elementary school and junior high, sometimes I knew the answers to questions, but I didn't dare raise my hand. Boys and girls danced up and down, waving their arms, with right and wrong answers. It was hard for me to chance being wrong. Also, I found it difficult to share my feelings; but I always broke the silence and stepped in if someone was being mistreated.

Now, as I sat alone, looking out the window of a Greyhound bus at 1:00 a.m., I felt like an initiate who had gotten cold feet and was hightailing it back to some privileged safety zone. I began to count the figures sprawled on the concrete still warm from the sun's weight on the city. There seemed to be an uneasy equality among destitutes: indigenous Americans, Mexicans, a few blacks and whites. Eleven. Twelve. I thought, a massacre of the spirit.

The sounds of the machines were still inside my head. The clanging punctuated by Frank's voice: "Are you ready to will your body to this damn beast, my friend?"

"No, Frank. I never told you I am going to college," I heard myself saying. Did education mean moving from one class to the next? My grandmothers told me again and again that one could scale a mountain with a good education. But could I still talk to them, to my parents, my siblings? I would try to live in two worlds—at the very least. That was now my task. I never wanted again to feel that my dreams had betrayed me.

Maybe the reason I hadn't spoken to Lily was I didn't want to talk about the war. I hadn't even acknowledged to my friends that I'd been there.

The bus pulled out, headed for L.A. with its headlights sweeping like slow yellow flares across drunken faces, as if images of the dead had followed Lily and me from a distant land only the heart could bridge.

The Blood Work of Language

There are few voices as urgent as Thomas Glave's. In *Among the Bloodpeople*, he neither hesitates nor attempts to prepare us for the unsayable "that" which divorces some men and women from their Jamaican families. No sooner than a quick leap, we are wound in the bloody, necessary realities of Politics and Flesh. We learn the cold, hard, naked facts up front, and Glave's profound dialectical relationship to these subjects. He writes:

> Speak with them [the locals] about the more than 1,500 people murdered in Jamaica in a recent year, one of these years in the early millennium—many of the victims eviscerated by machetes and otherwise butchered—but have the courtesy and common sense not to mention that at least one of those people so brutally killed was both a beloved friend of yours and a political comrade in the fierce struggle those people (your people) constantly have to wage for their survival on the island.

A graphic horror opens under the sky of a place once defined as a paradise, and through the passion of language and acute imagery we feel anger and rage. But Glave's voice resonates in the plucked string holding each sentence together, an echo of James Baldwin and Jean Genet; his language carries the full freight of witness. Where Baldwin writes of being "condemned" to speak, Glave seems to race forward to accept the mantle of all the lusty details of human love and existence—arms spread wide—nimble as some guardian angel of reprobation. He writes out of need, every trembling detail unmasked. Little escapes

---

Introduction to *Among the Bloodpeople: Politics and Flesh*, by Thomas Glave (New York: Akashic Books, 2013).

the hawk's eye driven by a prophetic heart in the deep mix of essential renderings. Glave is a seer in the old-fashioned sense and dimension: each essay here is a body-and-soul affair. His language is seductive and regenerative, critical and humanizing, almost mathematically gauged and encompassing, and it never fails to hold us accountable. But alongside the terror we witness, moments of sheer beauty seethe out of the landscape—not as a balm, but as needful epistles of reflection.

Among the Bloodpeople is woven with a similar muscular spirit as the poetry of that other famous Jamaican, Claude McKay, in a protest sonnet such as "If We Must Die":

> If we must die, let it not be like hogs
> Hunted and penned in an inglorious spot,
> While round us bark the mad and hungry dogs,
> Making their mock at our accursed lot.

Yes, these essays pulsate with the same charged lyrical, moral authority. No one easily wriggles off the hook. But here's one agonizing difference: McKay's poem is carefully aimed at the bigotry in the United States during the fiery 1920s; Glave's *Among the Bloodpeople* is calibrated toward the provocateurs of violence against Jamaican gays and lesbians. And in this anthem of we, Glave portrays this confrontation with the history one carries within:

> For this moment, as he ponders that beckoning water into which scores of his enslaved ancestors leapt off ships to their deaths three hundred years before, he unremembers the fact that this country, for the most part, has never loved him.

In this sense, Glave's voice is a show of force for the twenty-first century—sparked by a moral imperative. This writer calls out by name those citizens with governmental and juridical obligation who hide behind cloaks of cultivated silence, evasion, and sanction. Each is hitched to a rhetorical whipping post and shown the power of the word. At times it seems the girth and grit of language come close to curses hurled at those whose immoral violence has harmed these brothers and sisters. In so many ways, this is deep family business made of pain.

These essays are artistic and pragmatic, and Glave uses superb style as a device to ensnare those who would brutalize the people he loves and trusts in a world of scales rigged beyond any due process. He crosses borders of corporeality, timely and artfully, moving through painful territories of personal history that go back generations to his great-great-grandfather, and then he offers an elegiac embrace of the intangible "sound of all of them in the wind-language." Through this lyrical pursuit of truth that humanizes and subverts, the essay is Glave's weapon of choice.

The fleshed-out revelations here engage these contemporary realities: the inability for some Jamaicans to acknowledge a gay son, or daughter, or sibling; an open letter to the prime minister; a graphic insinuation of forbidden homosexuality; tributes to five literary forerunners; a poetry of deep reckoning with love; language as overlays to maps of facelessness; repression in the ivory towers of Cambridge University; picturesque moments in London as metaphor; poetic memory as the basis of empirical meaning.

The tension of poetry lives in Glave's language. And this conceit is especially highlighted in "Against Preciousness" through tone and form. He questions with honed exactitude:

> People who, across the centuries, were forced to admit into their bodies the engorged parts of those who owned them for centuries. There, one's own infinite and deeply personal catalog of memory against the ultimately offensive, dishonest, precious stink and artifice of preciousness.

The experimental moments seem naturally holistic. Glave has done a heroic deed. Now that the cultivated climate of mayhem and violence has been clearly articulated, one sees this body of work as the blueprint for change in Jamaica. Now that the situation has been laid bare, with bones of the past edging through, there should be only one undeniable action: laws must be constituted on behalf of gays and lesbians in the Caribbean. This blueprint—this layered treatise—begs action. Clearly, something must be done in a place where violence seems so regimented and codified that it has become belief. Something has to rout the terror.

Some know of the play *The Laramie Project* based on Matthew Shepard—a twenty-one-year-old gay college student who died in 1998 on a fence in a small Wyoming town—but few people know much about what happens to these men and women in the Caribbean. Once, we could feign ignorance, but not after Glave's sharply rendered *Among the Bloodpeople*. He has gone wherever wrongheadedness goes, always focused on what seems to be the underbelly of violence in worldly localities. His is a poetry of knowledge, of body and mind, which acknowledges and confronts tribulation, a longing for gestures woven through language, baring intimate details and vows of the night nudged into the broad daylight of knowing compassion. The problem of violence seems to be located in a false, symbolic manhood still situated in a concept of colonization of the heart that should prod us to the mirror.

With U.S. president Obama's fierce compassion for equality in his inauguration speech of January 2013, we know significant changes are in the forefront of the global psyche. Of course, especially after taking in Glave's raw and eloquent language, one hopes that there are sobering turns in the compendium of hearts and minds gathered on the edge of the Caribbean Sea. And we know there's no clemency now for passivity. There's no slipknot for escaping responsibility as witnesses. We know who the enemies of truth are, and in our silence they look like us in life and dream. But deep within each of us resides an unrelenting sense of freedom, and it is from this place that we must move forward.

Son of Pop

Floyd D. Tunson's Neo-blues

And the mind that has conceived a plan of living must
never lose sight of the chaos against which that pattern
was conceived.
—Ralph Ellison, *Invisible Man*

I have known Floyd Tunson since Colorado Springs, 1975. Even
then as young artists we must have seen something in each oth-
er, in our work, something that may have sounded like "Yeah,
man, I understand where you're coming from." And, for me,
this reintroduction to Floyd's work is a roundabout. Now, sitting
here in New York City almost forty years later, what has seemed
like several lifetimes ago suddenly feels very present. I rejoice in
celebrating this important retrospective on Floyd D. Tunson's
uncompromising plethora of images that illuminate a many-
sided vision.

When Floyd and I first met, we spent time talking art, ideas,
and states of being. And I cannot deny our discussions on the
realities of social history. We were two black men attempting to
engage the world through art. But that wasn't the only thing that
connected us. Yes, we did possess audacity, didn't we? From the
onset, I recognized Floyd's in-depth understanding of American
history and popular culture, and, now, decades later, it isn't sur-
prising for me to see in his vision the two fields intertwined into
fantastic dreamscapes and mirrors that expose the underbelly
of our modern psyche through popular and personal iconogra-

From the exhibition catalog *Floyd D. Tunson: Son of Pop* (Colorado
Springs Fine Arts Center, 2012).

phy. He knows the fine art of constructing worlds that change us. These installations challenge us to participate; one cannot approach a painting or installation by this artist with passivity or apathy. His psychological landscapes provoke narratives that are active, complex, textured, as well as essential.

Tunson is a master of visual satire, but, from the moment we met, I also sensed his gift of cool deliberation. He seemed to know how to slow down time. Back then, we gazed up at Pikes Peak and tried to lose ourselves among the natural sculptural formations in the Garden of the Gods, we took forays through Manitou Spring's penny arcade, and perhaps everyone there thought he or she could bend time through creative meditation.

Now, I recognize the "coolness" captured in his work as earned confidence in skillful know-how and execution. Perhaps Tunson has inherited or been nurtured into coolness; even in those depictions of the artist's father (finished in 1976 and 1977), he perfects a sense of eloquence and dignified ease that argues with time, as best described in "An Aesthetic of the Cool" by Robert Farris Thompson: "Manifest within this philosophy of the cool is the belief that the purer, the cooler a person becomes, the more ancestral he becomes. In other words, mastery of self enables a person to transcend time and elude preoccupation. He or she can concentrate on truly important matters of social balance and aesthetic substance, creative matters, full of motion and brilliance."

I haven't seen Tunson's studio in Manitou Springs, but the monumental scale of his work suggests that it is probably spacious. Some of his works occupy the full width of a room— perhaps an unconscious attempt to capture the overwhelming emotional canvas of the surrounding landscape. I sense how his space becomes a temple of articulation. And I can almost imagine how he moves in that space, applying strokes to the canvas with gestures both controlled and improvisational—like a jazz musician jamming. In his abstract works, such as *Nubian*, the colors break and swirl into (e)motion; we are there even before we're there. Silences and pauses are threads in the language and movement. The feeling is a dance. Or a destiny.

His images exist just on the other side of an idealized beauty, just across the mountains, barely or rarely out of reach, in a place in the world, but also outside of the world—a place of great vulnerability. Even if this zone houses the illusion of control, it is still a place of dominance over one's self—a place of supreme meditation. We usually think of such a state of mind as a space where miraculous, even magical, things occur.

Floyd grew up in the Rockies, in Denver, but still the migratory spirits of the Deep South shape his artistic personality. A premodern world interrogates a postmodern world by existing side by side. His contemporary portraits embody the affects of early American history. They are, in a sense, visual sorrow songs that continue to trouble our hearts and minds. In *Adrift*, the bare skeletons of dream boats illustrate a kind of wreckage, or blue limbo—in the juxtaposition of materials and the tactile atmosphere of hues and textures. And in works such as *Pop-Up Rodeo* or *Hearts and Minds* the Western frontier's contradictory worship of violence dovetails with iconic portrayals of folk heroes or gangster culture. His images—fully anointed—know something about survival, and we can see this knowing in the eyes of the young black male in *Endangered 8*. Tunson's incorporation of pop culture within his motifs sometimes seems natural, sometimes deliberate, where pop references create an almost poetic tension.

Tension. Pressure. Performance. His work doesn't lie merely on the canvas or on large American Standard plywood sheets, but it seems to rise, walk around, and challenge us. His collages are sculptural, and they often convey a sense of "madeness." The fine-arts critic Kyle MacMillan says in the *Denver Post*, March 4, 2005, that "Tunson is wonderfully adept at painting and sculpture, with his on-going 'Synchro-Mesh' series of wall and stand-alone pieces incorporating all kinds of found objects, including many with telling nostalgic and social connotation."

His pieces come alive, and move in the space of history. His works are often paintings within paintings; for the most part, each is multiple within one. They possess physical and intellectual heft, and also demand our attention as an intimate conversation does. Layered and complex, *Hearts and Minds* pulls the viewer in until one endures a self-interrogation, or at least a dialogue. What narrative do all these images add up to, what do they mean to us, how do they depict the inner cities and interiors of our national psyche, and who do they hold responsible for the inherited violence and malevolence?

Floyd's work—wrought with robust humility—seems intent on creating awareness that challenges and persists. His visual agglomerations—whether symmetrical or asymmetrical—always possess an architectural or crafted certainty. And, as viewers who encounter these structures, textured paintings, and iconic montages, we experience a momentary dislocation, a fracture in the psyche, and, in dialogue with the work, we begin to invent narratives in order to stabilize ourselves. For instance, in *Canary Metaphor* the viewer imposes a dialogue between the repeating images of the canaries and the close-up portraits of the black males. And has the artist painted himself in among them? Do these men represented here become sacrificial birds like the canaries in the mines?

At this turn in the road, one may consider the correlation between Tunson and Basquiat. As one compares the two black male artists, it is inevitably realized that their works have incorporated or transformed into pop iconography. Yet Basquiat's black figures appear distorted, maimed, wounded, or diminished to little more than caricatures or half-broken symbols. Tunson's black figures—especially black males—are fully rendered, intimately exacted, serious, and at times dignified, at times heartbroken. And is this heartbreak personal or public? Were they born into it? Condemned? One could easily say that perhaps this is an unexpected parallel between Floyd's Denver and Jean-Michel's Brooklyn (via Haiti). Both painters capture psychological and physical chaos—the urbanization of the canvas, but Tunson seems to have been driven by a mature coolness and compassion, which is in turn invoked in the viewer when encountering the works. There are, however, also elements of insinuation in Tunson, especially when pop images bleed through the naturalistic. Both artists possess moments of the improvisational, but one could say that Tunson's vision seems cooler, more reflective, and thus more controlled.

Where Basquiat dies at the magic-tragic number of twenty-seven, admittedly leaving behind a cache of impressive, enigmatic body of work, Floyd stays in the cut, never losing rhythm in a long, substantial gig, and uses natural light to expose what resides in the psychological weather of dreams and nightmares. Floyd has been creating and teaching art for over thirty-five years, and he's still surprising himself, knowing the configuration of the zone and aesthetics of the cool. The Fine Arts Museum in Colorado Springs celebrates Floyd D. Tunson's works, which challenge us across decades and cultures.

Tunson has made an implemental, slow, sustained impact in the Rockies, amassing a phenomenal body of work, and eking out an impressive presence in the arts, especially in galleries and museums in Denver and Colorado Springs, with seasoned art critics such as John Hazlehurst challenging us to see the complex beauty and social reality in the breathtaking twists and turns of this American genius. Hazlehurst says in his January 27, 2005, article in the *Colorado Springs Independent*: "Tunson, a modest man who taught a generation of students at Palmer High School, may well be one of the most distinguished American artists of his generation." I'm not the only one who believes it is high time for Floyd's work to move beyond the shadows of the mountains to touch Cleveland, Chicago, Los Angeles, Brooklyn, Manhattan, Venice, etc. Floyd is a loyal homeboy with fans and critics; he's always in his zone, situated in the philosophy of the cool, but now, with "Son of Pop," this neo-blues man has earned the right to challenge the larger art world to catch up to what he has captured on canvas, sheets of American Standard plywood, on whatever he gets his hands on. Of course, time is a part of Tunson's equation, and no one can deny this artist his necessary vision, and that he has paid his dues.

His works provoke our "ways of seeing" because he's aware of what has shaped us as social and political beings, and his work captures John Berger's philosophy: "The more imaginative the work, the more profoundly it allows us to share the artist's experience of the visible." Yet this artist is able to reveal something—again and again—hiding slightly below the surface of things through his layered juxtaposition of images nudging each other ever so slightly, baring something truly disconcerting within us. And perhaps Floyd has intuited something else Berger underscores:

Yet when an image is presented as a work of art, the way
people look at it is affected by a whole series of learnt
assumptions about art. Assumptions concerning:
Beauty
Truth
Genius
Civilization
Form
Status
Taste.

We could add to this list "Self" as an assumption—a sense of self.
"Know thyself" is biblical but it is also elliptical, especially in our
modern age of the visual as a compass.

Tunson knows what is truly meant by "Beauty" in Western art
when he proclaims:

> As Aristotle said, learning is the greatest of pleasures. My work
> reflects my journey to acquire knowledge. Along the way I
> have become a Janus. Looking at life from one direction, I
> see the terror of chaos, man's inhumanity to man, mortality,
> and the vastness of the unknown. From another direction,
> the human condition seems like a magnificent, orderly evolu-
> tion of extraordinary beauty. The totality of my work reflects
> my quest to comprehend and express these forces and their
> interconnectedness.

Some works, like epic poems, give the viewer the task of un-
tangling multiple paths that converge within a frame, or within
a frame of reference. These montages are often constructed of
still lifes. The artist goes on to say, "Even my nonobjective paint-
ing is based on this dialectic, where uninhibited strokes play
against geometric order." Where Aristotle reproaches the paint-
er for attempting to play God by creating the representational,
Tunson has found a way to fracture the shape within the design,
or reshape the "geometric order" by what appears as improvi-
sational contrast. He has also given the viewer the freedom of
participation through the art of interpretation.

The "Janus" strategy works double time in Tunson's remixes,
where the old and new converge to form a *new* way of seeing.

The contextual frames in his remixes, such as *Remix 1 (allusions to Matisse and The Adventure of Tintin in the Congo)*, *Remix A*, *Old School Remix*, *Remix H*, *Where in the Hell is Batman?*, and *Remix E*, all create artistic tension—even unspeakable anger—out of a satirical juxtaposition. If one thinks about remixing in regards to music, he or she may view the musician as merely a servant of technology. But any way one may approach this dilemma philosophically, one must admit that it does take a cogent talent for an artist to make the "remix" work, or flow, and Floyd has that ability.

Of course, since Floyd Tunson is a natural disciple of the aesthetics of the cool, remix seems to mean something different in his hands. His execution is painterly, and beauty resides just below the surface, like the tonality in a great delta blues singer after spending a few years in the city—something rough, something easygoing in the same frame. And in a certain way even Floyd's *Delta Queen Installation* is a remix: the agency of time pulls everything together. Even the 1930–1950 chair invites the viewer to become a part of the piece—the cigarette ad, the two black women whispering to each other, the white couple gazing off, amused, the delta queen (a figure of ambiguous gender) peering down from the top at the viewer. Is this androgynous person homeless in an unnamed city or a rural survivor? Or is this character a great blues performer that time has had its way with? And who are these onlookers? Is the viewer the couple positioned in the foreground of the seemingly segregated psychological landscape?

In a time when much art-making seems whimsical, Tunson gives us works shaped by a great need. For him, it seems, the making of art is a necessary *action*. Each installation is a composite of extended insinuations. His vision is masculine, robust, but tinged with the romantic. And at times he masters transforming tragic realities into iconic portrayals where blues rise out of the textured collages to say, "We're still here."

Conundrum

For some reason, when I think of Africa, I think of the matador in the bull ring planting feathered lances into the creature to wound, infuriate, and corrupt its spirit. Perhaps this is a metaphor for colonization. Yet if one compares Africa to India or a number of other places that have been colonized, one might see that it wasn't Africa's heart colonized, but its spirit. And one may argue back and forth, asking, What is the more brutal or complete colonization, the heart or the spirit?

Of course, Frantz Fanon's *The Wretched of the Earth* has eloquently articulated numerous facets of colonization. In his psychological-political opus, he says, "When we consider the efforts made to carry out the cultural estrangement so characteristic of the colonial epoch, we realize that nothing has been left to chance and that the result looked for by colonial domination was indeed to convince the natives that colonialism came to lighten their darkness." After reading the *Wretched of the Earth* several times during my late twenties, I dared a moment of blasphemy. I wondered if this radical seer would have felt differently today, but *if* is the largest word in Webster's, right? And now, decades later, gazing out at the New York City skyline, I feel doubly cheated: the loss of Frantz Fanon, the man, the world citizen, seems beyond question; but also, the loss of a sober retrospection from such a knife-edged intellect. What concerns regarding the haves and have-nots would he articulate today at Pen International, or the UN, in regards to Africa? I believe that his critique would still be brutally straightforward and clear without a touch of sentimentality or emotional dishonesty. No, he wouldn't back off from his systematic discrediting of cultural im-

From *Imagine Africa* (Brooklyn: Island Position, 2011).

perialism or capitalistic maleficence. He would read the riot act to those bent on perpetual excursions into Africa with eyes on obscene profits and the bottom line (countries like China holding on to eighteenth- or nineteenth-century beliefs that Africans are only three-fifths of a human being). And what would Fanon have said to those who suffered social and political aftershock in countries emerging out of colonialism? Yes, he would have openly condemned those new African leaders who sock away billions in Swiss banks while the people starve in squalor and wretchedness. And would he assess Africa's present leaders any less straightforwardly? In what humanistic critical light would he see the Congo, Kenya, Zimbabwe, etc.? Which countries and leaders would escape his ironclad scrutiny? How would he react to the constant turmoil and bloodshed, the nonstop gunrunning enterprises throughout enclaves of the motherland? Would Africa itself get off the hook?

Growing up in America, especially in the Deep South, in the black community the idea of "the dark continent" was always negative. The propaganda of skin color was a primer for the harsh realities of the social order and false hierarchies, even within the black family. So, in the 1970s, when I began to question every received system of thought, I read whatever I could get my hands on concerning Africa. But it was another Martinican, Aimé Césaire, who focused my attention in a slightly different way on the motherland. His concept of negritude beckoned to me, though Fanon questioned the term, saying:

> Now, turned toward Africa, the Antillean is going to hail her. He discovers in himself a transplanted child of slaves, he feels the vibration of Africa in the deepest regions of his being and aspires toward but one thing: to plunge into the great "black pit." It seems then that the Antillean, after great white error, is now in the process of living the great black mirage.

Despite being half wide-eyed with Fanon's feelings toward the idea of negritude, I momentarily lost myself in Césaire's body of work, especially in poems such as "To Africa," and was taken on an emotional voyage with lines such as: "strike peasant strike / on the first day the birds died / the second day the fish beached

/ the third day the animals came out of the woods / and formed a big very strong hot belt for the cities / strike the ground with your daba / there is in the ground the map of transmutations and death's tricks." Surrealistic, incendiary, and at times even polyrhythmic, Césaire's is a voice that has repeatedly engaged artists and thinkers, especially to black voices worldwide.

In retrospect, however, as I think of Césaire's fervor and revolutionary intentions, I find it difficult not to wonder if some of his most celebrated poems at times aren't facsimiles of Leo Frobenius's fantasticalness. Still, I refuse to believe that this poet's passion is anything but authentic. Two other voices of the negritude movement, Leopold Senghor and Leon-Gontran Damas, also came under the influence of this German ethnographer's rhetoric and his imagination in conjuring Africa. But it is Senghor who shines a light on this fact in his "The Lessons of Leo Frobenius":

> We had to wait for Leo Frobenius before the affinities between the 'Ethiopian,' that is the Negro African, and the German soul could be made manifest and before certain stubborn preconceptions of the 17th and 18th centuries could be removed. One of these preconceptions is that the development of every ethnic group, and of humanity itself, is linear, univocal, passing from the Stone Age to the age of steam and electricity and to the atomic age of today. . . . Frobenius tells us that, like individuals, ethnic groups are diverse, even opposed, like the Hamites and the Ethiopians, in their feelings and their ideas, their myths and their ideologies, their customs and their institutions; that each ethnic group, having its own paideuma—once again, its soul—reacts in its own peculiar way to the environment and develops autonomously; that though they may be at different stages of development, Germans and 'Ethiopians' belong to the same spiritual family.

In 1996 in St. Louis I fell into the ritual of visiting a smallish antique store displaying thousands of odds and ends because I became fascinated by a number of leather-bound books the storeowner kept in a safe in the rear of the shop. The books were very expensive and I almost purchased one or two several times but couldn't bring myself to fork over the money. These books were works of art displaying (exhibiting) a number of brightly hued plates depicting imagined Africans, colorfully untrue and fanciful. In fact, I think it would be safe to say that these were fake travel books on Africa—usually of a fabled Timbuctoo or scary netherworld populated by lions and tigers—sources of entertainment from the seventeenth and eighteenth centuries. When one reflects momentarily back to those fanciful, pricey editions based on the private fantasies and personalized iconography of the writers and artists, one sees an Africa that didn't exist. Each plate depicts only an illusion of colorful garb and stylized rituals that become, for the visual artist, commodity—tourism through written and visual texts. And mostly this happens without laying eyes on a single, flesh and blood African.

But even today, the real Africa isn't confronted; in fact, Africans continue to live in our imagination primarily as objects of pity and derision on the six o'clock news and late-night infomercials. We are in denial about the complexity of the continent's history and psyche. Sometimes we may even glimpse in other parts of the world such as Haiti, with age-old conflicts and tragedies, an image or a moment that reminds us of Africa's parallel dilemmas. And, of course, technology seems to exist for constructing numerous virtual realities and suggestions that bleed into each other.

At this moment, thinking about Africa, my question is this: Now, a decade into the twenty-first century, it is paramount for Africa to dream itself whole. I would risk saying that Africa has not been whole for a very long time, and perhaps it was wounded even before 1544 when the Portuguese arrived in its interior because of the various allegiances to the culture and politics of the numerous tribes. So when the Europeans arrived Africa was easy to conquer because there was not a united front against imperial aggression. It was lacking psychological infrastructure, not to mention physical infrastructure, and in so many ways was fractured—divided from within by tribal customs, languages, and dialects. The ship captains and merchants of flesh said to the conquering chiefs and proxy envoys, "We will barter for your prisoners, just march them to the holding pens, or to the gangplank." Of course, that was a perverse collaboration that affected Africa's past, and still discolors her present, and future.

As someone who has thought long and hard about histories and realities of Africa through the years, I see how it is imperative at this moment to confront history with truth and emotional exactitude so one can envision a healthy future for Africa. First, it is unquestionable that technology has rapidly changed the idea of time and space. Today, the borders between cultures and countries have been compromised. It doesn't take much to have the camcorder or the eye of the satellite scrutinizing the latest bloody scrimmage with hardly any guesswork. Because of this illusion of both closeness and distance simultaneously, even the names of political rivals chosen for assassination can be received in a text message.

Regarding Africa, attempting to dodge sentimentality, I think we have come to a point where we must go through the bedrock of the ultimate question and arrive at a place of responsible query. And at this way station, at *this* time, while dreaming Africa whole, one may wonder if allegiance to the tribe perpetuates an atmosphere of conflict and fragmentation throughout the continent. In thinking about the future of Africa, one may conclude that obligation to the tribe may serve best in the background. It's easy to keep a country constantly at war with itself from participating in global advancement, let alone collective advancement within the continent. When a country is divided at the root, disunity can permeate even the air breathed and corruption grow so thick one can cut it with a knife.

After arguing with Ryszard Kapuscinski's *The Emperor*, its troublesome depiction of Ethiopia's Haile Selassie and a host of characters through caricature, I was prepared to question *The Other*, but instead discovered pages of cogent thoughts and observations. He says, "The world is merging and becoming multicultural, and Otherness is becoming not just a negative reaction between white Europeans and those they have dominated, but a positive encounter between liberated peoples on every continent." I want to, or I need to believe this—that people have been liberated beyond inherited allegiances, that the world has embraced a humanistic ethos where culture is more than commodity; but it is also impossible not to acknowledge "Otherness" in tribal conflicts. Kapuscinski continues, saying, "The nationalist treats his nation, and in the case of Africa, his state, as the highest value, and all others as something inferior (and often deserving contempt). Nationalism, like racism, is a tool for identifying and classifying that is used by my Other at any opportunity." I think it is easy to see how tribalism fits this paradigm, especially since *contempt* often means bloodshed.

Perhaps there are still some benefits of tribal existence—traditions, rituals, and a communal system of laws and practices. Yet, even this can be destructive when accompanied by an us-against-them mentality, rather than an attitude of collective togetherness whereby tribes retain their distinctions yet coexist with an overall attitude of unity that bring the nations of Africa together as a means of making progress, and not just in the formation of an armed presence. I'm not suggesting that Africa should reconstruct itself on the recent European model of a unified continent, but perhaps a negotiated model based on such a prototype could be beneficial and advantageous.

Also, as a conglomerate of nation-states, Africa could pragmatically protect itself from encroachment from abroad. Presently it seems crucial for Africa and Africans to enter into a dialog concerning fundamental questions regarding its relationship to countries such as China. For example, how is the African defined by the Chinese today? Could it be possible, as the literature suggests, that he is still considered only three-fifths of a human being, still defined by an addle-headed anthropological supposition that goes back to the eighteenth and nineteenth centuries? If so, perhaps this is hardly different from the objectification of Africans depicted in those brightly colored fantasy books produced by the West as collectibles. And if there is an approximation of this myopic view within the Chinese psyche in the twenty-first century, one doesn't have to speculate about the imbalance of such a skewed perspective. One can only envision blood at the root of every tree growing near an oil field or diamond mine in Africa. Because anyone who believes as a principle that money is goodness and/or that people are impoverished because of some flaw innately in their character or race (where white is always seen as virtuous) will be unable to recognize the humanity of the African in such a lopsided equation. Consider the simplest reality: Isn't two-thirds of the world's most poverty-stricken located in Asia—not Africa, Latin America, or the Sub-Sahara? This kind of maniacal philosophy based on currency is sparked from a distance but quickly travels across borders, or oceans, especially to a continent as richly varied and unorganized as Africa.

Some would argue that the West and East exist in states of decadence worsening daily through economic tactics and technological advances. If so, I do wonder how Africa can survive such an onslaught. Can the individual exist in a culture of tribes, or is a form of government that favors natural socialism more applicable to Africa? In this sense, the only pragmatic advancement for Africa seems to be through a systematic moderation— somewhere between a democratic governance and applied socialism. In other words, Africa must learn from our shortcomings here in the West, whereby human beings are often viewed as commodities, or merely exist as clogs in a system of endless acquisition. I believe Africa has to resist the idea of the tribe in a time of globalism, that she must learn to construct things that last, including governments; she has to know the alluring swarm of modernity in mega cities cannot inform her future.

Perhaps the village life, or a matrix of villages with advanced systems that can produce green energy, or medical advancements, or clean and efficient transportation is what Africa should be dreaming itself toward. Imagine leadership academies for young men and women. Imagine seminars on solar energy, irrigation techniques, conservation, etc. Traditional customs and practices shouldn't be discarded, but should be discussed and debated in symposiums and community meetings. Let both the advancements and downfalls of the West become a source of instruction through observation; notice how we continue to wrestle with some of our obsolete practices and dogmas. The numerous shortcomings of the industrial nations are indeed instructional; change occurs through painful but fruitful deliberation. Being the mother of us all, wherever we may exist on this earth—without any cultivated arrogance—Africa has to love and treasure again those positive things it has given the world.

Clarence Major's
Cosmopolitan Vision

There's no other voice in American poetry that sings quite like Clarence Major's, and his new collection, *From Now On: New and Selected Poems 1970–2013,* elucidates ample proof. Of course, some poets and critics have attempted to trace the lineage of Major's voice and vision to the objectivists (because of his unembellished language), especially to Louis Zukofsky and George Oppen, and even to Denise Levertov; others associate him with the jazz-influenced poets aligned with the Black Arts aesthetic, and still other critics and poets have intoned Ezra Pound as a primary influence. However, anyone who knows contemporary American poetry, especially African American poetry, knows that Clarence Major, an iconic wordsmith, is also a gifted painter, novelist, essayist, and anthologist; but more than anything, he's always himself. And this new collection speaks for itself.

Major has artfully resisted being pigeonholed. In fact, here's a poet we can call a school of one; he fits that bill but not because he's trying to be different. I believe his work is naturally different. Highly personal, yet universal, Major's poetry is usually serious but playful through technique and tone. His work achieves a middle register—not high or low—like some of our great jazz stylists searching for the grace note, always dependable but edgy and democratic, someone who adapts a phrase or melody, and then bends it until it is completely theirs, through feeling, Major knows how to make profundity seem accidental; his almost casual phrasing makes this possible. His poems are

Foreword to *From Now On: New and Selected Poems, 1970–2015,* by Clarence Major (Athens: University of Georgia Press, 2015).

not consciously trying to be poems in an imagistic or rhetorical sense. And, of course, this concept of easeful engagement is an aspect of the poet's genius.

I think that Major's practice as a painter at the Art Institute of Chicago informs his craft as a poet, his method of weaving and dovetailing elements of sound into his unique way of seeing the world. At first, reading a poem by Major, one may think he or she knows the narrative but then realizes this poet is no tool or fool for the expected. His work embodies echoes—language as feeling. An example of this is the last poem of the book's first section; the title, "Something Is Eating Me Up Inside," makes one think he or she already has a clue to the poem's meaning. But let's see if that's truly the case; the poem opens this way:

> I go in and out a thousand times a day
> and the fat women with black velvet skin
> sit out on the front steps watching.
> "Where does he go so much?"
> I think often, not "much."
> I look like a hood from the 1920s
> in my Ivy League black shirt with button-down collar.

We may not know where we've traveled, but we know we have been on a voyage pushed and guided by feeling by the time we get to the phrase "There is a tapeworm inside philosophy." And, moreover, we may be that "tapeworm" because of our bloated assumptions about each other. But also, for me, "the tapeworm in philosophy" could be about Major's poetry, the mechanics of the speaker's psyche, or perhaps the line is about the artist compelled by language as a system of thinking. Major's poems articulate the quotidian, but they are also naturally philosophical, and each defies any narrow-minded trajectory; all the senses are employed—mind and feeling as organism. "Something Is Eating Me Up Inside" ends with the following lines:

> The sun is blood in my guts
> as I move from gin to sin to lakesides to sit down
> beside reasons for being in the first place.
> In the second place?:

in the second place looking outward
for a definition to a formal ending—.

And, yes, that dash is so instructive. Major's poetry relies on what is said and remains unsaid, and one enters his vision at the risk or the obligation of becoming a participant, an interloper within spaces of casual preciseness. The playfully simplistic is always more; in fact, it is a dynamo when queried by a feeling, thinking reader. And that is how Clarence Major seems to always be having fun in each poem, but never simply funny, slapstick, or bravura. Edgy and Socratic, his poems often posed questions through short declarative phrases, amassed-syncopation.

Major has a way of making a poem accrue. "Beast: A New Song" seems like a template for reading many of his poems composed of longer phrases. Here's the poem in its entirety:

The cage. Tiger. Stripes. From sun up to midnight the
    pacing tiger steps
softly. Caged. Soft traction. Across. Turns. Back. Up. Down.
    Turns.
Back across. Eyes? Headlights. Dark clues. Turns. The way
    things go
on. Pacing. Trapped. Absolute. Absolute cage. Absolute
    song.

Here, we see the underbelly of process and meaning converge. And it seems that pace and rhythm—words—almost work like colors laid down on a canvas in brushstrokes. Much of the music in *From Now On* whispers to us; it beckons, seduces, and then holds us accountable for what we are thinking. We childe ourselves, and might even find ourselves mouthing that almost edible conjunction: "But . . ." This poet teaches us there are few buts and ands when reading or hearing his poetry. One enters an emotional-psychological contract with a voice that can be defined as Clarence Major. His language is himself. We are challenged to grasp his style. This voice is bold and straightforward, as in "Conflict," the astute reader is with the speaker when he proclaims:

I claim that knowledge—
outside and beyond Verlaine, Baudelaire and Rimbaud.

That conflicting disorder
was not disorder—it was order.

In many ways, like the jazz musician, or any other artisan or craftsman who has earned the salt in his or her daily bread, Major has honed a cosmopolitan style that belongs to him, though in fact it may have been shaped out of the earthy stuff of Southern blues. Always measured, paced, and syncopated, each poem in *From Now On* makes us feel and know language is music, and of course, style is shaped through practice until it is earned. Insinuation and humor are always at the center of Major's poetry, and it seems appropriate that the final poem, "The Things You Hear," in this fine collection ends on this trope:

It doesn't come in a bottle
but it's also an effective medicine to drink.
Drink it slowly.

Dark Waters

Our civilization poisoned river waters, and their contamination acquires a powerful emotional meaning. As the course of a river is a symbol of time, we are inclined to think of a poisoned time. And yet the sources continue to gush and we believe time will be purified one day.

—Czeslaw Milosz, from "Rivers" in *Road-side Dog*

I grew up in the Green Empire. Magic City. The place was there, brimming in its mossy quietude, before the axes began to swing—cutting down the virgin pine forest on July 4, 1914, when the town was incorporated. The name comes from the Native American–named creek, "Boge Lusa," where smoke-dark waters flow through the city.

The Great Southern Lumber Company was established by someone from Buffalo, New York, connected to Goodyear in 1906. By then, the presence of the Native American had been virtually erased; now there was a killing to be made from the great, towering pines.

During the 1950s Bogalusa seethed, a hotbed for racism. Segregation, enforced by a minority, imposed inequality upon the majority of this city's population. There were no black doctors, lawyers, postal workers, police officers, firefighters, bank tellers, salespeople, machine operators, et cetera. Those who did go off to college returned as public school teachers to segregated schools. Everyone else faced making a living, and no matter the skills, the work involved perpetual hard labor.

From *The Colors of Nature: Culture, Identity, and the Natural World*, ed. Alison Hawthorne Deming and Lauret E. Savoy (Minneapolis: Milkweed Editions, 2011).

As a matter of fact, a metaphor for the daily realities of life in Bogalusa was manifested in the graveyards of the black and white inhabitants. Whites lavished monuments of granite and marble on their dead over acres of plush, green cemeteries. The graveyard for African Americans, half-hidden near the city dump, was visited by vultures and scavengers that used to linger between the smoldering hills of garbage and the graves, whose keepers fought off the constant encroachment of saw vines and scrub oak.

This hellish symbol was analogous to the town's psyche. It reflected an attitude that had been cultivated over many decades. It was the law—social and legal—a way of thinking that ran so deep that it went unquestioned each generation. Bogalusa was frozen in time.

The same attitude that allowed settlers to produce smallpox-infected blankets for Native Americans seemed alive in the psyche of our city. One could almost hear Sweet Medicine of the Cheyenne lamenting: "Some day you will meet a people who are white. They will try always to give you things, but do not take them. At last I think you will take these things that they offer you, and this will bring sickness to you."[1]

The first known settlers in the area were Scottish and Irish pioneers from the British colonies of Georgia and Virginia, as well as North and South Carolina. The Treaty of Paris, which briefly created British West Florida in 1763, also attracted Loyalists fleeing the American Revolution. By 1906, when the Great Southern Lumber Company was established—and before it was to grow into what was boasted to be the world's largest sawmill, the Native Americans had been suppressed to near extinction.

Their ghosts remained evident in some faces, as my poem "Looking for Choctaw" suggests:

> we dared him to fight,
> But he only left his breath
> On windshields, as if nothing
> Could hold him in this world.[2]

I grew up with the feeling that the Choctaw lived in our presence, in a half glimpse, somewhere among the trees as elusive, nocturnal souls.

Many Bogalusan blacks believed that "a good education" would lift them out of poverty and make their lies more equal to those of whites. They saluted the flag and trusted the Bill of Rights. Some had returned from World War I, World War II, and the Korean conflict, but they were still waiting for things to change. Some were counting the decades and years, making promises on their deathbeds, getting restless. A few were dreaming aloud.

In January 1964 the KKK burned crosses throughout Louisiana. Also, fifteen black people registered to vote in Tenses Parish, the last parish to enforce total disenfranchisement of blacks. In November the Deacons for Defense and Justice was founded in Jonesboro, Louisiana. The group advocated armed self-defense against the Klan. In December KKK members from around Natchez, Mississippi, burned a shoe-repair shop in Ferriday, Louisiana, owned by fifty-one-year-old Frank Morris. He died in the blaze. In January 1965 black protesters picketed Columbia Street stores in Bogalusa, a Klan stronghold. In May the Klan held a large rally in the Magic City, their Green Empire. On June 2, O'Neal Moore, African American and a sheriff's deputy in Washington Parish, was murdered by a white man who drove by in a pickup truck near Bogalusa. Ernest Ray McElveen, a forty-one-year-old Crown Zellerbach lab technician and member of the Citizen's Council of Greater New Orleans and the National States' Rights Party, was arrested not far from the murder scene. In July protests by the Voters League and the Deacons for Defense implored the Justice Department to enforce the Civil Rights Act through suits against city officials and the Klan. In 1966 Clarence Triggs, a bricklayer, was found dead after he left a civil rights meeting sponsored by the Congress of Racial Equality.

I have a love-hate complex with Bogalusa. The place still affects how I live and think. Its beauty and horror shaped the intensity of my observations, prompting my father to say, "Boy, you have a mind like a steel trap." Now, years after my book *Magic City*, I realize that I had attempted to present how toxicity taints the social and natural landscape. For me, the millpond—a hundred or so yards from our house—was always a place of ritual. We fished there. And sometimes we even swam in the dark water.

But in the back of my mind, I was always suspect of this slow-running pond. I think the poem "The Millpond" attempts to focus on my apprehensions:

> Gods lived under that mud
> When I was young & sublimely
> Blind. Each bloom a shudder
> Of uneasiness, no sound
> Except the whippoorwill.
> They conspired to become twilight
> & metaphysics, as five-eyed
> Fish with milky bones
> Flip-flopped in oily grass.[3]

I was aware of the hard splendor of this small, semirural city. I knew about cutting and hauling pulpwood because I had done it, as I attempt to describe in "Poetics of Paperwood":

> We pulled the crosscut
> Through the pine like a seesaw
> Of light across a map
> Of green fungus.
> We knew work
> Was rhythm,
> & so was love.[4]

Well, at least, I knew I loved nature—I sought so many hours in its solitude. It was the engine of my imagination. Maybe this is what Sophie Cabot Black projects in "Nature, Who Misunderstands" when she writes, "Nature loves and makes you love."[5] Perhaps we haven't learned nature's greatest instruction: we are connected. Everything's connected.

When it comes to wishing a "divine paradise" or an earthly Eden into existence, human history and imaginative literature are a web of contradictions and bloated wishful thinking, as when St. John of Damascus says, "In truth, it was a divine place and a worthy habitation for God in His image. And in it no brute beasts dwelt, but only man, the handiwork of God."[6] Following this line of thinking—does God invent God's own death through humans? Is commerce the death of God, since humans seem more deadly than so-called brute beasts?—a deacon might ask, "Doesn't God give people dominion over everything?"

Everything adds up to capital. Living from birth to death involves commerce. The poor, disenfranchised people grew up with couldn't afford fancy tombstones and divine-looking burial plots for their loved ones. Some seemed born diminished—cogwheels of flesh in a monumental system that stole and sold even the airspace overhead as if they were part of an experiment that had gone wrong.

Or, as I listen to Don Byron, an experimental jazz clarinetist, I read again from the notes that introduce his CD:

> And the album title "Tuskegee Experiments" refers to two experiments conducted on Black American men at the Tuskegee Institute.
>
> In 1932, the U.S. Public Health Service, with generous assistance from local Black medical professionals, initiated the longest human medical experiment in American history. More than half of the four hundred men chosen had syphilis, while the rest formed a non-syphilitic control group. None were informed of their condition, and they were observed for over 40 years, but NOT treated, just to document the physical effects of syphilis left unchecked. In the Tuskegee Aviation experiment, over-qualified and under-compensated Black men endured unnecessary indignities simply to "prove" they could be trusted to fly military aircraft.
>
> To me, these two experiments are metaphors for African-American life. In one, we see once again that black life is cheap, and that a person of color can be enlisted to work against the best interests of his group, for nothing more than a brief "vacation" from the pain of invisibility or the pressure of being seen as part of an "inferior" group.[7]

In essence, Byron points out that it takes a cultivated, sanctioned attitude to design a project that dehumanizes and kills people. It is the same attitude that prompted certain settlers to distribute smallpox-infected blankets to Native Americans. It is an attitude of war. A few decades ago, the same kind of stance advocated that the U.S. should bomb the Vietnamese into the Stone Age. A similar attitude drives the marketplace: the so-called Third

World countries often function as a dumping ground for numerous products that are harmful or banned in the U.S. and Europe. Some of the brainiest among us serve as reckless juggernauts geared up for another margin of profit, as if a capitalist must always sell his or her soul, that he or she isn't capable of compassion and morality. After all, by using simple deductive logic, since the Civil Rights Movement occurred less than four decades ago, with institutionalized injustices as a way of life, as law and custom, it should be no surprise that there are people in positions to whom minorities cannot entrust their lives and well-being. Hatemongers are still among us; some wield power and make decisions as to where harmful chemicals are stored and toxins dumped. All of this may be done with an almost unintentional malice—a way of thinking linked to the imperatives of an unjust history—without second thought.

We don't have to think of Nazi Germany to know that some humans have experimented on others for insane reasons. In my mind, all this connects. What about South Africa's Dr. Death: Dr. Wouter Basson? As I read "The Poison Keeper," this exposé grew even more frightening:

> We nonetheless know that, at Roodeplaat, Basson's scientists were working with anthrax, cholera, salmonella, botulinum, thallium, E. coli, ricin, organophosphates, necrotizing fasciitis, hepatitis A, and H.I.V., as well as nerve gases (Sarin, VX) and Ebola, Marburg, and Rift Valley hemorrhagic-fever viruses.[8]

Chet Raymo says in *Skeptics and True Believers,*

> Some of the criticism of science has come from inside the scientific community and is informed by a thorough understanding of scientific process. As such, it is especially welcome and useful. For example, Dai Rees, secretary and chief executive of Britain's Medical Research Council, writing in *Nature,* makes a startling claim: Science has "contributed massively to human misery" by undermining traditional stables societies without offering any compensating vision of what human life might be. It is time for scientists to pay their dues, he insists. . . . Scientists must accept responsibility for the application of their discoveries—for good or ill.[9]

Like a true American pragmatist, Raymo attempts to chastise Rees, and goes on to conclude,

> The conflict is not between science and society, as such, but between the two segments of society which I have labeled Skeptics and True Believers. . . .
>
> Certainly, it is not the sole responsibility of scientists to show the way to accommodation of empirical knowing and spiritual longing. This is a task that must occupy scientists, philosophers, theologians, poets, and artists.[10]

We must pay dues to ourselves and each other. Perhaps this is why Robert Oppenheimer questioned his heart and mind in the creation of the atomic bomb. I agree with Raymo's insistence that the larger intellectual community should pose questions and create a dialogue about ethics and technology.

It is scandalous, but the citizens have to create organizations to protect themselves from vicious practices by businesses going beyond the bounds of free enterprise. When we look at the preamble established by the delegates to the First National People of Color Environmental Leadership Summit held October 24–27, 1991, in Washington, D.C., the gravity of the problem is telescoped:

> We, the People of Color, gathered together at this multinational People of Color Environmental Leadership Summit, to begin to build a national and international movement of all peoples of color to fight the destruction and taking of our lands and communities, do hereby re-establish our spiritual interdependence to the sacredness of our Mother Earth; to respect and celebrate each of our cultures, languages and beliefs about the natural world and our roles in healing ourselves; to insure environmental justice; to promote economic alternatives which would contribute to the development of environmentally safe livelihoods; and, to secure our political, economic and cultural liberation that has been denied for over 500 years of colonization and oppression, resulting in the poisoning of our communities and land and the genocide of our peoples, do affirm and adopt these Principles of Environmental Justice.[11]

For me, the first and last of the seventeen principles under-
line the overall importance of the summit:

1. *Environmental Justice* affirms the sacredness of Mother Earth,
ecological unity and the interdependence of all species, and
the right to be free from ecological destruction.

17. *Environmental Justice* requires that we, as individuals, make
personal and consumer choices to consume as little of Moth-
er Earth's resources and to produce as little waste as possible;
and make the conscious decision to challenge and repriori-
tize our lifestyles to insure the health of the natural world for
present and future generations.[12]

When I was growing up in Bogalusa I could taste the chemi-
cals in the air. It was something we accepted as a way of life, but
it is also something one never forgets. I have tried to recapture
an image of my hometown in "Fog Galleon":

Horse-headed clouds, flags
& pennants tied to black
Smokestacks in swamp mist.
From the quick green calm
Some nocturnal bird calls
Ship ahoy, ship ahoy!
I press against the taxicab
Window. I'm back here, interfaced
With a dead phosphorescence;
The whole town smells
Like the world's oldest anger.
Scabrous residue hunkers down under
Sulfur & dioxide, waiting
For sunrise, like cargo
On a phantom ship outside Gaul.
Cool glass against my cheek
Pulls me from the black schooner
On a timeless sea—everything
Dwarfed beneath the papermill
Lights blinking behind the cloudy
Commerce of wheels, of chemicals
That turn workers into pulp

When they fall into vats
Of steamy serenity.[13]

One cannot miss Bogalusa's acid smell, but Louisiana State University Medical Center's Bogalusa Heart Study seems to suggest that overall health concerns are limited in a town that has been, for the most part, silent in its demands for industry to clean up toxic sites. Here are two troubling items in the Bogalusa Heart Study:

- Autopsy studies show lesions in the aorta, coronary vessels, and kidney relate strongly to clinical cardiovascular risk factors, clearly indicating atherosclerosis and hypertension begin in early life.
- Environmental factors are significant and influence dyslipidemia, hypertension, and obesity.[14]

The disparity in economics is at the center of the racial and cultural divide that influences environmental politics. Unfortunately, this is doubly true in places such as Magic City where the economic distance between black and white citizens is immense, and this chasm encapsulates and underscores history's imperative. For instance, present-day statistics (1990 census) verify the situation: the highest percentage of African American residents lives in north-central and southeast Bogalusa, with an annual income of $5,000 to $17,000; northeast Bogalusa has the highest white population, boasting an annual income of $40,000 to $51,000.

Even food products can be measured with dollar signs: poor communities usually pay more for their inferior food products. Also, it is more likely that chemical- and pesticide-free products are sold in high-income areas. An attitude permeates the relationships between merchants and certain communities, as is the case of American companies marketing questionable products in parts of the so-called Third World (tobacco products distributed in Asian countries and the former Soviet Union). Or we only have to look at the proliferation of billboards and other advertisements in minority communities for alcohol products—with the help of celebrity endorsements. Such things aren't accidental; everything is planned and perfected with the same attention as is given to any weapon. An argument can be made, as many have done previously, that the availability of drugs in certain communities is no accident; to the degree that it is planned, this offers yet another example of how communities are violated.

Our fears become our worst enemies. We need to trust each other. Otherwise, the mental health of the society wears to a fragile state. Distrust diminishes our emotional lives on a personal level and further deepens the chasm of misunderstandings among our communities.

I grew up in a climate of distrust. Blacks didn't trust whites, and it was sometimes difficult to disentangle truth from myth and folklore. For example, no black person could sell illegal, homemade liquor, but there was a white man who sold his brew to blacks. Not only did he sell "stoopdown" under the nose of the law, but it was rumored that he doctored his corn whiskey with pinches of Red Devil lye. We believed that some among us were slowly being poisoned. This is the kind of thing that fosters mistrust, when one doesn't know where the truth begins, similar to a *Sixty Minutes* scenario. Since many of the whites citizens of Bogalusa have kept blacks economically disadvantaged for generations, during the 1970s and 1980s, some blacks believed that well-off white families were redeeming food stamps at the local supermarkets, that some even paid their black domestics with government food stamps. "There's nothing a white man won't do to keep a black man down," they'd say. "If he can't legally keep you in chains, he'll connive some way to keep his foot on your neck."

This was the folk wisdom from my community. So, when it came to the politics of pollution and dumping of hazardous waste in the black community, many of us understood it was business as usual—a reflection of the national psyche. When we learned that white families were draining their toilets into Mitch Creek, we assumed that it was done only because blacks swam downstream on Sunday afternoons; we weren't allowed to swim at the Y.

"Bogalusa? It seems familiar. Where have I heard that name? It's on the tip of my tongue."

Oftentimes, that's the reaction I'd hear to the word "Bogalusa." Sometimes I'd add, "The 1960s?"

"Yeah that's right. The Civil Rights Movement."

Most times, I'd leave those words hanging in the air.

Louisiana has a bad record when it comes to civil rights and protection of the environment. But Jim Motavalli's article "Toxic Targets," in *E: The Environmental Magazine* suggests that there's a deeper problem. He writes:

> On September 10, 1997, Environmental Protection Agency (EPA) head Carol Browner issued a simple but unprecedented order: She disallowed the state of Louisiana's approval of an enormous polyvinyl chloride (PVC) plant in Convent, a small, mostly African-American community already inundated with 10 other toxic waste producers.[15]

One can see that a pattern had been already established, that the Japanese-owned Shintech plant must have been surprised by the federal government's directive. Motavalli states:

> The term "environmental racism" wasn't in the vernacular until it appeared in a 1987 study by the United Church of Christ's Commission for Racial Justice entitled *Toxic Wastes and Race in the United States*. Ben Chavis, the commission's director, stated simply that "race is a major factor related to the presence of hazardous wastes in residential communities throughout the United States," and a new field of study was born.
>
> The pillars that allow pervasive environmental racism are beginning to crumble. In April, the Nuclear Regulatory Commission denied a license to a uranium enrichment plant impacting the African-American communities for Forest Grove and Center Springs, Louisiana.[16]

I cannot stop thinking of these two lines from Antonio Machado's "He andado muchos caminos": "Mala gente que camina / y apestando la tierra" ("Evil men who walk around / polluting the earth").[17] Sooner or later, our cultivated attitudes force all of us to pay our dues. Agriculture Street Superfund site, where houses sit atop a polluted landfill. South Memphis's highly toxic

Defense Depot, suspected of causing a cancer cluster among the African American residents. But there are stories that garner even more news coverage, because the dream isn't half buried, a slow kill.

In *Dispatch*, Shirley Ayers writes:

> When a city's fire chief is the very first casualty of a hazardous materials explosion, you can be pretty sure that it is going to be a bad day. Such was the scenario in Bogalusa, Louisiana, last fall when a railroad tank car holding nitrogen tetroxide (rocket fuel) exploded at the Gaylord chemical plant, releasing a mushroom cloud of poisonous gas that sent thousands of people, including the Bogalusa Fire Chief, to an area hospital.[18]

When people from across the country called me and asked, "How's your family down in Bogalusa?" I said that I had my fingers crossed. I didn't say that my fingers have been crossed since the late 1960s, since the Civil Rights Movement, and since the 1970s, when I became aware that I had grown up across from a millpond filled with chemicals that "seasoned" logs.

I have never been sentimental about nature. I have accepted it in the same way as these lines by Emily Dickinson:

> A Bird came down the Walk—
> He did not know I saw—
> He bit an Angleworm in halves
> And ate the fellow, raw,
>
> And then he drank a Dew
> From a convenient Grass—
> And then hopped sidewise to the Wall
> To let a Beetle pass—[19]

Nature teaches us how to see ourselves within its greater domain. We see our own reflections in every ritual, and we cannot wound Mother Nature without wounding ourselves. She isn't a pushover.

94

Notes

1. Geoffrey C. Ward, *The West: An Illustrated History* (Boston: Little Brown, 1996), 30.

2. Yusef Komunyakaa, "Looking for Choctaw," in *Magic City* (Middletown, Conn.: Wesleyan University Press, 1992), 25.

3. Komunyakaa, "Mill Pond," in *Magic City*, 17.

4. Komunyakaa, "Poetics of Paperwood," in *Magic City*, 50.

5. Sophie Cabot Black, "Nature, Who Misunderstands," in *The Misunderstanding of Nature* (Saint Paul: Graywolf, 1994), 54.

6. Saint John of Damascus, *Writings*, trans. Frederic H. Chase Jr. (New York: Fathers of the Church, 1958), 230.

7. Don Byron, introductory notes for Don Byron, *Tuskegee Experiments*, WEA/Atlantic/Nonesuch, 1992, compact disc.

8. William Finnegan, "The Poison Keeper," *New Yorker*, January 15, 2001, 62.

9. Chet Raymo, *Skeptics and True Believers* (New York: Walker, 1998), 173–74.

10. Raymo, *Skeptics and True Believers*, 177–78.

11. Washington Office of Environmental Justice, "Principles of Environmental Justice" (Washington, D.C., October 1991).

12. "Principles of Environmental Justice."

13. Komunyakaa, "Fog Galleon," in *Neon Vernacular* (Middletown, Conn.: Wesleyan University Press, 1993), 3.

14. Bogalusa Heart Study, *American Journal of Medical Sciences* (Supplements) (December 1995): 310.

15. Jim Motavalli, "Toxic Targets," *E: The Environmental Magazine*, July–August 1998.

16. Motavalli, "Toxic Targets."

17. Antonio Machado, "He andado muchos caminos," in *Times Alone: Selected Poems of Antonio Machado*, trans. Robert Bly (Middletown, Conn.: Wesleyan University Press, 1983), 16–17.

18. Shirley Ayers, *Dispatch* 7, no. 1 (Spring 1996).

19. Emily Dickinson, "A Bird came down the Walk," in *The Complete Poems of Emily Dickinson*, ed. Thomas H. Johnson (Boston: Little, Brown, 1960), 156.

The Method of Ai

Infect your partner! Infect the person you are concentrating on! Insinuate yourself into his very soul, and you will find yourself the more infected for doing so. And if you are infected everyone else will be even more infected.
—Konstantin Stanislavski

I remember sitting in that Greystone apartment in Colorado Springs, gazing out over Monument Park, Pikes Peak looming there, as I turned from Ai on the cover of the *American Poetry Review* (July–August 1973, vol. 2, no. 4), back to the poems printed in those pages, poems that would appear in her first book, *Cruelty*. Ai's poetry found me when I was repeatedly reading Ted Hughes's *Crow*, momentarily taken by the poetic strangeness of this mythic bird; but her raw imagery and the stripped-down music of her voice seemed even stranger, more foreboding. Ai's poems are grounded in this world—naturally telluric—even when her characters are almost totemic. And back then her poems seemed like scenes from nightmarish movies imprinted on the eyeball, yet the images were revealed so matter-of-factly, so damn casually. Upon reading a poem or two, I'd flip back to the *APR* cover and take another look at Ai. From the onset, she knew how to infect her reader through insinuation. There was an air of innocence or coquettishness in her, and this seemed incongruous to the bold, raw, sensuous, bloody imagery entering my psyche that summer afternoon.

I searched literary magazines for other poems by Ai. She was born Florence Anthony, and I learned that Ai means "love"

Introduction to *The Collected Poems of Ai* (New York: Norton, 2013).

in Japanese. Each monologue I discovered made me feel that her speakers were tinged with an unusual, rural reality. They haunted me, and never again would I think of poetry quite the same way.

When *Cruelty* was published 1973, I read the collection repeatedly, transported by the mystery in the poems, and by the politics of gender on almost every page. The way the first poem in the collection, "Twenty-Year Marriage," opens is a clue to this poet's psychology: "You keep me waiting in a truck / with its one good wheel stuck in a ditch, / while you piss against the south side of a tree. / Hurry. I've got nothing on under my skirt tonight." The speaker's insinuation is calculated. The intentional, invented tension breathes on the page. She has our attention. But Ai knows—like any great actor—that language and pace are also crucial. Sometimes a poem may seem like personalized folklore, a feeling culled from the imagination. The characters hurt each other out of a fear of being hurt, and often they are doubly hurt. Do we believe her characters because they seem to evolve from some unchartered place beyond us but also inside us? They are of the soil, as if they've always been here; but they also reside on borders—spiritually, psychologically, existentially, and emotionally—as if only half-initiated into the muscular terror of ordinary lives. All the contradictions of so-called democracy live in her speakers. Most of the characters in Ai's poetry are distinctly rural, charged in mind and belly with folkloric signification, always one step or one trope from homespun violence and blasphemy.

What first deeply touched me in *Cruelty* is this: Ai's images felt as if I'd heard, seen, and felt them before, resonating from some deep, unsayable place—something begging from long ago to be put into words—tinctured by an unknown folklore translated from some prelanguage of knowing or dreaming with one's eyes open. Let's look at the third stanza of "Warrior":

> When you are standing in the river,
> you grab a fish,
> tear its flesh with your teeth, and hold it,
> until the bones in your fingers buck up
> and fly about you like moth.

Is the warrior African, Native American, an unnamed aboriginal, or some mythical citizen of an unknown place, from the misty mountains of the imagination?

We believe Ai's various speakers even when we don't wish to. The speaker in "The Rivals" is a perfect example of such an aversion, highlighted by the poem's ending: "Just try it. Fall! I don't give a damn. / You're hurting, so am I, / but I'm strong enough to let you cry alone." If we believe this speaker, do we also possess a similar capacity for malice? In a sense, we enter into a dialogue with each character that she's created; and we not only argue for our own humanity but also for the speaker's. Such a discourse through the unsaid does the job of poetry. Silence, pace, rhythm, the whole tonal shape of a poem is important to Ai.

The power in her poetry isn't rancor, but the terrifying beauty of pure candor. The second stanza from the last poem in *Cruelty*, "New Crops for a Free Man," underscores Ai's ability to create characters that challenge us morally:

Behind me, another fire, my woman,
under sheets wrinkled and stiff from heat and sweat,
throws them back and rises.
She cracks her knuckles, leans from the window and yells,
but I keep my head turned toward the thing I understand.
She's hot from a match I never lit
and strokes her breasts, cone-shaped candles,
whose wicks, her nipples, aflame, burn holes in her hands,
    in me.

Ai's characters uncover their sense of self as they speak, baring themselves physically, psychologically, and spiritually, and the music of telling seems to bring them to the cusp of being transformed. Each poem is a confession.

Could she be for real? Even if she hadn't personally experienced directly what she conveyed in her poetry, image after image, character by character, I believed and felt every word on the page. I thought I knew the violence and terror humans perfected and exacted on each other, but reading Ai's poems that afternoon so long ago, I felt that I had only tiptoed to the perimeter of a terror Ai depicted with such graphic ease. Many of her most memorable characters exist in the heart of an American frontier situated in a static passage of time that seems slanted. And, thus, she knew how to be in this world by existing out of this world through a supreme candor and honed toughness that approach transcendence.

Six years later I cracked the spine of Ai's second collection of poems, *Killing Floor*, and I encountered the same provocative passion as in *Cruelty*; I already knew she was indeed singing a deep, instinctual blues, but not because the book's title made me think of Skip James. She could carry her own tune. It wasn't just a tune plucked on the gutstring that made one's teeth chatter; her blues didn't rise out of fear or the rage of unrequited love, but by brushing up against more expansive moments of universal truths. Ai's title poem, "Killing Floor," isn't located in the Mississippi Delta or the Chicago stockyards, but in an extended nightmare in Russia (1927) and Mexico (1940), and it ends with the speaker facing his wife's mirror in a dream as a cross-dresser, saying:

> I lean forward and see Jacques's reflection.
> I half-turn, smile, then turn back to the mirror.
>> He moves from the doorway,
>> lifts the pickax
>> and strikes the top of my head.
>> My brain splits.
>> The pickax keeps going
>> and when it hits the tile floor,
>> it flies from his hands,
>> a black dove on whose back I ride,
>> two men, one cursing, the other blessing all things:
>> *Lev Davidovich Bronstein,*
>> *I step from Jordan without you.*

Some poems in *Killing Floor* are for Yukio Mishima, Yasunari Kawabata, Marilyn Monroe, Ira Hayes, and the poet even dedicates "Pentecost"—a poem with Emiliano Zapata at its center— to herself, ending with these two lines: "If you suffer in the grave, / You can kill from it." A frontier philosophy seems to touch all sides and angles of the poet's vision.

For Ai, the page was always her stage, and the voices in her poems were hers and they weren't hers. She mastered the shape-shifter's voice; not as a form of ventriloquism, but through a unique personification, where the most unspeakable acts still speak to us, and where we are frightened by our own most secret thoughts and daydreams through acts of imaginative participation. She created characters that earned our attention. The voices were mainly rural, but also tonally antipastoral; her characters are at home in the silence of the landscape, but always have something to say about life and death matters. We believe Ai's voice because it transports us to a place shaped by the old brain, that terrain located in the right hemisphere.

There are battles beyond the mind and flesh, yet purely of the flesh. Ai's images refuse to let us off the hook; she keeps us fully situated in the dynamics of modern life, holding a magnifying glass up to our most wounded moments, as she does so expertly in "The Kid" (he's not Billy the Kid—our antihero of the Wild West—but just as vicious); after the speaker kills his father, mother, sister, and two horses, the poem ends with these lines:

Yeah. I'm Jack, Hogarth's son.
I'm nimble, I'm quick.
In the house, I put on the old man's best suit
and his patent leather shoes.
I pack my mother's satin nightgown.
and my sister's doll in the suitcase.
Then I go outside and cross the fields to the highway.
I'm fourteen. I'm a wind from nowhere.
I can break your heart.

This character comes out of the brutal silence of America. The word *your* in the last line makes us the speaker's accomplice.

I think it was Stanislavski who said, "If an actor thinks he is the character, the director should fire him." In many ways, Ai is a proxy actor in the various characters she creates through the agency of the monologue, but she also remains the conjurer, the maker of the most tantalizing imagery in American poetry. Her work has always had an audience. The voices she creates are of her, and also outside of her. Though she once created a voice for Jimmy Hoffa that she'd read in a few times, Ai was always the poet, first and most importantly.

Recently, as I reread Adrienne Rich's smart, compact, little book, *Poetry & Commitment*, I thought of Ai, especially in the following paragraph: "If to 'aestheticize' is to glide across brutality and cruelty, treat them merely as dramatic occasions for the artist rather than structures of power to be revealed and dismantled—much hangs on the words 'merely' and 'rather than.' Opportunism isn't the same as committed attention. But we can also define the 'aesthetic' not as a privileged and sequestered rendering of human suffering, but as news of an awareness, a resistance, that totalizing systems want to quell: art reaching into us for what's still passionate, still unintimidated, still unquenched." Ai's *news of an awareness* is what corners the reader. She lets her characters betray themselves by what they say and don't say—imagistic and brutally honest.

Ai was a believer, in the old-fashioned sense of good and evil, and this seems to have directed the unmitigated passion in her poems. One only has to look at the titles of her eight collections to glimpse the moral equation of Ai's work: *Cruelty, Killing Floor, Sin, Fate, Greed, Vice: New and Selected Poems, Dread,* and *No Surrender.* Some of her poems at times seem like excerpted passages or facsimiles gleaned from the book of Revelation. Hidden in the praises are curses—from the mouths of seers, soothsayers, and shape-shifting prophets posing as everyday citizens. She also gives us the voices of J. Edgar Hoover, James Dean, Jack Ruby, Lenny Bruce, General George Armstrong Custer, Jimmy Hoffa, Walt Whitman, Richard Nixon, Joe McCarthy, The Good Shepherd, etc. And some of the voices let us in on secretive thoughts, on moments that betray the speaker and the listener (reader). But some of the most political moments are in the unsaid. Ai mastered signification because she knew our history, what we are truly made of.

The complexity of her own lineage perhaps shaped her outlook—privately and publicly—on the reality of American culture. She embodied both conflict and harmony as conveyed in the title of her 1978 essay "On Being 1/2 Japanese, 1/8 Choctaw, 1/4 Black, and 1/16 Irish" (*New York Times,* March 27, 2010). In an interview for *Standards* (Spring–Summer 2001), it becomes clear that race and skin color formed the psychological axis of her most intimate feelings and thoughts. Speaking about her unpublished novel, she says, "The novel is called *Black Blood*, and it turns on how much Black blood these people have, in the novel. [laughs] So how did they get mixed? By having sex with somebody in another race; that's how! But I think my memoir is really gonna be good. [laughs] If she ever finishes her research!" Ai seems taunted and haunted by blackness in her life and her work. Elsewhere in that same interview, she says, "I told one reporter that night, 'Well, score one for mixed race!'"

"Passing Through," the last poem in *Vice* (which won the 1999 National Book Award), shows Ai overtly addressing race and skin color. The monologue opens with these lines:

"Earth is the birth of the blues," sang Yellow Bertha,
as she chopped cotton beside Mama Rose.
It was hot as any other summer day,
when she decided to run away.
Folks say she made a fortune
running a whorehouse in New Orleans,
but others say she's buried somewhere out west,
her grave unmarked,
though you can find it in the dark
by the scent of jasmine and mint,
but I'm getting ahead of myself.

The story the poet gives us is woven from blues shaped out of American history. The voice is so clear and layered that it seems the story has been lived. And we believe these lines when the poem ends, after the twists and turns of a rueful, relentless life:

When I got off the bus,
a hush fell over the people waiting there.
I was as white as my mother,
but my eyes were gray, not green.
I had hair down to my waist and braids so thick
they weighed me down.
Mother said, my father was a white musician
from another town,
who found out her secret
and left her and me to keep it.
Mama Rose knew me, though, blind as she was.

"What color are you, gal?" She asked
and I told her, "I'm as black as last night."
That's how I passed, without asking permission.

This moment of passing in reverse says much about the poet's sense of politics and history.

Ai spent her last years teaching creative writing and literature, and assaying her personal history, searching out her Native American roots. *No Surrender*, Ai's last collection of poetry, takes on a different voice, one that's determined to create an echo of the past that commemorates the indigenous peoples. She says, "This book is dedicated to Northern Cheyenne chief and tribal historian John Sipes."

In the end, Ai becomes a pronoun, but remains a one-of-a-kind voice that refuses to plead for mercy. In the last section of "The Cancer Chronicles" she says, "Her thoughts clattering around in her head like marbles, / Their sound echoing down the long road of suffering / She must have chosen, / Although she couldn't remember doing so." The slanted directness in this poem is vintage Ai. And, of course, this posture of resistance and acceptance echoes through everything she's written. Ai is still a hard act to follow, and her illuminating poems accentuate her true identity and presence. She has created a body of work that endures, that questions who we are and what borders we cross.

I believe Ai will continue to engage readers who are brave enough to face her vision. Her "method" was being alive. Giving us numerous hints along the way, she instinctively captured the nature of being in this world. She gave us clues to her spirit—as a human, as a poet, as a woman—sometimes with only a few lines. Ai, the method actor-poet, who superbly insinuated through a passionate language of the frontier, may find a home with actors who are searching for unique monologues to hone their voices with truth solid as whetstone. I can still see Ai stepping from the page to the stage. There's no voice like hers in American poetry; her unusual characters bear multiple truths.

II

Interviews

Collaboration and the Wishbone

Interview by Michael Collins

1. On Collaboration

MICHAEL COLLINS: You have been involved in many collaborations.
You have collaborated with musicians and with visual artists.
The results have included stage and radio performances and
CDs. In general, what attracts you to collaborations with artists
working in different media?

YUSEF KOMUNYAKAA: The ideal collaboration is a dialogue and
negotiation. Of course, one has to carefully select his or her
partner in crime; one has to select someone whose sense of
aesthetics is interwoven into the character of each endeavor.
But also, most importantly, someone who can grow with you,
so that the two of you are like two or more dancers entangled
in a tango of the heart and brain. However, the moves are not
agreed upon in advance; the collaborators must be able to
negotiate that sway of the imagination. That is what interests
me the most; how one's vision expands into a collaborative
action. Ideas speak to each other; they sing and fight together
until they make each other whole.

Natural or unnatural, they belong together, and they create
a fluid insinuation, a tension that speaks to us. Life itself is such
a dialogue.

Of course, each collaboration is different. Like friends or
lovers, each has wandered into my life uniquely, each bearing
inherent differences and similarities. *Testimony* came to me
out of nowhere, after I presented a reading of my poetry on
radio in Sydney at the Australian Broadcasting Corporation.
Christopher Williams, a radio producer there, asked me

From *Callaloo* 28, no. 3 (2005).

107

in 1995, "Do you think you can write a libretto on jazz for radio?" There was an immense moment of silence. Finally, I said yes. But what would the libretto address? Within the hour, I committed myself to writing a libretto on the infamous Charlie Parker. I would work with a wonderful saxophonist and composer, Sandy Evans, whom I heard playing at local gigs around Sydney. At the time, I think, she was performing and traveling with three of her ensembles, each configured to produce a unique sound. I knew she would write some striking music. But how could I shape Parker's life into a libretto? Why had I said yes? Instead of plunging into *Testimony*, I began to pen some lyrics for an American jazz singer, Pamela Knowles, which grew into the CD *Thirteen Kinds of Desire*. When I returned to Bloomington to teach at Indiana University, *Testimony* was still on hold.

How could an opera assume the shape of Parker's chaotic life?

In thoughtful desperation, I wrote a series of poems that possess an illusion of symmetry. Christopher said, "I thought we agreed on a libretto?" But he forwarded the series of linked poems to Sandy Evans and she said, "Thank God. This is what I'd been hoping for." It seems that the words had given her the space in which to write her music. *Testimony* was broadcast in 1999 on ABC Classic FM. This radio airing created a buzz about it in Sydney that did not go away until, finally, the official world premier of this performance piece was sponsored by the Sydney Opera House and Sydney Festival in association with the Melbourne Festival. The premiere itself took place in early 2002 and featured the Australian Art Orchestra.

Meanwhile, in 2000, Pamela Knowles had recorded and produced *Thirteen Kinds of Desire*, and the CD had gone on to generate something of an underground following.

With me, there's always a beckoning, and if I keep my heart and mind open, as I suppose is true with all of us, one thing leads to another. For instance, after I presented an April 1998 reading at the George Moses Horton Society Conference, hosted by the University of North Carolina, Chapel Hill, the marvelous composer T. J. Anderson walked up and introduced himself. In retrospect, it seems I immediately found myself nodding my head and saying yes to his wonderful idea about writing a libretto based on a slave named Arthur who was born in 1747 and hanged in 1768. He had refined himself, saying,

"I'm almost free," and it was this trope that excited me. I had to say yes to T. J., to Arthur, and also to myself. Tim Breen, a historian at Northwestern University, had written a monograph on Arthur; otherwise, the main character in this new opera would never have existed. I began to assemble an emotional landscape for Arthur, after attempting to locate the language that would best serve this venture, and then *Slip Knot* began to slowly take shape. From the onset, I worked very closely with Rhoda Levine, a prominent director who has overseen approximately three hundred operas, and, of course, T. J., a senior American composer who's very inventive and structured. Now I felt like I was on solid footing. We traded ideas, and I began to develop an emotional terrain where Arthur could dream, live, and die. I worked very hard on *Slip Knot*, going back to the drawing board time and time again, searching for clarity and dramatic tension, and a staged workshop of this operatic work-in-progress was presented by the Northwestern University School of Music on April 26, 2003.

Another of my successful collaborations can be traced back to 1990, when I and five other American veterans were invited by the William Joiner Center (the Institute for the Study of War and Social Consequence) in Boston at UMass to return to Vietnam to meet with members of the Vietnamese Writers' Union. I immediately said yes. But, flying out of Indianapolis, my plane was delayed and I missed my connection with the other American vets headed to Southeast Asia. Delayed four times, I wondered if some greater power was intervening on my behalf; however, two days behind schedule, I was determined to make the trip to join my fellow veterans, who by now were waiting in Bangkok and making bets that I would turn around and head back to Indiana.

Somehow they had been able to monitor my trip. Finally, I arrived in Bangkok, with my baggage lost, and was taken (a bit later) to a place called the Black and White Club, located in the hotel where we were hosted.

It was there that I encountered three dark-skinned Thai waitresses dolled-up in gowns, kneeling before their male clientele. Then to my surprise they strolled over to three microphones and began to lip-sync a song by The Supremes. I excused myself from the guys and went upstairs to my room, feeling disgusted and confused, wondering if my bags would arrive before we took off for Vietnam the next morning, and somehow unnerved by the whole sex-trade scene in Bangkok. I filed away my observations and fell asleep.

Eight years later, a friend, Radiclani Clytus, gave me a copy of an article from a popular magazine—I think it was the British edition of *Esquire*—that highlighted the problem of some Western men visiting Bangkok on plastic money and killing themselves later on because of their inability to disengage from this illusion of paradise. So a couple years passed before I found myself sitting in a café in Chicago telling the musician Susie Ibarra about my idea for a performance piece called *Saturnalia*. Susie kept nodding her head yes, and before we knew it, we had agreed to collaborate. I wrote a libretto and Susie wrote a score that is classical and innovative. *Saturnalia* has since been workshopped at three locations: Passage Theatre in Trenton, New Jersey; Union College in Schenectady, New York; and The Kitchen in New York City. The whole experience confirms my sense that seemingly different worlds occupy the same frame, and that simultaneity is a great place for collaborations to begin.

Another piece with a long gestation period was *Ish-scoodah*, which came after *Saturnalia*, but probably began over a decade earlier when I first saw images of Edmonia Lewis's sculpture in *A History of African-American Artists*, edited by Romare Bearden and Harry Henderson. I knew I wanted to write something on her; and, finally, I wrote a long poem, "Hagar's Daughter," about this woman of Mississauga and African American ancestry who attended Oberlin College and later exiled herself in Italy. One day, I found myself talking to Aleta Hayes, who taught dance at Princeton, about Edmonia Lewis, and then I knew that I wanted to write a performance piece for Aleta. She possesses a great presence on stage, a full voice. Also, William Banfield's music kept playing itself in my head until I called him and asked if he'd consider composing for *Ish-scoodah*. He said yes, and our trio went to work with support from Toni Morrison's Atelier at Princeton University. We wrote this performance piece during the course of the term and taught students, who also wrote and prepared their own performance pieces to be staged along with ours at the end of the semester. At this moment, I hope to return to *Ish-scoodah* and refine it before the year ends.

A piece whose development overlapped *Saturnalia* and *Ish-Scoodah*'s began, in effect, in 1998, when I read a *New York*

Times article by Ann Waldman entitled "A Pianists' Final Piece: DeWitt's Descent." I remember tearing out pages of the paper and folding them inside a book, *The Art of Romare Bearden*. The article opened with "He had marvelous hands, magical hands. DeWitt White grew up poor in a Bronx neighborhood where piano lessons, not to mention pianos, were in short supply. But at 12, he discovered classical music and a prodigious talent for playing it." I read about his mother dying of AIDS, his homelessness, his drug use and involvement in the drug trade, his violence, and his death at seventeen on a desolate Staten Island street.

Then I came to the paragraph that cut into my heart: "DeWitt's absorption was total. He 'borrowed' bags of music from the Lincoln Center library. He composed, imitating Beethoven and Bach; he would improvise on the piano, then write in pen, scratching out changes like Beethoven, whom he worshipped. He identified with the strength and defiance embodied in his music. He said he was Beethoven reincarnated." I knew then that I'd write something about this remarkable young black man who was cut down so early. I told T. J. about DeWitt, and we began to meditate on *The Reincarnated Beethoven*. He talked to the director of the Harlem Boys Choir, and finally one day I sat down and wrote act 1 and sent it to T. J., and he seemed happy that we were breaching this important story. But I didn't want this piece to be melodramatic or sentimental in any way. Very slowly act 2 began to solidify in my mind, but without words on paper.

And then another collaboration, *Wakonda's Dream*, rode in. Hal France, who was the conductor of Opera Omaha at that time, left a message on my answering machine to call him about a project. I hesitated. Days passed. Then finally I dialed his number and found out that Opera Omaha was interested in me writing a libretto on the trial of Chief Standing Bear. Until 1876, Native Americans couldn't appear in court or own land because they weren't considered human beings. Standing Bear had to prove that he was a human being to appear in his own defense, and of course that paradox immediately interested me. Anthony Davis and Rhoda Levine were my collaborators, my coconspirators. Again, I had to find the dramatic plot and the language. I knew that I didn't desire a step-by-step depiction of Standing Bear's biography. We had to find a way of centering Standing Bear inside a contemporary narrative. Early on, the

111

three of us were invited to visit Omaha and attend a few Ponca rituals, to speak to members of the Ponca tribe and establish a dialogue, but only Anthony could attend at the time. He came to our next meeting with a story about a small boy who was a seer, someone who could see into the past and future. And our question was this: How does such an individual fit into present-day society? This conceit is at the heart of *Wakonda's Dream*.

As I've said before, topics for collaborations tend to seek me out. Even before *Wakonda's Dream* was finished, seemingly without a beat, Chad Gracia was talking to me about adapting *Gilgamesh* for the stage. Actually, at times I found myself working on *Wakonda's Dream* and *Gilgamesh* simultaneously. And now, after completing those two pieces, I'm ready to return to *The Reincarnated Beethoven* and finalize it.

MC: In retrospect, how do you see your collaboration with Dennis Gonzalez and the CD that resulted from that collaboration? And what are your memories of the performance with Gonzalez?

YK: I had the freedom of suggesting to Dennis members for this unique ensemble. I wanted a blues feel, but also something different. I could hear in my head the instruments playing off each other to create a provocative sound. Each musician is a master, and Dennis is the voyage's sexton. At the rehearsal in Chicago, there were some tense moments because of the egos on stage. Of course, I began to question my wisdom concerning this collaboration. But then the musicians began to listen to each other, to add their own colors to the canvas, and I knew we had something different from any time where poetry and music had come together to speak to each other. We weren't there to be unique or different: I hope we were there to challenge our hearts and minds, to try and make something whole from parts that belong together. Music and words were part of the same dialogue, the same narrative.

MC: You and the band enter into a tremendous groove on "Jasmine." Did you feel at the time that something magical was happening?

YK: By the time we worked out way into "Jasmine," I think we knew something special was happening between us. Maybe we didn't want to show naked feeling on stage, still halfway inside our armor, but at that moment we let the music and the words live inside the space we created for them. We listened to each other. I wasn't fully aware of how well we'd gotten into the groove till

I head the recording. Nothing technical, just the raw stuff art is made of: the only sample we had were each other and that was enough to make "Jasmine" almost magical.

MC: How would you compare the work you did with Gonzalez to the work you did with John Tchicai?

YK: Both have a thread of the blues woven through them. But there seems to be more bop in "Love Notes from the Madhouse," by John Tchicai's ensemble. John and I came together to record the first CD for the record company 8th Harmonic Breakdown.

Plus, their backgrounds in music are different. I wanted the contrast because I'm interested in the quality of surprise in each collaboration. Perhaps that is why rap and hip-hop don't interest me. No, I don't crave the same beat. In an ideal collaboration, all the players are willing to follow each other into a tonal inner sanctum, and John's path to that place is slightly different than Dennis's.

MC: Who thought of the title "Love Notes from the Madhouse"?

YK: Both titles were decided by the founder and producer of 8th Harmonic Breakdown, Tony Getsug.

MC: Are the poems you produce when collaborating with a visual artist different from the poetry you produce when collaborating with musicians, or when you collaborate on projects like your current one, the play *Gilgamesh*?

YK: Each collaboration is different. Matter of fact, each poem is different. Of course, poetry always begs connective tissue, especially since each reader or listener is a collaborator because he or she helps render the poem's meaning. Language is music, so when poetry embraces the sounds made by instruments, the two shouldn't collide; they should work together to produce a whole sound if the musicians are listening to the words, and vice versa. I'm not talking about harmony; I'm thinking about lyrical discord that creates tension and thought. This happens when two or more voices are reaching for a resounding *yes*. And, sometimes the yes comes to us in their ways. Take *Gilgamesh*. I had read parts of that Sumerian epic years ago, and remembered how the two central characters, Gilgamesh and Enkidu, were linked through grief. When Chad Gracia approached me about writing a *Gilgamesh* for the stage, I didn't readily embrace this daunting task. But there was something in Chad that I trusted. I had never written a full-length dramatic piece, but I knew this man would usher such an effort to a fruitful conclusion. I said yes to the idea of *Gilgamesh*, and then I went to work to find the appropriate language. It had to sound different from anything that I'd written and yet possess the essence of my aesthetics. Often, Chad was the engine behind this piece, asking all the right questions and making sure that I kept abreast of the tone and dramatic intent: "Suppose this word was changed? Suppose this passage was shifted up here for dramatic effect?" This collaboration was a dare, a challenge. Why not start at the beginning of our literature? I knew this story needed poetry as its emotional spine, but it had to linger slightly beneath the skin of the piece.

MC: Before we leave the subject, can you comment on your collaboration with the visual artist Rachel Bliss? For instance, what did the two of you see in each other's work that made a collaboration seem possible and desirable, and did your collaboration develop as a call and response?

YK: I saw images from Rachel Bliss's work before I met her, in a catalog entitled *A State of Bliss*, curated by Dr. James Dickinson at the Rider University Gallery. I was struck by the originality in her work. Also, I kept returning to the following paragraph in the catalog:

Many small works depict strange, demented and surreal animals. However, to interpret the exclusively in a traditional manner, as evidence of an imaginary world of dreams and fantasy would be a mistake, for an intense realism informs Bliss's depiction of this menagerie. As Bliss recalls, a neighbor, Farmer Jim, began collecting exotic birds and animals, keeping them in an alley that connected with Bliss's house. For a while, the collection made for an unbelievable sight, contradicting the grimness of surrounding conditions: "Here were these animals—which at the beginning were so wonderful and totally out of place—in the midst of drunks smashing bottles against factories the local vandals were busy burning down, the screams of female prostitutes being beaten up by men under the El, loud car stereos, which set off car alarms all down our street, empty crack vials, dirty needles and used condoms that I swept up every morning off my front door step." The family enjoyed "waking up to the animals . . . the rooster cock-a-doodle-dooing, the pigs oinking, and the huge peacock staring at us curiously through our bathroom window." But neglect and abuse made it necessary to call in the

S.P.C.A. to rescue the surviving animals. Thus the surreal imagery of the animal paintings records a real situation. As Bliss puts it: "I use fantastic color to remember the beauty of the animals but if they also look sad and somewhat demented it's because they were."

Who was this woman, this painter, and why did I feel somehow connected to her vision? *Night Animals* has been a recurring title in my head for more than ten years, long before I saw an image by Rachel. I knew I wanted to write poems about nocturnal creatures, animals and human beings. So, in this sense, we were already walking on a similar landscape before our paths crossed.

At times, the realization that we have been on the same page in so many ways is daunting. Her background dovetails with mine, linking in some strange fashion her Rochester, New York, with my Bogalusa, Louisiana. We both love jazz, and the music has instructed us in the pursuit of our work. And it didn't seem extreme to ask her to consider painting twelve portraits of jazz musicians, titled *Madrigals*. In other words, we have chosen to collaborate on topics of mutual interest.

Most of Rachel's works are portraits, which seem to me the most difficult, time-consuming avenues or approaches in creating visual art. Faces demand differences, even if they are only slightly varied, such as identical twins. Each portrait is a concise study—an active meditation and/or approximation. Rachel is a natural surrealist. Authentic surprise is interfused into the character of each piece—a personality. It seems that her highly developed graphic skills give her the ability of a gifted psychologist who can capture a mental landscape through visual depiction: the mind made flesh through paint and texture. Some of her most provocative pieces appear as chimeras that have wandered out of a state of mind. But because of her technique and process, nothing is an accident. Everything's deliberate, and intensively deliberated on. Intention bends to her control; a tough beauty emerges from the thoughtful hues. In this sense, Rachel's ability to find beauty and celebrate it is what drew me to her work. For her, destiny is often a reality: the crippled songbird lands on her shoulder because she has the heart to help it. If one detects or glimpses violence in a piece of hers, it isn't accidental or ornamental: it underlines the state of affairs in America—personal and public, urban and rural. Together, as collaborators, we are interested in creating dialogue.

MC: You told Toi Derricotte that you tend to work on, I believe, if I remember correctly, two projects at once. What are some of the pairs of books you have worked on? Do the pairs have antiphonal relationships to each other?

YK: Actually, I'm usually pursuing three collections simultaneously. In the summer of 1981, I returned to Bogalusa to live with my grandmother, and I found myself working on *Copacetic*, *Magic City*, and *I Apologize for the Eyes in My Head*. One can see parallels or hear antiphonal echoes in the first two, but some of those poems in *I Apologize* began when I was in graduate school at UC Irvine, and they seem to have come from a different zone. I completed *Copacetic* and *I Apologize for the Eyes in My Head*, but I had to put *Magic City* aside, and it was only after writing *Dien Cai Dau* that I could return to this collection about my childhood and hometown.

After my new and selected poems, *Neon Vernacular*, was published, I began working on *Thieves of Paradise*, *The Chameleon Couch*, *Talking Dirty to the Gods*, and *The Wishbone Trilogy*. Sometimes a collection seems to demand its own completion. Of course, *Thieves*, *Talking Dirty*, and *Taboo* (part 1 of *The Wishbone Trilogy*) have appeared, but the in-progress collection that most parallels *Thieves* is *The Chameleon Couch*, which has assumed its own pace. Plus, *The Autobiography of My Alter Ego*, a monologue spoken by a white Vietnam veteran, began to take over my psyche. So all these ideas and projects occur side by side. And I think it is tone and subject matter that assure a single collection's integrity and continuity. This working method helps me keep surprising myself. I've been thinking about writing a novel, *Confessions of the Minotaur*, but I know that other projects would have to be put on hold.

2. On *Taboo* and Other Subjects

MC: You use a stepped, mostly three-beat tercet form for the poems in *Taboo: The Wishbone Trilogy, Part One*. Commenting in *Blue Notes* on the very similar form of your poem "Trueblood's Blues" (which is actually included in *Taboo*), you write that you discovered that the form "could incorporate information that enhances the text without undermining the poem's fluidity and music." Are the reasons for using the form the same in *The*

Wishbone Trilogy as a whole, or is there an additional symbolic significance? Is the form itself a kind of wishbone?

YK: I adapted the tercet form in *The Wishbone Trilogy* for basically the same reason as that in "Trueblood's Blues," discussed in *Blue Notes*. Also, I am attracted to the shape of each poem, how each one enhances the book's visual flow—a falling shape—a surge and descending. Of course, I still wish for the text's fluidity and the emergence of music alongside meaning.

MC: In "Lingo," the opening poem in *Taboo*, you take up a tremendous subject—a subject that has long been present in your work, but which is very explicit here—the subject of the way language prefigures, prefixes—puts the fix in, so to speak— on thought, and therefore, to some extent, on action and even on history. One of my favorite passages in the poem reads as follows:

> There's a reason why the dead
>   may talk through a medium
>
> about how Aryans drove cattle
>   along the seven rivers & left
>   dark-skinned Dravidians
>
> with tongues cut out, sugarcane
>   fields ablaze, & the holy air
>   smelling of ghee and soma.
>
> These ghosts know the power
>   of suggestion is more than body
>   language: white list, black
>
> sheep, white tie, black market.
>   Fear climbs the tribal brainstem
>   or wills itself up an apple tree,
>
> hiding from the dream animal
>   inside. The serpent speaks
>   like a Lacan signifier,
>
> posing as a born-again agrarian
>   who loves computer terminals
>   better than cotton blossoms . . .

Could you comment on this passage, which to me suggests that poetry is a strange tangle of divination through language, and struggle against being controlled by language?

YK: Language often prefigures feeling and action, especially when it comes to race. There are certain traits and values assigned to colors. In our culture, the adjectives *black* and *white* tell us how to feel, what to think, and how to exist. In that sense, these words are existential. And they are woven into our literature. I wonder if references to color of eyes and hair occur more in American literature than in other cultures. Or maybe it has to do with the complexity of our society. Sometimes, I do have my students think about this. What are the symbolic differences when a character wears a white hat or a black hat? How do we depict the outlaw and the hero? Even if one isn't taught or told the symbolic value of a word or image, how long is it before one feels it, how long before the unconscious references enter the psyche and work their way into the gene pool? Of course, I see this as something more than mere subliminal suggestion. After all, language is what underscores how special and complex we humans are.

MC: Apart from history and language, a major subject of the poems seems to be the unconscious, as you suggest with the remarkable simile of the serpent speaking "like a Lacan signifier." Lacan, of course, famously said that the unconscious is structured like a language. Would I be wrong to claim that the poems in *Wishbone Trilogy* are an archaeology of the unconscious as it speaks, ventriloquist-like, through the prefixes that, you write, "cling like hookworms inside us," and through fixations, too, such as those of some of the troubled characters in your poems?

YK: Poetry gives itself over to language, to what it is made of and resists, and in this sense, the tension, the struggle within the embrace, says everything about why poetry exists. Poetry could be defined as a dialogue with the unknown and the unknowable. That is, we might say, poetry exists because of the human ego we crave to know the unknowable, anything to facilitate our illusion of control. Gods and religions grew out of poetry; thus, it is defined by mystery. So, yes, there seems to be divination at the root-heart, at the gut of poetry. In many ways, *The Wishbone Trilogy* is a dialogue with the Self, with all the bits and pieces I've taken in through the years, an attempt to form a composite, to compose a shape to the questions.

Also, the trilogy became a way of reminding myself that black existence is a very complicated canvas. Indeed, we are a great deal more than song and dance, than football and basketball, and a hell of a lot more than hip-hop and rap. To oversimplify is to systematically dehumanize. I don't know if the unconscious is structured like a language, as Lacan suggests, because this merely seems like an attempt to quantify the unquantifiable through words. How do we know when the unconscious speaks for itself, when the ego isn't riding herd? I believe this: in our capacity to be aware or conscious of our changes as organisms, we are exalted and condemned. Perhaps that is what makes the human a sacred creature. We possess the capacity to create gods.

MC: I'm intrigued by your reverence in "Lingo" to computers as the new cotton, so to speak. Do you see global capitalism as the new agrarianism, planting fields of computer terminals and harvesting low-wage workers?

YK: Yes, those fields of computer terminals are scary. You know, I don't know if this is a fact or if I dreamt it. But in my mind, in that unruly catalog, I remember that we were constructing a monument to J. Edgar Hoover, that essentially the building would be a monolithic computer or a system of computers that would control information. Yes, indeed, those low-wage workers are manning telephone banks through the world. However, for me, what is even more scary is how we wholesale our neuroses around the globe.

MC: Going back to the image evoked by the title of your trilogy, the image of a wishbone, one can say that a wishbone always breaks in two ways. Are words, with the deeply ambiguous functions you portray, wishbones?

YK: If we think about how language cuts or breaks, it has much to do with what each of us brings to it. Language is what humanizes the species, and yet we have a thousand ways to corrupt it and make it lie. We also cast wishes through language. We bless and curse with words. Some of us may speak to gods through silence and/or signs, but our most damnable gods are summoned through songs, chants, prayers, and incantations. Language is also used to conjure, to make whole, and to beckon us back into the world. Said or unsaid, we think in symbols and signs associated with language. The tongue is a gift.

MC: You have a number of poems that touch on the subject

of Western slavery in general and on the subject of artistic perspectives on slavery and/or race relations in particular. Among these poems are "Sunset in Surinam," which takes us into William Blake's studio as he composes his illustrations for John Gabriel Steadman's *Narrative of a Five Years Expedition against the Revolted Negroes of Surinam*; also in this group are "Jeanne Duval's Confession," which appears in *Blue Notes*, and "Unframing a Triptych," which takes us out beyond the margins of a work of visual art into the world and works of Alexander Dumas. These poems accomplish many artistic tasks simultaneously, but I wonder if the tasks include the examination of signifiers of race from perspectives different from those of our time? Are the works in some sense a history of these signifiers?

YK: Yes. How could I not address the specifics and vagaries of that peculiar institution that was the backbone, at least part of the foundation for, prosperity here in America, in the West? I'm not so egocentric or out of touch with reality that I'd demand restitution. Mainly, because I do know my history, and I also know how complicated this history is. Last year I was in Ghana, standing there in Elmina and Cape Coast Castle, thinking about the recent wars and acts of genocide in Africa. To know and feel history, one can't grab a sliver and bite into it and expect to know its full quality and terrible taste. That is why I admire South Africa's attempt at Truth and Reconciliation. First, there has to be a facing up to, then a passing through, and finally an embracing of the future. *The Wishbone Trilogy* deals with personal and public histories as a place of reflection but not as a mirror of victimhood. I, myself, am not willing to be a victim. I think that many of the early blacks throughout the world didn't view themselves as victims, and they achieved moments of great personal and public freedom. I don't deny the social reality of racism, but I'm also keenly aware of the fact that the flimsy walls of many urban enclaves are held up by excuses. Self-deception is more tragic and deadly than the echoes of slavery from the past. Presently, I'm writing poems on Chevalier de St. Georges and Aleksandr Pushkin, and it's hard to believe that either one thought of himself as a victim. In America, especially since a victim doesn't have responsibility, he or she is often free to victimize others within the community. The culture of victimization isn't merely within the African American psyche. I have said numerous times that it seems as if even the ancients were more inclusive than us moderns, and signification through race possesses different nuances because of time and circumstance. We don't have to venture back that far: I think the ghosts of Martin and Malcolm couldn't survive the shock of riding a bus through urban America today.

MC: When you write a poem like "Captain Amasa Delano's Dilemma" or "Lament and Praise Song" (about Phillis Wheatley), do you intend to comment in some way on, say, Melville's story and Robert Lowell's play, or on Robert Hayden's poem about Wheatley?

YK: No. Not exactly. I have read those pieces, but I hope that my takes are slightly different. I'm different, having benefited from their works. Perhaps my poems reflect theirs, and a dialogue is established. A call-and-response through images. An acknowledgment, rather than a comment. Sometimes, I find myself rooting around in the same emotional minefield as my precursors, but I still attempt to make it new.

MC: In *Blue Notes* you write, "I have never purposefully written a poem for a select group of people. Generally, I just find myself writing a poem." Is your poetry then a "letter to the world" like Emily Dickinson's, and do you see no significant difference between the African American literary tradition and the mainstream American literary tradition?

For instance, in poems like "Chiaroscuro," you step without hesitation or awkwardness into the European tradition. Is the world of your poetry, then a borderless world where, as you write in "Chiaroscuro,"

Carnival / is in my head, & Robert Schumann calls for Clara . . .
I see brownshirts / searching Paul Klee's / house, confiscating
Love / letters to his wife / Lily, Everything begs / remembrance.

Is the poet's duty to be, as Kafka said, a memory come alive? A memory not only for himself, but also for his culture?

YK: First, each poem is a letter to myself. It is a moment in a continuous personal discourse. In that sense, it's a letter to the world because I'm part of the world. The brain is an organism, when it exists outside the restrictions and limitations of culture—if this is possible in our contemporary world of information as commodity—it is indeed borderless, with the innate power to traverse varied social and cultural terrains. The brain is inclusive, and perhaps that is why enduring cultures are a composite of influences from various time periods. The brain is a perfect little machine because it is gluttonous and has the capacity for unbelievable adjustments. Otherwise, would human beings still be king of the mountain? And yes, I believe that Kafka is partly correct. The poet's quest is rooted in memory alive in flesh and myth, but also the act of discovery is part of that quest. The poem is an action that journeys beyond the stasis of pure memory. Plus, I don't believe that memory arrives when we arrive into the world. Mainly, we humans are a tutored species. But our capacity to project and imagine is what defined early poetry. It began as a meditation on possibility.

MC: Your poem "Oil" appears to have a strong political resonance. It opens as follows:

Now, when I hear Horace
    Silver's "Baghdad Blues"
        the sandy sky blooms

smart bombs. Live
    footage of an old man
        on a yellow bicycle

trying to outpedal
    the apocalypse—
        the film runs till

he's my Uncle Buddy
    who turned to mist
        after his father hocked

two hundred acres to go
    his bail. He'd killed a man
        who cornered him in Biloxi.

I am surprised to see
    my grandmother's twin
        riding out of war fog.

Though written before it, this poem, read in the wake of the ongoing Iraq conflict, has tremendous political resonance. It seems to connect the American Jim Crow era with American interventions overseas that some have characterized as driven by concern for oil. Was that intentional? Is this in some sense a protest poem?

YK: For me, "Oil" wouldn't exist without the personal, that story about my great-uncle disappearing after my great-grandfather put up the farm as bail. My grandmother, Mama Mary, always talked about her lost brother, Buddy. The story of oil lingered beneath her words, how it was discovered shortly after the farm was seized. There are other similar stories in my background. But with "Oil" I can't deny the importance of Horace Silver's "Baghdad Blues" in giving the poem its tone. That piece was playing as I visualized and wrote "Oil," moving through the images that came to me. Also, I couldn't get the phrase "sand niggers" out of my head, how Arabs are seen as the other. The cultural enemy. We only have to look at some of the images in our literary canon. What does "El Cid" mean to us? And, of course, Othello's first crime is that he's a Moor. If one is truly thinking, all these moments link and create a composite, and such thinking is an action that could be considered political. In this sense, in "Oil" the personal may possess a political resonance. Perhaps the poem is addressing an attitude, an American style of thinking that has gotten into the blood. We need to dust off our copies of *The Ugly American* and change a few adjectives and nouns.

MC: You told Vincente Gotera in 1990 that poetry "has always been political." Does this fact make overt protest writing superfluous?

YK: Human beings are social and political animals, so how can one of our oldest artistic expressions not reflect that? Language itself is political, but what troubles me about many so-called political poems is that the politics are on the surface, that one is told how to exist and what to think. How can any beauty and celebration survive in such contention? I'm not suggesting that the poem should be a verbal sucker punch, but I am saying that, for me, the ideal poem is layered with numerous nuances, that it even risks beauty.

MC: I know you do feel strongly about the importance of subject matter in poetry; in a 1990 interview with Vince Gotera you described much American poetry as "a poetry of evasion." Just last year you threw down a kind of gauntlet to the writers of such poetry in your introduction to *The Best American Poetry 2003*. Has there been no progress in the thirteen years between 1990 and 2003?

YK: There have been some stunning individual voices to emerge during the past decade. Anyway, I don't relate to schools and movements. I do trust individuals. I don't have to call names, because I think that we know who they are when we read and hear them. But I'll say this; they aren't from spoken word or *Def Poetry Jam*. I believe there are some powerful young voices out there that are destined to endure. They are writing poems that cut to the interior, outside entertainment and hype. And neither are they overly experimental and opaque. One has to journey into the poems to grasp their meaning, and this is one quality that makes so many of these recent voices so damn enjoyable and meaningful. Also, there's some gut and deep singing inside the language. I believe that the poetry of evasion cannot give life, even if it fattens itself on illusion and pretense.

MC: In "Lingua Franca," the speaker and a woman on the far side of a color line that must not be crossed connect, at least psychologically, by listening "to Afro-Cuban / because we both can move / to the drum." Here music as lingua franca makes me think of the lingua franca of clichés you once said helped soldiers from diverse backgrounds communicate. Can poetry like yours, in which any one, any culture, and any ear is welcome, work as a lingua franca for diverse poetry audiences? Is a new lingua franca what is needed in American culture right now?

YK: I hope so. If there's a lingua franca of the soul, of human spirit, an existential lingua franca, then poetry and music provide the alphabet. Bridges are erected and crossed in the flesh. Is that why Othello damns himself through the agency and language of poetry? There are so many moments in poetry where feelings and insights cross borders, creating an understanding beyond words. Not denying or forgetting Walt Whitman's lapses into exoticism, I think that he creates a terrain in *Leaves of Grass* where people coexist side by side with grace. He says in the first stanza of "Song of Myself": "I celebrate myself, and sing myself, / And what I assume you shall assume, / For every atom belonging to me as good belongs to you." Whitman's concept of language seems cosmic and carnal. I hope to achieve a voice just as inclusive as his, or Pablo Neruda's, and maybe this is possible if I continue to search. Until recently, African Americans produced a music that brought people together, and perhaps poets should return to that source for instruction. Today, with rap and hip-hop, with the violence and the love-hatred of women that have influenced much of the spoken-word scene, we'd do well to return to the lyric, to a lingua franca that humanizes us as citizens of the world. We need more than rant and rave. And there are some young voices out there that know where to journey to find good poetry.

Three Shades of Past

Interview by G. F. Mitrano

1. Childhood and Apprenticeship

MENA MITRANO: Memories of your childhood in Bogalusa,
Louisiana, often crop up in your poetry. In your well-known
"Venus's-flytraps," the child protagonist at one point wonders
why "the music in [his] head" makes him scared. I wanted to
ask you about the connection between that child and the poet
you grew up to be. What is that "music in [the] head"? What
made it so overwhelming for the child, and what makes the
music—if this is still the case—overwhelming for you?

YUSEF KOMUNYAKAA: Well, I think of the music as a point of
departure, the moment of awareness. And perhaps music is also
the sounds of life. If one thinks about laughter, how it can shift
and drift into cries—cries of pain, of pleasure. So, I'm thinking
about music played on instruments as well as the music of life.
I did listen to music growing up. It was always through the
radio, at a distance—the surprise happens inside this immense
distance. So, there are different kinds of music I am addressing.

GFM: In that poem, particularly, music is such a powerful metaphor
because the child is trying to patch up and balance different
sets of things, different worlds: the whispering of adults,
which he cannot totally decipher, and the facts, the music of
the natural world. Music as it returns, if I'm not mistaken, in
"Rhythm Method": the pulse, the basic throbbing of a natural
law.

YK: Right. A lyrical insistence. A music that defines itself, says what
it is.

From *Callaloo* 28, no. 3 (2005).

GFM: One of my favorite poems is "My Father's Love Letters." Your father comes back home from the mill; he is in his carpenter's apron bulged with nails and he is transfigured, it seems to me, into a model for the writer. He is laboring over simple words, focusing on wooing back his reader—your mother. The poem strikes me as the masculine version of Alice Walker's *In Search of Our Mothers' Gardens* or Paule Marshall's "The Poets in the Kitchen." In other words, it stages—in the best sense of the word—a scene of apprenticeship in which a parent or an ancestor who sometimes can only sign his name, nevertheless becomes the young writer's mentor and first teacher. That seems to happen in your poem. As he stands there, "redeemed by what he tried to say," the father transmits a core knowledge about language to the child. The achievement of the poem to me lies in its capacity to preserve the power of this transmission despite the violence of the father, which is very clear in the poem. Is your father—was he—a mentor to you? How much of his world of labor has made its way into your philosophy of composition?

YK: Growing up, I don't think I was actually conscious of that influence from my father. But in retrospect, as a matter of fact, years after writing the poem, I realized that yes, as an untutored mentor, his precise ways of looking at the world and his techniques as a carpenter were instructive. I think the first thing I remember him building was a birdhouse for me. It was a replica of a larger house, everything in place and so fine-tuned. I think he taught me something about revision: how to go back. If something didn't work for him, he would dismember it and approach it again. Maybe that's how I learned to return to a poem and look at it in a different way, to tear it apart.

GFM: This is a wonderful way of talking about revision: this idea of taking the experience of labor and then making it work for the composition on the page.

YK: Also, when I think about my father, though, I think he was ashamed of not having been educated, so he used physical labor to measure himself against the ones who, particularly, had been to college, for instance, and came back to Bogalusa as teachers. He built for himself three houses. I think he began to measure himself in material things, to at least make himself feel that he had achieved something in his life.

2. *History*

GFM: You trust words. That is clear to me when in some poems you make words paint things.

YK: Yes, sometimes I wish I were a painter. I love art. Giacometti, Beauford Delaney, Bourgeois, Bearden—artists have influenced my care for imagery.

GFM: I was struck by "The Whistle": the men capping their thermoses and switching off Loretta Lynn, the blue jays and redbirds, your father in overalls wading through the field of goldenrod and mustard weeds, his lunch of "red beans & rice / with ham hocks & cornbread. / Lemonade & peach jello." Words are good enough to convey a sense of place, of location, and a sense of the culture in which that place is drenched, for better or for worse. Words are good enough to describe rituals. In the same poem, after the five o'clock whistle the men go home and the women wait for them, setting the table with flowered oilcloth. But there is anger boiling under this rich canvas of which "The Whistle" is only one example. In that particular poem the anger is conveyed by the image of your father caressing a .38 on the seat of a pickup. Now, if words are good enough to describe—almost painterly—a sense of place and culture, do you trust them equally when it comes to writing about conflict and violence?

YK: I suppose we have to trust words. Think about laws or principles of ethics relying on verbal symbols, think about sacred texts, think about prayers and curses executed through language. One of my rituals growing up in Bogalusa was the church, and I remember "the Word made Flesh." This phrase stuck with me, foremost in my psyche. So, I suppose we have to think about language as tangible, that we can trust language when it is very concrete, the names of things. That was very important from early on. Not to name things in order to own or control them, but to name things in order to understand them and learn how those elements fit into one's life.

I remember early on when I was about five, six, seven, going out to play in the woods. I didn't want to know that a tree was a tree; I wanted to know what kind of tree it was, and how there were differences, even in the leaves, in the texture of the bark and so on. That's how I began to name things as well as the scientific names. Sometimes in rural Louisiana there might be two or three names for a given object, and one has more tonal value than the other. I do think that in trying to understand conflict and violence language has power. Now, I'm thinking of that poem by Claude McKay, "If We Must Die." The poem was written in 1919, of course right about the First World War. I think the poem is about the brutality visited upon black Americans after soldiers returned from the First World War. But it is ironic that Churchill recites "If We Must Die" to the British people during the Second World War. I don't know if he credits McKay, but I do know it has power: "If we must die, let it not be like hogs / Hunted and penned in an inglorious spot, / While round us bark the mad and hungry dogs. / Making their mock at our accursed lot. / If we must die—oh, let us nobly die, / So that our precious blood may not be shed / In vain; then even the monsters we defy / Shall be constrained to honor us though dead!" That's powerful language. And it is interesting that this is a sonnet, whereas usually we think of sonnets as poems about love, nature, or metaphysical inquiry. But this is a different take on the form; it is a protest sonnet. I think what Churchill realized was that he could trust the language to deliver—not just to the masses—the passion of determination to stand firm against the Germans.

GFM: You mentioned Claude McKay's poem on war. You wrote your own sequence of poems about war, about the Vietnam War. You were in Vietnam; you wrote for *Stars and Stripes*. If there was an inkling of history and violence in "The Whistle," in your acclaimed collection *Dien Cai Dau* these themes, which are acknowledged as *your* themes somehow, take on national proportions. It is as if we could finally get down and talk about the political without the power of words—the dazzling materiality of words—getting in the way. And yet I am very struck by the extent to which you engage in a very political matter such as the war in Vietnam through the filter of intimacy and sexuality. For example, in "Tu Do Street" issues of war and race are almost drowned in a quiet nonargumentative interiority, with a Vietnamese woman's body that is kissed by both black and white soldiers who, in kissing the same woman, breathe each other's breath. So is the body—female, foreigner, and perhaps, from the reader's point of view, exotic—the most capable cultural historian? What is this body saying?

YK: Well, in a certain sense, that is a moment of humanization because there's conflict not only out in the field, there's also conflict back in the rear areas where the soldiers should be getting along together as fellow citizens who have put their lives on the line. But they are divided by race and the culture of social apartheid in America. They brought it across the sea with them. And, yes, they are divided within their collective psyche, but brought together, without them being conscious of it, through this nameless person, this lady of the night. They relied on her to keep them human.

I went back to Vietnam in 1990, and I remember a Viet Cong commando saying that oftentimes missions were made easier because of the women, the information they collected. That was quite revealing and quite frightening at the same time.

GFM: So, what would the women do?

YK: They provided information to the Viet Cong and NVA [North Vietnamese Army]. Troop movement, intelligence, et cetera. But also, I think that some lasting relationships were established as well, even though there was a tussle in the middle of the minds and bodies of many American GIs. How could one say the word *love*—and I think some did—and the next day aim guns at the same people? This isn't the first war where Americans were divided. In fact, race has entered every military conflict we've been involved in: the American Revolution, the so-called Indian Wars, the War of 1812, the Civil War, World War I and World War II, the Korean conflict, and the Vietnam War. I don't know about future wars, but I won't be surprised if race isn't at least a part of the psychological character of such conflicts. When considering our history, we can look at a single incident out of many: during World War I when American black soldiers were fighting in Europe, General "Blackjack" Pershing issued a statement to young French officers suggesting that they should not treat black Americans better than they would be treated when returning to the United States. So, there is this long, ugly history.

GFM: It is almost as if psychically, in that space of the poem, race disappears but only to exist even more reinforced in the social sphere. It's like moving between a dreamy world and the real one.

YK: Yes.

GFM: In your Vietnam poems your voice sounds more like a murmur than a protest cry. But many of the Vietnam and post-Vietnam generations felt the pressure to say no out loud to the American establishment, to use a shorthand. I taught a seminar titled Introduction to Critical Theory this past year, and we read

Eve Sedgwick's account of herself as a poet who turns to theory, who becomes a theorist because she feels that poetry cannot say no, that no is better said in criticism than in poetry. How do you feel about the power of poetry to say no?

YK: I think it's the opposite of that. In fact, poetry says no in many different ways. It really depends on the reader, or the listener, how many different ways no can be said. The reader or listener isn't being told that this is no or this is yes, but one arrives at an approximate no through a connection to language—a language where the nerves are exposed, left bare and pulsing with possibility. In that sense, poems can be democratic.

GFM: It is interesting that you should say this because, in the same account, the poet turned theorist always speaks in melancholic terms of her first love, that is, poetry. And she sees an element of poetry in what has come to be known as theoretical writing. So, it is interesting that you should defend the opposite position, whereby, yes, it is possible to say no even out loud in poetry.

YK: There are so many poets who have written against war. Whitman comes to mind. And, of course, voices from World War I: Siegfried Sassoon, Richard Addington, e.e. cummings, Georg Trakl, Wilfred Owen, Yvan Goll, Anna Akhmatova, Eugenio Montale, Osip Mandelstam, and Isaac Rosenberg. Well, a good example, which isn't really a war poem, is that McKay poem, "If We Must Die." That is a poem definitely saying no, and is stated with a gutsy imagistic power. The fact is that, as I've said elsewhere, the reader, or listener, is the cocreator of meaning.

3. Women/Music/Aesthetics

GFM: The sensuality of women nurtures your writing. I can think offhand of "Jasmine" and "Woman, I've Got the Blues," but these are only two examples among many. I was leafing through *Pleasure Dome* the other day and I could see many others. At times women and their bodies belong in a signifying chain, so to speak, with the landscapes of your childhood, but also high art and African American music, and they seem to function as a buoy, keeping the speaker above water, still speaking with a sense of self-confidence. In "Woman, I've Got the Blues," for example, the voice asserts itself after the dizzying spells of the

MOMA high art and the mixture of glitter and pain of Charlie Parker's sounds with a final, earthly eulogy to a woman's ass. Do you ever feel you are walking a fine line between the celebration of women's sensuality and aesthetic abandon? Are you ever an aesthete in your poetry? Do you enjoy that?

YK: [*Laughter*] Well, I do think there is celebration. I think it has a lot to do with the presence of women around me when I grew up. They were the caretakers of ritual and the things that taught survival. I'm particularly thinking of my neighborhood. The image of the woman is always the image of desire. It is an attempt to integrate and make whole the psyche of the male as well as the psyche of the woman. There is a negotiation that is taking place. Since I'm writing within the context of my own time, I think about each word chosen. Some words are rather direct and, at the same time, there are elements of the sublime woven through vernacular expressions. I think there are layers of diction in the poems. I know it's true, because that's probably who I am. It has much to do with how I came to language, the spoken as well as the language I read in books. Language is acquired in numerous ways and all of those ways can embrace poetry. At least, I hope so, that there is a weaving of expressions without one canceling out the other.

GFM: The reason why I asked about the sensuality of women is that sensuality in general plays an important role in your poetry, and your tone is never argumentative; it is not confrontational. I don't know whether this can be said to be a trait of poetry, but it is certainly there in your poetry and it seems to me that sensuality keeps your voice short of an argumentative vein or a confrontational tone. Does this make sense to you?

YK: Well, I've defined poetry as a composite of celebration and confrontation. However, when I say confrontation, I mean it in an imagistic sense: not as statement, but as image. Statement is problematic in poetic expression; it becomes argumentative; it becomes reductive. I like to give the reader and the listener some credit for his or her own capacity to negotiate the images. Likewise, when I read a poem I wish to be propelled back up to its beginning and work my way down through it again. I want to savor the language, to feel it take over, to give myself to the sensation of discovery. For me, poetry would not exist without the image, so I rely heavily on imagery.

GFM: Yes, it does. . . . We started out with music as a metaphor in one of your childhood poems. But music, especially bebop and jazz, has had an enormous influence on you. You are known, in fact, as the editor of jazz anthologies, and your writing teems with references to African American music.

YK: Though jazz was invented by African Americans, I think of it as an American music. And, yes, it has influenced my entire character as a person.

GFM: In summing up this influence of music in your poetry someone has described your line as "a banjo gone electric."

YK: [*Laughter*] I've never seen that expression. Where did you find it?

GFM: In the *Boston Review*, a 1999 review of *Thieves of Paradise* that is available online. Could you explain the technical consequence of jazz on your writing?

YK: I suppose I admire the improvisation and the dexterity of the musician who is able to compose and play at the same time. I am still in awe of that ability. For me, its interest is in a certain kind of freedom and it makes me think about language as music, that the body is an amplifier. Language is our first music. Not that one attempts, as a poet, to imitate instruments or anything of that sort; but just being comfortable with language, and the sounds of words. And the other thing: the surprises. That's why we often hear the musicians say, "I've played that tune twenty times but I've never played it the same way." That means that he or she has the capacity to surprise him- or herself. And that is important in poems as well, where everything isn't so thought-out or plotted beforehand, where the form of the poem becomes the mold that we pour opaque expressions into.

GFM: Do you remember how we talked about revision, about going back to the poem to constantly readjust it. Does that relate to jazz at all?

YK: That's a very good point. Initially, a poem for me perhaps will be one hundred lines long and I'll go back and cut it to fifty or sixty lines. So, yes it's that kind of readjusting, not the music as much as the image. The images do not collide but they inform each other. And often, in the context of an improvisation, one isn't surprised by every phrase one writes, and one has to introduce silence as well. Silence is also part of music for me. So, if I scratch out a line or two or three lines, there is a silence, and it becomes a bridge from one phrase to the next.

GFM: I'd like to ask you about *Thieves of Paradise* (1998). In the Western tradition great geniuses have been thieves. I think of Picasso and African sculpture. In your book, among other things, you pay homage to the American and African American genius of Charlie Parker, "Testimony." Could you talk about your pieces on Parker and his artistic influence on you? How does Parker's genius depart from the traditional notion of artistic thievery?

YK: Well, I wasn't thinking of Parker as a thief of paradise as much as I was thinking about, maybe in the back of my mind, manifest destiny. The cover of the book is an image from Benjamin West's *Penn's Treaty with the Indians.* That painting is in Philadelphia. There is an idea of manifest destiny throughout *Thieves of Paradise.*

I am fixed on that question about Charlie Parker. I don't see Parker as a "thief." If he stole anything he stole from himself, in that sense. His demise is so early and he's left such a legend. He dies at thirty-four; that's amazing. I was just at the Charlie Parker festival in New York City on Sunday.

GFM: I wanted to ask you about Charlie Parker so that you could give a concrete example of the role of music in your poetry. This time I am not referring only to the technical influence but to the extent to which writing about the genius of musicians of the past crucially nurtures your language.

YK: In my book of interviews and essays, *Blue Notes,* I talk a little bit of how that Parker poem came about. I was in Australia at the time and the director at the ABC [Australian Broadcasting Corporation] asked me if I could write a libretto. I said yes. Then I came back to the States and I realized I couldn't write a traditional libretto, that I had to write this series of poems. And that has been made into a musical piece in Australia. It is interesting to hear the words. The words have been sung. So, it's a poem but also, in a strange way, it's a quasi-libretto. And I relied heavily on images. I didn't want to get away from the image; I didn't want to write song lyrics. I wanted to stay very close to the poem. It was a way of capturing the spirit of Charlie Parker, because I admire his musical dexterity, what he was able to accomplish in his short lifetime, coming from the Midwest and traveling all over the world. I have this idea about the Midwest . . .

GFM: Why?

YK: This might surprise you. I have this idea that in the Midwest—I don't know if it's still true—time and space are so important for individual voices. It doesn't surprise me that Charlie Parker comes out of the Midwest and he had his own self-expression, his own individuality. Miles Davis is from the Midwest as well, out of East St. Louis. Also, we could talk about writers who have come out of the Midwest. T. S. Eliot and William Burroughs from St. Louis, Missouri, Kenneth Rexroth from South Bend, Indiana, and Langston Hughes coming from Joplin, Missouri— all of these very individualized voices. Usually, when we think of culture in this country we think about the East Coast or San Francisco, but if we think of the Harlem Renaissance . . . that's why I began thinking about the question of time and space, because I was teaching this course on the Harlem Renaissance and I realized that most of the writers were not born in New York. They came there.

GFM: I happen to know that young poets starting out now admire you a great deal. Perhaps your blend of European experience and black technical experience attracts young poets, especially those who, while wanting to own the racial heritage as a very important source of their drive and their art, nevertheless feel uneasy about being classified solely as African American poets. And I was introduced to your poetry by one of them two years ago. I wanted to ask about the reasons why young generations trust your judgment. Is your ability to mix classicism and innovation the sole component of the trust they place in you as a poet and an authoritative figure?

YK: Well, in a way the ground was laid for me by Robert Hayden and the fact that he really saw himself as an American poet. However, one cannot get away from race as such, but it shouldn't be the nucleus of one's overall expression. It shouldn't define one, or confine one. I believe that there isn't any subject that is taboo. It depends on the aesthetics. And that's why, for the most part, one's impulse to insert statements into poetic expression can be problematic. One has to let the image, to let the language, do the work, and trust the reader. For a long time African American poets and artists were condemned to write a service literature and for the first time individuals can journey to the interior of themselves, to deal with that aspect of one's existence, and deal with the exterior as well. Does that make sense?

GFM: Oh, yes, it does. In fact, the question of aesthetics is so important because it seems to me—and I am speaking from the point of view of criticism—the temptation is still there to read, not only African American literature, but race-related or class-related literature in allegorical terms and therefore to control the aesthetic side of the text, whatever it is, prose or poetry, and translate it into ideological issues. Not that that should not be done but . . .

YK: . . . that should not be the sole purpose of the work.

GFM: For many years people have talked about minority literature. Minority literature has been exposed to the risk of being read allegorically. Do you think that what you said about race—about it not having to be a confinement—is true of class as well? Or are the two issues different?

YK: Class is an interesting one. Recently I've been particularly interested in exploring the poet Nancy Cunard. She is really known for an anthology she edited, *Negro*, that was published, I think, in February 1934. She comes from England. She is part of an aristocratic background. Her grandfather I believe was a shipbuilder, so she grew up on this huge estate. She was very conscious of class, I think. She really bridged class and dealt with the problem. Especially in the 1930s, class was very much intricately interwoven with race. When I think about class now . . . it's a difficult one. Class is the major problem. W. E. B. DuBois talks about the color line, and today I think it should be reclassified as the class contrast. In fact, when we think about race, especially in this country, the bridge has contracted— the distance, I should say, between the two. I don't know how to approach that as a poet, but I do know that I'm looking at a number of poems that even use the word "homeless." So, poets are quite aware. And it seems to me, just that word alone will keep at least some of us abreast of what's happening in our cities especially. In some cities, and New York is a good example, San Francisco is another good example, I cannot see how it is possible to live on minimum wage. So, class is going to be even more of a pressing problem in the future.

Coda

GFM: A personal curiosity. I read that you acknowledge Elizabeth Bishop among your influences. You said her poetry is important. Could you say a bit more about that?

YK: Well, her care for the image is important to me. I don't care if it's "Man-Moth" or "The Fish." That's such an interesting poem to me because of what takes place within the context of those lines. I don't think I've ever counted the number of lines. But the number of images . . . just the fact of this survivor—that's what the fish is actually—with all the hooks in its mouth that has broken so many fishing lines. And yet in that poem the fish is almost beckoning for its own demise; it's almost given up inside. The poem is about endurance. It becomes a metaphor for human endurance, in a way, because it is almost depicted as a warrior, and yet we realize that humanity has a lot to do with this aspect of giving up inside for the fish because of that rainbow on the water—it's an "oily rainbow." It's a poem about nature.

GFM: Last question. On looking back at the way you made yourself into a poet, what do you consider as the most innovative aspect of your work?

YK: Innovative? The most innovative?

GFM: Yes, I know once you said that you'd like to be remembered for your persistence. [*Laughter*]

YK: Maybe the most innovative is subject matter. At the moment. I don't know about next week, but at the moment I would say subject matter. I'm going back to the idea that there isn't any topic that is taboo. So, I don't have to keep reminding myself about it, it's just part of who I am. We have to embrace many points of view in order to keep ourselves whole.

Excursions

A Conversation with Kyle G. Dargan

KYLE G. DARGAN: I was talking to Jericho Brown yesterday and he told me you two had already gotten started on this conversation.

YUSEF KOMUNYAKAA: [*Laughing*] Oh really?

KGD: He was telling me about how you saw hip-hop, and the negative effects it has, as linked to a larger structure—what seemed like possibly a larger plan, which was implemented on black communities. I am wondering if you could recount that for me or just give me a sense of how you see that web being woven.

YK: Well, I hate to attempt to align hip-hop with something that has been planned, a conspiracy theory or anything like that, but the effects seem so negative. Of course, most likely, a conspiracy happens within the heart and soul of the community itself. Our entire critical apparatus has been undermined. One reason is because we were always, or rather I have always, seen black Americans as caretakers of positive vision and a kind of music which linked us to the past, present, future. The music produced prior to hip-hop I see as the music of inclusion. It was a music that beckoned for people to come together and that's why the music has functioned as a choice of weapon against the larger problems of black existence.

KGD: I agree with you; and one thing I see is that the slave spiritual was Negro in the sense that it took a Christian, European religious concept and infused it with an African musical sensibility and created something new that ultimately was used

From *Callaloo* 29, no. 3 (2006). This conversation took place August 24, 2005, during the Bread Loaf Writers' Conference, Ripton, VT.

138

to subvert the system. In a lot of ways, I see hip-hop as the same in the sense you had these urban communities where resources were being taken away from the people—you weren't getting music instruction, you weren't getting any introduction to the arts. What the kids did is say, "All right, if you are not going to give me the opportunity to do this, then I am going to make my own instruments. I'm going to take a turntable and make that an instrument, I'm going to take a sampling machine and create some new music from it."

YK: But at the same time, if we want to speak of the "us"/"them" syndrome, it still uses their technology to underscore our shortcomings. What I mean is that black Americans were playing music long before it was institutionalized in schools. Before the drums were banned in the Congo Square in New Orleans. Even when we couldn't buy instruments, we made them—we were very vibrant in our imagination. It does take a certain lifelong commitment to play an instrument. It's not easy. Sometimes Charlie Parker or Coltrane practiced ten or twelve hours a day. To play one's mouth [*laughs*], it can happen overnight. This illusion of shortcuts can undermine us. A good example of this—I was talking to someone who said, "You know, there's money available for young people to play music in Trenton." I said, "What do you mean there's money?" He said, "Well, it's there and we can't find anybody to play instruments." That is one of the problems, you know.

KGD: But what age group were they talking about?

YK: They're talking about elementary students and teenagers.

KGD: That's the thing, though. Because if you're not getting kids when they're little and they have no introduction to arts at all, to give them a trumpet at age sixteen . . .

YK: No. At one time, the music happened within the community, regardless. Within the family. The passion to excel was woven into the fabric of the community. There were always instruments—people instructing each other. If the instrument is there, one finds a way to play it, to perfect that instrument. But if that precision is de-emphasized, the music isn't going to happen. Instead, our allegiance to that which appears easy is perfected. We can get over. We can do it overnight, you know? We'll write it—not even write—we will *say* a few rhymes and get over. I think that's the attitude. I don't think this is what Lee Morgan's sister was thinking when she gave him a trumpet when he was fourteen.

YK: And the misogyny is very problematic. Rap is a music of put-downs.

KGD: Generally?

YK: Yes, generally. If we consider folklore, African American folklore was so damn inventive. I don't care if it's "The Signifying Monkey" or some of the jailhouse toasts. These rhymes were relentless. They were rhymes of insinuation, innuendo. When you heard one, you had to participate. It was an act of inclusion. So there's a simple meaning, a surface meaning, but there's also a larger, deeper meaning and I don't think that's the case with hip-hop or rap.

KGD: I agree that right now that may be the case, but I feel like, in terms of black music, every genre of black music at some point hits that place where it gets absorbed into popular culture in a way that those types of demands that were initially put on it by the community, to have that creativity, to have that brio, get lost. I remember when I was growing up, most of what I got in relationship to jazz was smooth jazz. And I know, now that I've gone back and listened to what was closer to the inception of jazz, that that music and smooth jazz are nowhere close and I don't even think should be considered in the same vein.

YK: Right, I agree.

KGD: In the same way, I'm not sure that the hip-hop produced now is much different. I feel like the hip-hop being produced is the equivalent of smooth jazz. It's something that's easy to be reproduced, it's something that's commercial and that you can sit back and listen to without having any investment in at all.

YK: Well, true listeners of jazz never listen to smooth jazz. They know the tradition. Of course, that became the question, "Where can jazz go?" I think that jazz has always been an international music—now we have to become aware of what Cuban musicians are doing, what's happening in Japan, and what's happening with Polish players such as Tomasz Stanko or Jannsz Muniak. For the most part, jazz lost the black community in the U.S. when it was divorced from dance, when one had to listen and not compete. I do think, with the African American culture, we do possess the capacity to embrace that which involves reflection. This is what I believe and feel, maybe some will disagree, but the listener does not have to compete with the musician. I feel our emphasis has been primarily on interactive entertainment. Modern jazz requires one's attention. One can get booted out of the Village Vanguard for talking. Rappers and hip-hoppers need to exist within a zone of noise.

YK: Already, through our folklore, we possess the equivalent of rap and hip-hop. Also, during the 1970s, we had groups such as the Last Poets, the Funkadelic's, and James Brown and the Famous Flames. Some of the poetry of the Black Arts Movement could, in a way, be aligned with today's hip-hop and rap—without the trite rhymes and "*un*heroic" couplets. It was more positive and sophisticated. Also, underlying rap and hip-hop is a—I want to say, or if I dare say—buffoonery. Even the names of the groups in a way make me think of "Pigmeat" or "Dolemite."

KGD: I agree. I totally believe that groups like the Ying Yang Twins are minstrels.

YK: Yes, they are minstrels. For anyone to appropriate the desperate history of the Siamese twins is problematic. But, of course, minstrels don't seem to have a sense of history.

KGD: But I also feel that you get acts like the Ying Yang Twins when you sport with something like hip-hop, something that was functional. Like you figure the blues came out of the spiritual because you had these black people moving north and having a new experience that they needed to articulate which the spiritual was not necessarily satisfying in the same way. So in that same sense—

YK: But the blues is still different. They rise out of the soil and sweat of the South, carried along by the motion of the Great Migration. Spirituals and blues remain basically black. One is sacred and the other is considered profane, basically coming out of the same tonal, cultural expression.

KGD: True, but both are functional in a way because the spiritual was physically used as a code to facilitate slaves' escape whereas blues was used to help people mentally escape the idea that "Wow, we've 'escaped' to the north and in some ways it's not that much better" or "We're dealing with a whole other set of problems that we didn't anticipate." I feel like these young people in the '80s, in the late '70s, really, when hip-hop was starting, they were trying to articulate that, but they didn't have the same things.

YK: I think some were escaping responsibility and the reason I'm saying this is, you know, for some urban—not even urban—for some, especially, African American youth, the only thing that they inherit is an excuse. That's what's passed on to them—

this illusion that they are one step from slavery. That isn't true. Matter of fact, when talking with many people about hip-hop or rap and one asks them about their African American history, ask them, "Who's Paul Robeson?" They'll say, "Who? Who's he?" They may know Langston Hughes. Very few know about Baldwin. None know anything about Marian Anderson.

YK: The turntable—who can create music on a turntable? If one knows an instrument and then he or she ventures to the turntable, that's a different thing, but to try and play the turntable as an instrument, somewhere along the line that's a shortcut, a defilement of the human spirit.

KGD: Well, I wouldn't say anyone plays the turntable as an instrument. You have to know music in order to be a good hip-hop DJ. You have to know the music that comes before you or else you won't know what to sample.

YK: See, to sample something is to steal something that one doesn't have the talent to fashion from one's own know-how and breadth.

KGD: But Bearden's not a thief.

YK: Pardon me?

KGD: I said Romare Bearden is not a thief.

YK: Well, Romare Bearden is entirely different. If one looks at his wide range of work, one realizes that he knew his craft. He could draw! He could paint! He received his degree in mathematics and I think mathematics influenced his collages. Many try to duplicate Bearden, to steal from his idea, but they can't do it. You look at Bearden's early work, his more impressionistic period, when he is just putting paint on the canvas, and you'll see that he is a great draftsman. He could draw a hell of a lot better than Jean-Michel Basquiat, who, interestingly enough, many who are drawn to hip-hop and rap embrace. I was talking to a friend of mine, Steve Canon, an African American poet and writer who was instrumental in starting the magazine *Yardbird Reader* with Ishmael Reed and Al Young. Steve was born in Louisiana and he has a clear relationship with jazz and art. He knew Basquiat early on and he said, "Basquiat wasn't fully formed," and I understood exactly what he was talking about. He paints for ten years—this whole big body of work. He wanted to be famous more than he desired to be a good artist, and consequently he was drawn to Andy Warhol. Through that whole industry of art, he does become famous. I think that his fame has more to do with his lifestyle as opposed to what he was actually producing. In the same way, I wonder sometimes if a rapper or hip-hopper can carry a tune. I hear some whispering in my ear, "He couldn't carry a tune in a bag." How can one sing and not know anything about harmony? Rap is just one syncopated beat, syncopation by default. I feel that one should know and feel melody.

KGD: But there are groups like, say, the Jurassic Five. I don't know if you have ever heard of them. They are a West Coast group, a combination of a couple groups, but they do tend to use a lot of harmony in their refrains, in their songs. When they do rap, it is often with an attention to how their voices come together as one and split off and do different things.

YK: Well, they are trying to drift back to the source, to something that has already been accomplished. One only has to hear a minute of Marvin Gaye to know the mountain that he or she has to climb.

KGD: One thing my father always says is that he doesn't listen to hip-hop because he feels that it confirms for him that musicianship is dead. And for me, I always have to do a lot of work to bring him a record, bring him something else, to show him that there are people out there doing this who are really musicians. In hip-hop, the problem now is that the majority of those doing hip-hop are not musicians because the majority of them aren't doing hip-hop because they want to make music. They're doing hip-hop because they want to live a certain lifestyle, they want to be a part of a certain culture.

YK: They want to wear bling.

KGD: And that's the problem. I feel like, initially, rap music—before there was hip-hop and there was just rap and there was breaking and there was graffiti writing—that in that place, the art was dictating the culture. Now, I feel with these young people today, we have the culture dictating the art, and when the culture is dictating the art then the art aspires to little.

YK: I think built into hip-hop, having listened to some of it, not very much, is limitation. The musician who's very efficient on an instrument, such as the saxophone or trumpet, though there are limitations there, there's also this need to reach for the blue note—the impossible note, which is pure challenge, and I just don't think that basic concept inhabits hip-hop or rap, this need to transcend. I was listening to a recent documentary on Stevie Wonder, I think he was eleven or twelve, and he brought so much musicianship to his phrasing, I said, "Damn, where can a singer go from here?" There was so much there. I think listening to the lyrics of Curtis Mayfield, the protest, the concern with community, all of that is right there in the man himself, and how do we take a step into the future with that reality, that achievement, already intact as the foundation? Do we take a step backward or do we take a step forward? That is the challenge.

KGD: Well, don't you believe every generation has to take a small step back before it can take the next step forward?

YK: [*Laughing*] But not a step where one finds oneself in the well, where one finds oneself falling so far back one says, "God, am I in hell?" You know, I live in Trenton, and rap surrounds me. I see two year-olds dancing to this crap—"bitch that" and [*laughing*] "nigger that." I see what people are taking in, what they live on. I think it's very detrimental. I was reading a book of short stories by a young Russian writer, Irina Denezhkina, and one of her characters is named "Nigger." I say, "What! How can she get away with this?" Then I realized what has influenced her, okay. I realize what helped to create the aggressive tone of *Give Me: (Songs for Lovers)* for this nineteen- or twenty-year-old writer. These stories have been translated into many languages [*laughs*].

KGD: You think that hip-hop influenced her?

YK: Yes! Especially with the "nigger" character in the collection's first story.

KGD: But the word "nigger" in the dictionary doesn't even mean—

YK: I know, but I do not believe this word came from her dictionary. Also, many of her stories were generated through e-mails. That tells us a frightening lot doesn't it?

KGD: Yeah, but I don't think hip-hop had anything to do with Webster's changing the definition of the word "nigger."

YK: But I think it is an attempt to legitimize something that has changed the collective psyche of black people. We have never been as divided as we are today. Hip-hop and rap have created an attitude that's dangerous. If one looks at the history of minstrelsy, one sees the word "nigger" a lot, sometimes coming out of white mouths that have been blackened up. I think the 1960s and 1970s were moments of timely confrontation. My hero—people often ask me, "Who's your hero?"—is not a basketball or football player. I say, "Actually, my hero is Paul Robeson." But, recently, I was asked by a friend of mine,

Goutam Datta, to travel to India, to Kolkata, because of the negative view of black Americans.

KGD: I think I've heard this. They thought that black people didn't write poetry.

YK: Many thought black poetry was hip-hop and rap because that's what's publicized. They think 50 Cent—I think we should be refunded forty-nine cents—and that's a real problem because this is what's promoted worldwide. It's important to note that Paul Robeson's name occurs in a proper song in India. Hip-hop and rap have helped to undermine and erode the positive image of blacks in America. This is psychological warfare.

KGD: But I don't see 50 Cent—because of what he is, he's a character—as really any different than, say, Little Black Sambo, and in the same way that they made Little Black Sambo comics, they make 50 Cent tapes.

YK: It's interesting you mention Little Black Sambo because, initially, that character, coming out of the British psyche, referred to the Indian.

KGD: To go back to what you were saying about jazz and it being international, it is the same thing with hip-hop. Hip-hop in Cuba, hip-hop in Japan—it is spreading because there, it's new. One thing Questlove, drummer for The ROOTS, I don't know if you know the band The ROOTS, but one thing he says is that right now it's 1980 in Cuba in terms of hip-hop. They're in that phase where they haven't yet had that commercial influence.

YK: I hope it does not affect the Cubans because right now as far as I'm concerned, if there is a new face to jazz, it would come out of Cuba. I see great potential for Cuban jazz.

KGD: So you don't think the two can coexist?

YK: I wish rap and hip-hop would desist—overnight if possible—but, since it's so ingrained into the urban psyche, it's going to be there for a while and to our detriment because right now, when I look at the whole jazz scene, there are very few African American, young players mainly because very few are training on instruments. So now, the music is mainly coming from white America. It's coming from Europe. It's coming from the East. Even if you go to a gig at the Village Vanguard, you only see one or two black faces. I went to hear Taj Mahal at the Blue Note a few weeks ago and there may have been three blacks and there was only standing room in the place—one reason is Taj Mahal can play a damn good guitar. He can take it apart. He can talk about the history of the music with great articulation and verve.

145

He's a musicologist and a committed musician who doesn't expect to become rich overnight. Just before I came up here, I was in Trenton and a car passed by—the lyrics were so bad I did not believe it was being played on the radio.

KGD: Why didn't you believe they would be playing it on the radio? That's what the radio station wants people listening to.

YK: I didn't want to believe that we had sunk so damn low. We had a certain moral currency in the 1960s and 1970s. If there is a conspiracy, okay, I think it would be to undermine that moral currency. Especially since the so-called Cold War—the war of ideas is over. The United States changed its policy on civil rights because we were on the world stage with the Soviet Union. Perception means a lot.

KGD: It's funny for me—well not funny, but interesting—just in the sense of how seeing something as part of the past affects the appreciation for it. I mean, I feel like, right now, I'm in the middle of hip-hop. I was born at the beginning and I grew up through its maturation, so I know the good stuff. I'm here now for the stuff that I know most of which is detrimental. It is hard for me to make any general claim about hip-hop because I say, "Well, I know it was this and I know what it is now." So I can't say, straight up, hip-hop is a terrible thing, but I can recognize what it is now.

YK: What was good and what was bad about it, yes.

KGD: And the one thing I always question is whether we will ever get back to that point where hip-hop was something that was generating dialogues and being creative or will there have to be a new black music and what will the new black music be.

YK: Well I'll tell you one thing, it will never be the same after hip-hop. At one time, we produced music without being overtaken with concerns about money, fame, and all those things that come or don't come. The music was being produced because there was a need for it. There was a function, but also a kind of personal need, you know? One could be made to feel a certain kind of power, but one could also be to made feel like a whole person by what he or she was singing, playing on the piano— trying to get every note right, playing way deep into the night without worrying about if it was going to make a dollar. I would love to embrace the new music and I've tried. I've listened to it, but even going back and listening to the Last Poets . . . I couldn't believe I had ever listened to the Last Poets, and I did in the 1970s, you know, but I was listening with a different ear.

A lot of the concerns were different. I didn't necessarily want the entertainment because there were so many other things to entertain me. Just being alive [*laughing*] is entertainment enough.

Even with someone such as Miles Davis—I'm writing this essay now called "The Birth of the Uncool" playing off Miles Davis's *The Birth of the Cool*—Miles makes a statement. He says the reason he stopped playing ballads was that he loved them too much. When *Bitches Brew*, the first LP of the fusion records, came out I said, "Gosh, this is different," but by the time the third one came out I said, "Wait. I want to hear the lyricism, the lyrical bravado behind Miles's trumpet." I didn't want these little screams and squawks and relying on the wah-wah of the electronics to accelerate, to produce the music. I wanted his genius behind it, not some programmer, some engineer, sitting in a room somewhere.

Getting a Shape

Interview by Divya Ayyala and Rob Rosencrans

DIVYA AYYALA: What was your first experience with poetry?

YUSEF KOMUNYAKAA: Okay, the first two poems I memorized were Edgar Allan Poe's "Annabel Lee" and James Weldon Johnson's "The Creation." That encouraged me to read Paul Laurence Dunbar, and I ventured from his "Ode to Ethiopia" and "An Antebellum Sermon" to voices from the Harlem Renaissance such as Langston Hughes, Arna Bontemps, Anne Spencer, Claude McKay, and Countee Cullen. You know, the more I think about this, I'm certain that the Bible and Tennyson came my direction before Dunbar. That's right. But I never thought I'd write poetry. At thirteen or fourteen I discovered James Baldwin, a book of his entitled *Nobody Knows My Name*. Then I read what I could find of his. His work was very instructive, because there was a distilled elegance and confrontation in everything Baldwin wrote or spoke, and that's the circuitous route I took before writing my first words of poetry.

DA: When did you first know when you would become a poet?

YK: I attended my first poetry workshop in '73. Dr. Alex Blackburn had been living in England for almost fourteen years and he returned to the United States to teach literature at the University of Colorado, and I was lucky to have been in his creative writing workshop. Though I had taken with me two anthologies of poetry to Vietnam, Hayden Carruth's *The Voice Is Great within Us* and Donald Allen's *Contemporary American Poetry*, I never thought I'd actually write poetry. Before I arrived at the University of Colorado I had already begun to fall in love with language and what metaphors and imagery could do, which

From *Pioneer*, a publication of the Isidore Newman School in New Orleans, November 21, 2008.

jump-started my acute imagination. Early on I had read Phillis Wheatley's poem entitled "On Imagination," and what really held my attention was the power she allotted to the process of imaging distant worlds, as well as the haunting biographical facts of her life. She's an African who had been brought to Boston at age seven or eight, named after a slave ship, and was writing poems as a teenager servant that were published in a 1773 edition in England, and some of the poems were rather provocative and possessed audacity. So, I had already discovered the power of poetry.

ROBERT ROSENCRANS: So you seem to feel like there's been an evolution in your reading and you talk about the evolution of your life. Do you feel like your writing has evolved with it and changed from basic things like the way it's shaped?

YK: We are such complicated organisms, changing from day to day. You're not the same person today that you were yesterday. Each of us is constantly being challenged and shaped by complex stimuli. It seems as if there's always an element of evolution taking place. The brain is also such a gluttonous mechanism. That is, it is constantly being shaped and challenged by what we experience. In that sense, who I am as a person has changed, and consequently my writing has also grown.

RR: Do you think that growing up where you grew up is one of the things that shaped you?

YK: Yes, for me, Bogalusa was a mecca for inquiry. The landscape beckoned to me, forcing me to journey imaginatively and see deeper into things around me. I loved trekking out across the pastures, into the cornfields, the pear orchards, and losing myself in the woods, with thrashers and jackrabbits among the muscadine and saw vines. There was always an intense discovery going on in my boyhood. I think that internalized emotional terrain became a psychological overlay for how I see and experience the world. It's still active in my personality, still a part of me.

RR: "Venus's-flytraps," the first one in *Magic City*—when you wrote a poem like that, is that how you felt as a child or is that so much more retrospective?

YK: I think it's a combination of both: I remembered the image of the insect-eating plant, its brightness on the other side of the barbed wire, and this remained with me wherever I went. In a way, that image kept me connected to Bogalusa, always resurfacing, rising out of the psyche.

RR: The Venus flytrap?

YK: Yeah. The Venus flytrap, the idea of it definitely amazed me when I was four or five years old. In a sense, it was vegetable and animal, and I think it fueled my young imagination. That was the first image to connect me to nature, to that great beckoning mystery.

RR: Those images—how do you pick images when you're writing your poetry?

YK: I don't choose the images . . . the images choose me. For me the poem is really an act of improvisation. I write the first image or tonal idea, and then a fluid movement transports me to various places. I hope there's a register outside of a logical conceit. One has to practice one's craft until there's at least an illusion of control. So, yes, the images, they choose me.

DA: How hard is it to revise work?

YK: How difficult is revision? Well, I never add anything to a poem. Usually I'm extracting what seems extraneous, trying to refine the music and the imagery, hoping that the poem still surprises me through revision. But this is based on my composition process, the practice of writing down all the images, not worrying about the poem's shape or form until later. Then I try to revise the poem down to its most natural imagistic impulse, keeping in mind not to polish the heart out of the poem.

DA: So you pare it down to make it take a shape?

YK: Yes, to take a shape. Or, so it can discover its shape in the center of an extended possibility. Well, I'd like to believe it's an illusion of symmetry [laughs]. I like to think about it in that way.

DA: How important to you is the rhythmic sound of it?

YK: I read it aloud as I'm composing it. I need the music to enter my body. The ear is a great editor; it keeps us true and honest.

DA: On that note, when where you first exposed to rhythm?

YK: Well, I can journey back to that very first moment, when I became very conscious of music [pauses]. There was a mahogany radio in our living room, and it seemed as if it was this tall, about thirty-six Inches. I was three years old, and the reason I remember this so clearly—I can still see myself sliding behind the radio, and being very inquisitive, you know, hypnotized by the glow of the bulbs—

RR: The tubes?

YK: Yeah. The tubes. They were beautiful, so red, but I didn't realize they were so hot. Not until I touched one. I suppose that's when I discovered the essence of fire [laughs freely]. That's why I remember this moment so clearly.

DA: Two-in-one deal?

YK: Yeah, two-in-one thing. And also, I loved to sing along with the music. I wouldn't sing the recorded lyrics; I would attempt to sing my own words.

RR: The shape of poems? Is the old style dead?

YK: Well, for us Americans, anyone writing and thinking in English, there are some built-in limitations, especially when we consider the tonal limitations of those end rhymes. Sometimes the shaped performance of a poem becomes more important than its emotional architecture. How it appears on the page becomes more important than what the words convey.

RR: The meter of the poem?

YK: If one has encouraged the poem's music to enter the body, the meter is automatically present. In language itself—cadence, meter that isn't notated—the body and the mind work together to create the most natural rhythm. For me, internal rhymes seem freer than end rhymes in English. When considering literary conceits, I believe that one should write in one's own time. Even though there's a lot of rap and hip-hop, it still seems so contrived and unnatural to my ear. Perhaps that's my shortcoming. Being here in New Orleans at this moment, and knowing how important the playing of instruments and the history of music is to the soul of this city, it's difficult for me to even imagine a young musician here embracing rap or hip-hop. It seems this would be a total regression, unless one doesn't have the talent or wishes to take a shortcut. Recently, I did write some lyrics for a recording entitled *The Mercy Suite*. And, of course, in writing those lyrics I did turn to rhyming schemes that transported me back to that moment when I was five years old singing beside the radio. That's the nature of song lyrics. My poetry is different from my song lyrics; it's in free verse, more traditional. Of course, we usually don't think of it that way, that free verse probably predates all those literary conceits based in forms. However, if we were writing poems in a Romance language such as Spanish or Italian, our poetry could more naturally embrace typical forms. I began to rethink this idea when I first heard a recitation of my free verse poems that had been translated into Italian, how the rhymes were naturally embedded in the language.

DA: Do you feel like it loses or gains something when translated into a language?

YK: I feel like I'm lucky. I trust my translators, each of whom is keenly aware that I'm a fall guy for the natural music that resides in everyday spoken language. When I first heard my poems recited in Polish I was taken aback. Musically, to my ear, the poems sounded as if they'd been rendered into a Romance language. I was surprised by the lyricism captured in a different language.

DA: Do you think that speaks volumes about how language originated? The rhythm that we're prone to speaking in?

YK: I think so.

DA: That's what language is.

YK: Yes, that's what language is. Language is, especially when we consider poetry, an attempt to recapture that first moment when humans began to measure themselves against the immensity of things. At first, it was a way of speaking into the void. It must have been a resounding echo coming back. It must have been frightening.

RR: Do you feel like that as a teacher? Do you watch your students speak for the first time into their voids?

YK: By the time a student arrives to me, he or she has already been shaped by so much. But it's interesting to see and hear them discover their own voices. Because I suggest to each that one possesses his or her own voice already—the gift is to recognize it. And one has to be true to that recognized voice.

DA: When do you think that happened to you?

YK: Well—

DA: Or do you think it's still happening now?

YK: Maybe it is still happening [*laughs*]. Yes, it's definitely still happening. Otherwise, why would I still face the challenge? Why would any of us so-called artists surrender again and again to the muse? Perhaps the quest is indebted to the discovery within the voice, or what's revealed. One would hope to embrace a continuing passion. Otherwise I would do something else.

DA: On to another subject.

YK: Yes.

DA: When we read your poetry, well it's obvious that Vietnam has played a huge role in your poetry, but do you have a specific event from that time period of your life that you would like to share with us that just sticks out in your mind or epitomizes your stay there?

YK: Well, it's a moment. There are many moments, really. Sometimes everything seemed sped up, and other times things seemed slowed down, suspended. But—I want to go to a moment where I remember squatting in a grassy gully—it was a stolen moment of solitude. I could see the helipad at the rear of the division hospital in Chu Lai, on the edge of the South China Sea. I could see the medevac helicopters landing. I could see the stretchers being pulled off the helicopters. It's that moment—how do I say it? I felt lucky. Because at that moment I could see myself on one of the stretchers, you know? I'm so close—and I'm so distanced from it. Well, maybe it was the time of day, because it was twilight, and I'm daydreaming of a beautiful morning, in limbo. I was gazing at the sun setting, and then there's the line of helicopters in the midst of this very tranquil moment. The silence of the horror is what made this personal moment so surreal.

DA: Personal experiences have shaped you into who you are today. But do you have one or two poets or authors or people of really great literary works that have brought together who you are as a poet? Or do you think it's a very internal process?

YK: I'm in awe of numerous voices. Pablo Neruda's love poems and elemental odes, his poetic inquiry about the United Fruit Company, his prose in works such as *Passions and Impressions*, etc. Federico Garcia Lorca's concept of *duende* interests me greatly, how he embraced aspects of the Gypsy culture and mystique to inform his highly personal and national voice. The idea of the protest sonnet during the Harlem Renaissance by Claude McKay, Anne Spencer, and Countee Cullen, along with some of the more modernist voices such as Helene Johnson, and then to Melvin B. Tolson, Gwendolyn Brooks, and Robert Hayden. And, of course, I can't forget Charles Baudelaire's *The Flowers of Evil*. After reading those poems, how could one never regard dispossession and lice the same way? But to answer your question—yes, writing is always first an internal voyage that involves risk and discovery.

RR: Do you think there's such a thing as a good poet and a great poet?

YK: I'd rather not attempt the pin it down that way. I think if the work can continue to beckon and summon readers across the ages because a certain poet has been true to his or her time, the moment of history in which he or she lived, then that is a gift, and time is the point of that equation. Gwendolyn Brooks once told me that art is that which endures. I believe that. But there are some great poets that we tend to not embrace today, as well.

If time has kept the voice in the poem honest, with humble and brave attention paid to observation, experience, and imagination, and if there's a touch of enduring beauty, then it's great poetry.

DA: And do you feel that in order for someone to achieve that, they need a lot of time or experience writing poetry, or can that be something completely raw and free of formal training?

YK: I think so. Of course, the training of one's mind and heart doesn't necessarily arrive from formalized training in academia. Academia, however, can provide a community. The poetry workshop often is no more than an instant community of shared and contrasting ideas. But sometimes the artist needs something to push against, something that assists in forming or augmenting a necessary passion.

DA: Current events. Robert Frost, Maya Angelou at inaugurations . . . which poem by which poet do you think should be read at Barack Obama's inauguration as president?

YK: I don't know. But it was important to see President Obama holding a copy of Derek Walcott's *Collected Poems*. I love Walcott's poetry. His depth and breadth of vision are astounding. But I also love his plays, such as *Dream on Monkey Mountain*. Poetry, interestingly, also enters Walcott's plays, as it does in Tennessee Williams's dramatic works and short stories.

DA: Stage directions.

YK: But with Tennessee Williams we don't think of him as a poet. Most people don't read his poetry. I don't know, but perhaps that's because of the baroque style and embellished texture of his poetry. I think Williams viewed himself as a poet first, and it isn't surprising that the character Tom in *The Glass Menagerie* is a poet. Oh, how'd I go off on that one? [*laughs*].

RR: You touch a lot on racial issues in lots of your books. And you mentioned Adrienne Rich earlier, so it's obviously a big part of your life. What do you, what are your thoughts? At a time when we can simultaneously have a black lawyer be elected as president, what part is race of our identity now as a nation, as a people?

YK: Well, it's interesting from that perspective. I believe that black America has long been able to produce a person for the situation. It isn't the first time. At the moment, I'm thinking about Frederick Douglass—what Frederick Douglass comes out of, you know? He was amazing. And it's so interesting, especially at this moment in our history, to return to his infamous Fourth of July speech. And, of course, there's W. E. B. DuBois editing

Crisis magazine and writing books such as *The Souls of Black Folk.* He challenges the South's black apologist, Booker T. Washington; he's already questioning our retrograde concepts of race globally, already addressing the cultural pathos of double consciousness, clearly ahead of the times. In 1923 he published a book entitled *Dark Princess,* and I wonder what people think of *Dark Princess* today. Do you know that book?

DA: No, I was thinking about Black Reconstruction—that was in—

YK: Right. Something that was dead before it began. I was thinking of Jackie Robinson. In regards to the culture and politics of race, Jackie Robinson comes under the spotlight in the 1940s. Yes, race has always been at the epicenter of our culture, because of the continuing echo of that peculiar institution called slavery. America has always been a mecca of contradictions and double-speak. We only have to think of the term *manifest destiny,* broken treaties. Holy facades. When Thomas Jefferson was comfortable in his perceptions concerning politics and ethics of false biology and law, he could only approach Phillis Wheatley's poetry by saying that it was beneath his commentary. But George Washington did shake her hand and attempt to praise her words. I think she recited her poetry for him. Simply, Wheatley challenged Jefferson's beliefs about race and inherent hierarchy. But the United States is one of the few places, if not the only place in the world, that's constantly reinventing itself. And I feel that we are now at a most surprising juncture where it has reinvented itself again. I mean, that's why people from the world over—it's a beacon— for people around the world. I think it has a lot to do with the size of this country, its natural resources, but perhaps it's also an approximation of a democratic spirit.

RR: So that's race?

YK: [*Laughs*] Well, race isn't interesting anyway. In many ways, it's an artificial construction.

RR: Have you ever read *Passing* by Nella Larsen?

YK: Yes. Years ago. But now there's a different kind of passing. I'm thinking about how many newcomers to the United States have attempted to insinuate themselves into the dominant white culture because of perceived advantages. And many of these immigrants are the products of colonization, and at times it seems that their hearts and minds have been colonized through a brutal and precise system, and many of their forebears were yes-men and yes-women to some very tyrannical machines. So, yes, race still complicates the national psyche.

RR: It's just another denominator on your ID card.

YK: Right. And then it's kept us apart, but the Civil Rights Movement was a black *and* white movement. Most people forget that, you know. Many still want to believe that it was a black movement, that it was only a self-serving gesture. But that movement challenged a system of injustice. One only has to look at the photographs of those black and white students boarding the buses to the Deep South.

RR: Freedom riders.

YK: That's right. Freedom riders—eighteen- and nineteen-year-olds—that's amazing. They're challenging the system of injustice, but they're also challenging themselves as human beings, living in the United States—that's what.

LAURIE WILLIAMS: What advice would you give young poets (high school-, junior high-aged) poets? What advice would you give them as writers? Or as readers as well, too?

YK: Reading, that's probably what it is, isn't it? I would say read everything. Not only literature. I would say that one has to possess a healthy work ethic. I would also say that one has to be fully engaged in the ideas of the world. One has to learn the names of things. We should know the plants, the animals, their vernacular names and scientific names, rituals and needs. Everything. Nothing's taboo. One has to be inquisitive about life, about the elemental and unthinkable components of existence. Such questions keep us connected to who we are, and what our possibilities are as human beings. Not as writers, not as the audience, just as human beings.

The Wolf/Interview

Interview by Ishion Hutchinson

ISHION HUTCHINSON: You have written verse plays and have collaborated with other artists for staged performances in the past, but your *Gilgamesh: A Verse Play* is the first time you have adapted an existing work for both the page and the stage. Can you speak a little at how you arrived at your own dramatic language that reimagines the old narrative?

YUSEF KOMUNYAKAA: Well, when Chad Gracia asked me to consider writing a version of *Gilgamesh* for the stage, I had already read some translations, and I knew immediately that I didn't want to write a facsimile of all the other versions of the text culled and reimagined from the Sumerian cuneiforms where Iraq stands today. For me, a *Gilgamesh* for the stage had to come out of me, as well as from a borrowed landscape. I had to discover my own language to even attempt *Gilgamesh*, and it took a single sentence which was broken into six short lines: "Did I not put my head / with a god's for days, / asking why is there blood / and hair in the snares / and not even a ghost of prey / left behind?" This single question propelled me, because I had to confront what all the other translations and adaptations didn't have to—attempt to construct a narrative that could live on the stage. I knew I wanted the language stripped down. We had to invent, to see into things. We were lucky to work with some wonderful actors, to hear and feel the text read aloud on Sunday afternoons. There are some piercing translations of *Gilgamesh*; a few days after I finished our pages for the stage, I received a copy of Stephen Mitchell's version, which is terrific, but I must admit that I was thankful we already had our *Gilgamesh*, that I wouldn't be teased toward doubt.

From *The Wolf* (November 27, 2012).

157

Now, after a superb reading of *Gilgamesh* at the Ninety-Second Street Y a few years ago, the play will finally receive its first full production at the Constellation Theatre in Washington, D.C., from May 2 to June 2. I can't wait to see the play come alive on the stage, because I view the director, the actors, the stage designers, musicians, and everyone behind the scene as collaborators.

IH: The time between *Warhorses* and *The Chameleon Couch* is relatively close, yet the two collections differ significantly in form and content; to me they don't read sequentially or seem even to be in close dialogue; how do you handle or keep separate the different psychic and creative energy that went into each, especially within such a similar time frame?

YK: I like to work on a number of collections, usually three, side by side, moving through and shifting various states of mind, within a somewhat stable state of being. I attempt to honor the fact that we are indeed complex organisms, and time seems to always mediate and negotiate who we are, and as a writer this is right for me. Perhaps I like the dare within, the challenge. I feel each challenged moment is a part of the whole; that each poem engages my gut-level concerns regarding the natural and psychological worlds we endeavor to traverse intellectually. However, I do spend time organizing a collection after the poems have been written, to see if I can feel and understand how they live beside each other tonally, through images.

IH: It is clear that your numerous geographic shifts are part of the reason for the alacrity and elusive leaps in your poetry, jazz being another part of the reason; in a way, you, or your poet-persona, is chameleonic, chimerical, hard to pin down—where do you feel most at home? Do you feel settled/located in New York or is there restlessness, a search for home?

YK: Perhaps the alacrity has much to do with growing up in the Deep South at a certain in our history; it has to do with survival. I mean, well, one's internal landscape shifts or it becomes static, and for the dreamer we can easily guess which is the better path. The human is naturally inquisitive, especially the artist and the scientist. We love to engage everything. The earth is a mother lode of metaphors we live by, and I must say I have never been bored. Even as a boy in Bogalusa. My mind was always entangled with some humbug, trying to make sense out of things, and it is still difficult not to engage that which I have come in contact with, to not create some dialogue. For me, the poem is always a dialogue, not merely an attempt to transform, lay bare, or translate elements of an experience or feeling. So, all the doors are open. Nothing is taboo. And I love being alive. I think that's what Parker, Miles, Coltrane, and Mary Lou were getting at even when they played the blues. Not a longing, but a gutsy, sacred dreaming that refuses to be jailed by borders and conceits. I grew up dreaming myself away from Bogalusa, but the further I journeyed the closer I came to the Magic City. After all these years on the road—home? I want to say that home is where the heart is, but psychologically and philosophically I know it is more. I'm not a chameleon because I question everything around me, but I do believe that we are indeed affected by what we come in contact with, things that change us and mark our existence in some unique way. I'm not saying that malleability or amorousness is ideal, but that we are always becoming the shape of our imagined and lived dimensions. My voice was already shaped and seasoned when I came to the Big Apple, and I'm happy about that because we all are condemned to take some deep journeys. Such journeys need a sound footing. I'm lucky to have come to New York City as a mature person, but at the same time I feel that I'm not totally defined and/or confined by a voice. That's what I like about Sonny Rollins, how he transforms his sound from a place that is already his, already solid.

IH: Robert Hayden is one of your formidable influences, but rereading your work (and this is probably because I have really been struck by the poem "Blackbirding on the Hudson," in which Robert Lowell is the "unwilled" catalyst presiding over the poem's journey) I have been thinking Lowell is very important in shaping your own American voice, getting to what you say in *Blue Notes* is your "personal terrain . . . idea of trying to get underneath who I am"; do you agree and how would you contextualize your work with Lowell's?

YK: My personal pantheon seems swollen with many singular voices. And, yes, Robert Lowell definitely resides there. His is a robust reckoning with American history. I admit that history was my favorite subject in high school, with my own reading and research, because it armed me to challenge all the inherent contradictions. That can be troublesome for the poet. Perhaps this is why I admire Lowell's work; he could have so easily sidestepped or denied what he knew. Of course, someone like Stevens is so different from this upper-classed Bostonian, and one can locate the difference in their subject matter and aesthetics. Lowell not only argued with the Southern agrarians, but he argued with time and history, his inheritance, his ghosts. He challenged himself. How does he get from *Lord Weary's Castle* to *Life Studies*? I admire his journey, giving us poems such as "West Street Jail," "Beyond the Alps," "Fall 1961," and "The Quaker Graveyard at Nantucket."

IH: You once wrote that "the mood I desire in my poetry is one in which the truth can survive." It is a profound statement, and since there is an implicit artificiality about art, and though this might be a rather flawed question, but what is your falsity detector; how do you know the truth is on the page and that it will survive? A small confession: years ago when I first encountered your statement I wrestled with it for reasons I am not entirely sure of, perhaps it just seemed immense to me, a novice, and only after I had interloped it this way, "the mood I desire in my poetry is one that can survive the truth," I got some ease!

YK: Perhaps it was the word *truth* that put you ill at ease—that grand abstraction. Or, maybe it's the article, *the.* But I do think that *a* truth resides in a certain language because of the music, the tone, rhythm, which challenges the reader or listener. That's when the poem beckons; when it summons us into its reckoning. Or, maybe I was thinking of that line by Paul Zweig, when he says, "I speak, and I don't want to lie." I know the idea of art is artifice, but I don't believe it has to be artificial. I see art as an action. If it were merely a momentarily illuminated facade, or a moment of invertebrate wit, I would probably not write. I'd do something else. Perhaps psychology. Or I think I'd be a carpenter, like my great-grandfather and father. I have a friend, Ron, who was a navy helicopter rescue pilot in Vietnam, now one of the best carpenters in the world, who believes that it is pointless to build anything that doesn't last at least thirty years. One could say, yes, there's truth in what he constructs. I believe that there's too much planned obsolescence woven into everything—for a mere moment—life, art, cars, technology, sneakers, and et cetera. I wish to write poems that endure, without the idea of endurance in my mind as I write them, and I hope that comes close to a truth. Whether it's poetry or carpentry, I like the idea of passion, skill, beauty, and truth at the heart of one's work.

IH: Your vocation as a poet is marked with different degree of intensity with each new book, and that intensity has been even, steady; you do this while maintaining a university career and being active in many other fields; what is your writing process like? How do you make the time for the concentrated effort it takes to create?

YK: I suppose the internal rigging of my existence has always been rather complex. I began working manually at ten in Louisiana, but also found a way to engage myself intellectually, as well as play sports, going from one zone to the next, but remained psychically whole and consistent. I write even when I'm not writing because I feel engaged with the world through observation. I still continue to look at very small things and their function in the universe. I try to write and read daily. I love to lean from the bed and scribble down a few lines or a passage before my feet touch the floor. I write images on scraps of paper and in notebooks without order, hoping that an image, line, or short passage can later surprise me, can take me to some place that I didn't plan to go. My mind or thinking process isn't mathematical or errant, but it is definitely inquisitive, always searching for a metaphor philosophically and emotionally apt. I don't know if I always achieve that. I steal the time to create, to remain in dialogue with myself, with the larger world. How else can I feel whole?

IH: I was thinking of your brilliant address to Harold Bloom, "A Note to Bloom," and was wondering if you were to write a note to Helen Vendler and Rita Dove regarding all the talks that sprung up in light of Vendler's criticism of Dove's job on *The Penguin Anthology of Twentieth-Century American Poetry*, and Dove's subsequent response, what would you say?

YK: I don't know. But like most creative projects, scholarly or critical pursuits, each possesses a personal dimension. I am convinced that Rita Dove, who has an acute awareness of American history, literary and otherwise, chose poems—given her budgetary restrictions—that enlarge the so-called canon. Her expansive sense of voices that influenced twentieth-century American poetry is present in her introduction. In that sense, *The Penguin Anthology of Twentieth-Century American Poetry* is a worthy compendium shaped through a fair-minded vision. Of course, *The Penguin Anthology of Twentieth-Century American Poetry* does create a dialogue with what isn't in its pages, with those voices that appear in all the other anthologies of American poetry through the decades, when few, if any, critics or scholars

161

decried the configuration of those compilations. We all have our favorite poems and poets, and an anthologist as informed as Dove is, knows that we are also indebted to our literary history even as we question it. Like literary magazines, some anthologies possess hands-on personalities.

IH: The list of poets you have directly mentored is long and impressive, and yet one is faced with answering the question of whether or not poetry can be taught. What is your response? Having had the great luck of studying with you at NYU I am aware of your approach in the classroom, but tell me, what is it you like to do best with students? If you were not teaching what would you prefer to do?

YK: I don't think passion can be taught. I do, however, believe that the typical poetry workshop is usually a collection of voices that we grow to trust over days, weeks, months, through the years. It's a place of engaged, compressed intensity. Discussion is important. But listening and reading are also invaluable. In such an atmosphere of mutuality creative sparks can fly and great things can happen. It's a place of intense dialogue. However, I don't believe everyone should go away writing the same or similar poem. For the artist, ateliers have been going for a long time. And if we think of Dante and his friends listening to each other's new poems, perhaps that's one of our first poetry workshops. It's a place of fierce, beautiful dialogue, where each poet has the freedom to say yes or no to any given critique. Think of the traditional cantor poet of Ghana who creates a poem for the tribe to chant as a verbal weapon against its enemy—if not a workshop, it is still truly a group dynamic. The workshop isn't high ritual, but it is indeed a ritual. And magical things can happen there. Think of those exchanges where Socrates stood at the apex of philosophical inquiry among friends and foe. But our poets are never tormented to drink hemlock from the golden cup or coconut shell. For me, sometimes that one-on-one dynamic is what works best, where there's an exchange of ideas about poetry, shared readings, critique, and where discoveries spring out of contrasting realities and philosophies.

IH: Any recent discovery of poets that have taken off the top of your head?

YK: When Dickinson said "as if the top my head were taken off," there were few poets in America. Now, there are numerous young American and Caribbean poets who more than hold their own, but since there are so many perhaps it is difficult to say who stands out, especially because our contemporary poets are so well-versed in craft and poetics. I do think some of our more important voices come out of NYU's program because of the legacy of Galway Kinnell, Sharon Olds, Philip Schultz, and Philip Levine. However, there are also a plethora of voices—not that poets have to write the same, traditional-sounding poems like visual artists painting by the numbers—whose language have become fluffballs caught in a system of haze and jive. In fact, now, I'm often more drawn to those world voices, same as in world music, where content and skill coalesce. I think content and style are what truly make voices unique, such as Mahmoud Darwish—well, he's someone I wish I had met. I don't have to name names, because there's always someone left out. I am also rereading poets such as Etheridge Knight, Pablo Neruda, Lucille Clifton, William Carlos William, Hayden Carruth, Ai, Paul Zweig, and the list goes on. Cesare Pavese, a voice that made me run to the bookshelf and pull down Eugenio Montale's *Collected Poems*. It's difficult not to compare, isn't it? That's one great thing about poetry, oftentimes, it lives on, and we rediscover it again and again. And, of course, there are those American poets that are iconic, still writing great poems, book by book.

IH: The first of your *Wishbone Trilogy, Taboo,* has been out now for nearly ten years, you have published three collections since (counting *Gilgamesh*). Are you still at work on parts 2 and 3? What else are you working on?

YK: Yes, I'm still working on parts 2 and 3 of *Wishbone Trilogy,* still intrigued about the collision of cultures defining blacks and blackness in the ancient and modern worlds, and how those borders crossed inform contemporary existence. Some of the titles of recent poems written for the *Trilogy* are "The White Handkerchief," "Box," "I Am Silas," "Quicksilver," and "They Went Down into the Water." At the moment, I'm also working on the following collections of poetry, *The Emperor of Atlantis* and *Night Animals.* In 2013, *Testimony,* a compilation of music-related poems, accompanied by jazz CDs, is forthcoming from Wesleyan University Press. I have also been writing essays, plays, and other collaborative performance pieces. As you can see, my muse has been keeping me busy.

Celebration and Confrontation

Walt Whitman

A Conversation with Jacob Wilkenfeld

Yusef Komunyakaa is the author of fourteen volumes of poetry, including the Pulitzer Prize–winning 1994 collection *Neon Vernacular*. His many other honors include the Kingsley Tufts Poetry Award, the Ruth Lilly Poetry Prize, and the Wallace Stevens Award. His most recent book, *The Chameleon Couch* (2011) was a finalist for the National Book Award. He is Global Distinguished Professor of English at New York University. The absorptive, kaleidoscopic range of Komunyakaa's verse has led some reviewers to draw parallels between his work and Whitman's—a comparison Komunyakaa has modestly described as "an easy—less than critical—gesture."[1] However, while he may not be a "Whitmanesque" poet, Komunyakaa has long displayed a keen interest in Whitman's work, as manifested in the allusions contained within poems such as "Kosmos" (1992), "The Poetics of Paperwood" (1992), and "Praise Be" (2005), as well as references to Whitman that the poet has made in interviews, and his participation in the 2008 PBS documentary *American Experience: Walt Whitman*. At least one parallel between the two writers is worth preserving: both defy easy generalization. For example, Komunyakaa's work often explores the meanings of black experience. Yet race, unquestionably one of the major themes of his poetry, is not a connective thread holding all of it together. Rather, if there is a perpetual theme in Komunyakaa's work, it is the startling diversity that exists within both his own and the collective imag-

From *Walt Whitman Quarterly Review* 30, no. 3 (2013). Interview conducted in August 2010.

ination. Whitman's lines from "Whoever you are Holding me now in Hand" are a fitting description of Komunyakaa's protean verse, always disclosing the unexpected:

Even while you should think you had unquestionably caught me, behold!

Already you see I have escaped from you.[2]

JACOB WILKENFELD: What first drew you to Whitman? What were the most significant aspects for you of your first readings of *Leaves of Grass*?

YUSEF KOMUNYAKAA: I was in high school when I first came across Whitman's name. And at the time I was reading poetry from the Harlem Renaissance. Before that I had been reading poems such as Tennyson's "The Eagle," James Weldon Johnson's "The Creation," and Paul Laurence Durbar's "The Colored Soldiers." I went to check out Whitman's poems from the school library, but the volume wasn't on the shelf. The librarian had been instructed to keep Whitman behind the circulation desk. Yet somehow I actually checked out the volume. Of course, it was different from Tennyson. It was also different from the Harlem Renaissance poets, their protest sonnets, and it was definitely different from Poe, Poe's "Annabel Lee." I became immediately caught up in Whitman's language. In retrospect, what was instructive to me was the music in his poetry. And much later, decades later, I found myself reading him again, and it was almost like reading the volume for the first time— *Leaves of Grass*. But I think my body remembers the music more than my mind remembers the music. There was urgency, an experience underneath the language that surprised me. And his imagination was so huge. That was the thing. His imagination was almost otherworldly at times, but also seemed naturally insightful and encompassing. His references on democracy were interesting because I had never heard anyone speak so passionately about democracy except possibly James Baldwin, who I discovered at fourteen. And Baldwin of course was constantly talking about the possibility of democracy, and of the responsibility to ideas of freedom. I think Whitman in a certain sense speaks about responsibility, responsibility through, first, the imagination—that one has to imagine another person free before he or she can even see that person, feel that person in a moment of shared freedom.

JW: In the recent PBS *American Experience* program on Whitman, you single out the auction block scene in "I Sing the Body Electric" as an example of Whitmanian empathetic identification with others, regardless of their cultural origins. In your words, "For some reason I feel like he has the capacity to imagine himself on the auction block as well. . . . It really enters his psyche. I think he's wrestling with himself."[3] Could you speak some more about this dimension of Whitman's work and its significance for you?

YK: This idea of being empathetic is also embedded in the idea of democracy. For Whitman it is not an abstraction. His seems really intense empathy. I think what he basically believed is that one is not really human until he possesses the capacity of empathy through the imagination. Also, there are so many references to the body, as if language enters the body and becomes tactile and physical. So when Whitman speaks of the black man, such as the passage where he sees this black man driving a horse-drawn wagon, he seems to be sitting there beside him. He is not, at that moment, merely of compressed belief and passion. In the woven language of the poem, Whitman may even be that man. I think this is really an amazing kind of epiphany. Likewise, for this poet, the auction block seems more than a physical dimension, a part of his psyche. He's a witness.

JW: In another interview, you have said that Whitman's vision, like Hughes's, is "driven by an acute sense of beauty and tragedy in America's history."[4] This also seems an apt description of your writing. Like Whitman, you have written very profoundly about the tragedies of war, but also about other forms of American tragedy. Could you talk about the interrelationship between beauty and tragedy in your poetry and in Whitman's?

YK: Perhaps I borrowed the phrase from another phrase of mine, as it relates to nature, that there always seems to be an alignment of beauty and terror. Whitman doesn't back off from that which is beautiful. He celebrates it. Nor does he back off from tragedy. Death—he's right there, almost on the deathbed. And it is so tactile. It is so physical. At times, however, Whitman risks sentimentality. We can define sentimentality as passion without form, basically. But at the same time, Whitman can write about a mockingbird, almost as if this mockingbird has symphonic capacity, and I admire that, because he is also listening very carefully. In *Leaves of Grass*, that's the idea. The title relates to the simple beauty of nature, and then the pages morph into human complexity. One leaf is different from all the other leaves, and that multitude is always crowding Whitman's brain. So beauty is severe. Sometimes beauty is as severe as tragedy, and there is a marriage between the two in other places in Whitman. One reason is because of the meandering of phrases. *Leaves of Grass* is a heroic attempt to concretize passion, and I think this is why Whitman influenced so many other poets I associate with a similar directed passion, such as Neruda or Ginsberg. It's that same kind of earthy feeling. It's almost as if the poet connects directly to the earth. I grew up in a very small town, and my early rituals actually had to do with nature, with celebrating. I was celebrating without even being aware that I was celebrating. Of course, Whitman says in the opening lines of "Song of Myself," "I celebrate myself, / And what I assume you shall assume, / For every atom belonging to me as good belongs to you." And the way he celebrates is acquiring an acute awareness. He reminds us that it's hard to be aware of nature, its beauty, and not also feel a part of it, a respect.

JW: The critic Kenneth Price has argued that poets of color have a complicated relationship with Whitman. In his words, "There are complex issues involved when an artist of color acknowledges a white predecessor."[5] Do you see this a valid argument, and why or why not?

YK: In a way, from an opposite take, we could say that it dehumanizes one who doesn't have the capacity to embrace another. And that is what Whitman is all about in a certain sense. Yet to embrace the positive elements of Whitman, one has to also be aware of the negative elements. But that's true with each and every human being. Whitman is really a unique product of his own time. He responded to the obvious inequities in our country. The idea of slavery is rather complex, if we really want to get down to the facts. First, one tribe defeats another and sells its prisoners to merchants and ship captains. Now, that's already a complicated situation, right? And we know there are numerous demarcation lines drawn in the dirt, especially when we begin to argue with history, but sometimes we have to be brave enough to cross those lines and demand at least an approximated truth. And we know through inheritance all the old, ugly, pathetic stories of slavery. This is what I feel. Many of us, not only the descendants of former slaves, are constantly defining and redefining who we are as human beings. Look at those from immigrant backgrounds, excluding only the Native American. Whitman was wrestling with himself, because, let's face it, he is a product of that historical moment—a witness. To break off from Whitman for a moment, think of the complexity of a poet such as Phillis Wheatley. One moment she's defending herself before those eighteen Bostonians, and the next moment, in her poetry, she is casting an eye towards Africa that is not sympathetic, saying, "'Twas mercy brought me from my *Pagan* land." There is complexity in that glance, and in history as well.

JW: In the first version of your poem "Kosmos," you write that Whitman "heard primordial notes of jazz / Murmuring up from the Mississippi."[6] Do you see Whitman's poetics as analogous to a jazz aesthetic, and if so, what parallels are there?

YK: Improvisation. Many of Whitman's poems were improvisational. This doesn't directly parallel elements of passion, but it does parallel the idea of celebration. I think Whitman is really celebrating his voice. He's attempting to celebrate the mystery within himself, and I think that's what the jazz musician does. The jazz musician has a musical phrase or melody that expands, deconstructs musically, and he puts it back together, reconstructs. And I think that's what Whitman is doing. I don't think he's consciously saying, "I'm going to improvise." I don't see it as strategy. If anything, his is a voice shaped from need and driven by enthusiastic genius.

JW: He does have the poem "Spontaneous Me."

YK: That's right. And if we think about spontaneity, he's already there—ahead—alongside the Beats. Spontaneous necessity, spontaneous prose.

JW: In another interview, you celebrate Whitman for his attention to life rather than abstraction, his inclusiveness, and his willingness to treat aspects of life once considered inappropriate for literature. In your words, Whitman "didn't dodge anything."[7] Do you see today's poets as carrying on this tradition?

YK: Today's poets? It depends on the poet. As a matter of fact, I think there is a certain amount of erasure in contemporary poetry. And the erasure happens mainly through over experimentation. This is interesting because Whitman experimented to underscore content. His eyes and ears—his senses caught everything. And some of today's poets—now I don't want everyone writing the same poem. For me as a writer it is important to relate to my experiences, my observations and feelings, to dwell in a place of expansion. And I think that's what Whitman attempted. There are topics that I'm waiting for some young American voices to address. One of them is racism. And how does one address that? The reason I say this is that, just coming back from Paris, I feel like there is more of a racial ease there, people more comfortable with each other. I saw very young people, children of different races, playing together. Not that they had been instructed to play together, but just as what humans do. But at the same time I'm very much aware that there are problems of class and among ethnic groups in France, especially when we think of Muslims. Here we tend to sidestep that topic, as if we have already dealt with it. And I suppose the only way to deal with it is on a personal basis, not to have a political agenda, but just as human beings.

JW: In some ways race is the supreme fiction of American culture.

YK: Yes, it's an invention. And that invention has kept us apart, but also privileged others. And Whitman, I think, was very much aware of this, this divide that happens. Ironically, I do think that divide is beneficial to some citizens. We don't talk about class either. Recently, I was reading *Einstein on Race and Racism*, and I was incensed by some of the historical situations described. Einstein attempted to deal with what he witnessed while living in Princeton. He offended some educated people. I think it was Baldwin who, pointing out a difference of the South and North, said, in the South the black man is always the subject of discussion, in the North never, so denied in one sense and exaggerated in the other.[8]

JW: Like Emerson, Whitman views the poet as a representative figure who—differently from but also similarly to a political figure—speaks for a multitude. Do you view the work of the poet in this manner? Also, are there dangers inherent in writers' presuming to identify with or speak on behalf of others? And are there dangers in poetic attempts at inclusiveness?

YK: I think it is necessary in the twenty-first century. We have to think of when Whitman was writing. I think he was taking a risk. Now, there is a certain white poet, a contemporary of mine, who says that he writes for white people. I think that is so narrow-minded it's laughable and tragic—not necessarily for others so much as tragic for him. I believe we have the capacity, and one has to say the audacity, to carry each other in our hearts, in our minds as well, and write for anyone who dares to picks up our work, but first write for oneself.

JW: Some have argued that instead of letting different voices speak through him, Whitman imposes his poetic persona upon others. Critics have argued that his poetry is not truly multiperspectival.

YK: Whitman's definitely egotistical, and I think he had to be at that particular time to assume the voice of the great poet. We can see and feel him inventing himself. Is this the same thing that happened with Dante? Perhaps so. I think Whitman was taken by his singing. That's the way I see Whitman, as a singer, more than as the solitary poet sitting in a corner, going from phrase to phrase. I'm willing to bet Whitman read everything aloud as he was composing. I bet he was having great fun. He talks about dancing as well. He makes language dance. And in dance we think of celebration. Often poets confront certain things and celebrate other things. But sometimes a single line is a moment of celebration and the next line is a moment of stern, necessary confrontation. Sometimes it's a confrontation with oneself, not necessarily with the external world. There's an insinuation, suggesting that we don't have to have an argument with what's around us, but we can definitely have an argument with what we are made of.

JW: You have also alluded to some of the more troubling aspects of Whitman's poetic project. You have spoken of fetishism or eroticizing of characters in his work. You also touch on this dimension of Whitman's work in the second version of your poem "Kosmos," when you address Whitman as "locked inside / your exotic Ethiopia."[9] Could you speak more on this topic?

YK: Whitman's poems are very sexual. He was a sexual being. There's muscle inside his imagination. His lines. My belief is that Whitman also reacted to the general feeling embedded in the national psyche about blacks. Whitman definitely encountered that. How could he not? The slave on the auction block is always stripped down. Even the black man driving the coach is very physical through depiction. Whitman draws him with robust energy. That became very much a part of Whitman's psyche. It's interesting, because that is something that we, contemporary poets, celebrate as well. And sometimes, if we think of time and space, it is in just a glance. I think Whitman was trying to be truthful to himself, but at the same time, in fetishizing, there's a risk involved, to make that other human being into an object. I don't care if it's an object of adoration. It's still an object, and we're all capable of that to an extent. How can we not be? Because we're using the tools of language—symbols embedded in language. Poets have always existed in a visual culture, even if it occurs mainly in the head, through tonal imagery. And some of the definitions of those symbols carry all kinds of connotation, innuendo, insinuation, and it's hard to be outside of that. So I hold Whitman accountable as I hold myself accountable.

JW: Michael Baxandall has made a strong case for the misguidedness of critical approaches that look at influence in a traditional way.[10] In his view, critics should look more at what the second artist does to his/her precursor, rather than at how the precursor has affected the later artist. In this sense, it is proper to speak of a Whitmanian influence on your poetry, or is there a better way to describe your engagement with Whitman's work?

YK: In a certain sense when I first read Whitman I didn't think of a great distance. I heard an echo of a voice coming to me that was really a composite of other voices I had grown up with. And in that sense, when I started writing poetry, I don't think I had Whitman's voice in my head as much as I had the voices of others in my head, though I had read Whitman. I had read Tennyson. I had read the Harlem Renaissance poets. I think that what happened is that Whitman gave me a deeper hearing, which may be in concert with a deeper singing. Because I think it's all about listening. And sometimes if we have, even accidentally, listened, we can hear an echo of the singing. I don't think that Whitman really sets out to make sense of the world. However, we participate as listeners and readers, to make sense of Whitman. And in that sense, we are making sense of Whitman's world. Maybe what's most constructive, for me, is to continue to believe that there's mystery. Whitman I think taught me to accept mystery. Everything doesn't have to be explained. Everything doesn't have to equal a neat number. But there is this immense mystery.

JW: He says, "I and this mystery here we stand."[11]

YK: Here we stand. Yeah. I don't know if I answered your question, but I'm going to come back to it in a different way. I think the artist is always more directly influenced by what he or she isn't conscious of. If one purposely sets out to imitate another artist, there's a real problem. It's important to have a foundation and then to go through that, embrace that foundation, and go where one's imagination, one's experiences, one's passions can take him or her.

171

JW: Can we speak of a Whitmanian tradition, and if so, which contemporary poets do you see as belonging to it?

YK: Of course we could say, off the top of the head, Galway Kinnell, Phillip Levine, C. K. Williams, Gerald Stern, Allen Ginsberg. I know you're waiting for black poets [*laughs*]. No, I'm kidding. Michael Harper. Gwendolyn Brooks. But we can even say a voice such as Baraka.

JW: I would wonder what he would say about that.

YK: I wonder what he would say about that [*laughs*]. But also I think of Robert Hayden, especially some of the longer poems. "Middle Passage" comes to mind. Even someone like Jay Wright, his "The Cradle Logic of Autumn" possesses an echo of Whitman.

JW: Martín Espada has described himself as "a branch on the tree of Whitman."[12]

YK: Yes, Martín Espada does inhibit a similar facility for language and raw passion. The music—the rhetorical drive, the celebration, the common man and woman, it's all there in Martín's voice.

JW: In "The Poet," a lecture that had a profound influence on Whitman, Emerson exhorts prospective American writers to perceive, "in the barbarism and materialism of the times, another carnival of the same gods whose picture he so much admires in Homer."[13] Your own work, particularly your more recent verse, suggests the relevance of ancient narratives to contemporary life. Could you speak about the interplay you see between ancient narratives—both historical and mythological— and modern-day experience and poetry?

YK: I think I'm paying allegiance to the human brain, that fluid mechanism that exists by creating syntactic links—leaps. I'm thinking of all the things I've read, all the things I've experienced, all the things I've thought of. I don't think the brain attempts to create strict categories. Things collide and time dissolves. The old brain and the new brain is no more than a jump cut apart. Perhaps this has a lot to do with creating a poetic time, where the mythological, the present moment, even the future, all can live in the same moment of feeling and reckoning. I think Whitman talks about that, attempts to bring the future into the present.

JW: As in "Crossing Brooklyn Ferry."

YK: Yes. Although this is essentially a cityscape, Whitman is the unrelenting spirit of the frontier. He attempts to call together one great force—this huddle of humanity. For me, it's not so much the mythology borrowed from a different time, as that which focuses us on a necessary scrutiny of where we are. There is a certain ancient innuendo in a voice such as Catallus, almost the same kind of insinuation and intensity I see in the blues idiom. And that's a good example of how time is deceived, the idea of time is deceived, changed, redefined. I tend to cross bridges, and sometimes those bridges are in midair, and they sometimes don't necessarily go or travel a predefined direction. And there are some elements of mythology, and classical allusions, that can lead to some interesting, necessary surprises where the sun shines in an alley or on a mountaintop.

JW: Speaking of Whitman and Dickinson, you have said that "as a poet I embrace Whitman more, with his long lines."[14] However, your own poetry tends to be composed in shorter lines. Could you speak about the form of Whitman's poetry and any significance it has had for you?

YK: My poems are usually a composite of short lines. I think that it has something to do with contemporary time, a kind of vertical plunge, with the shorter lines coming out of the Beat movement, reading some of the poets associated with that movement. The long line for me invites more of a meditation, and not that same kind of vertical urgency. Recently, some of my poems seem to have longer lines. I'm particularly thinking of "Blackbirding on the Hudson," and some of my prose poems. Whitman invites a certain meditation with those long lines, and I'm very much interested in that. I remember Richard Hugo saying that a poem should have long and short lines. And I think he was talking more about the music, maybe influenced by elements of swing music, the kind of modulation that takes place. I still admire Whitman's long lines because they're almost biblical. And that was really my first introduction to poetry. I suppose that's what happened with Whitman. He takes me back to biblical verse, even though I have probably attempted to forget biblical verse. Maybe that's what it is. It's an echo of that which I first came in contact with.

Notes

1. "An Interview with Yusef Komunyakaa, Author of *The Chameleon Couch.*" *Farrar, Straus, and Giroux Poetry Blog* (www.fsgpoetry.com).

2. Walt Whitman, *Leaves of Grass,* 1867, 123. Available on the *Walt Whitman Archive* (www.whitmanarchive.org).

3. *American Experience: Walt Whitman,* dir. Mark Zwonitzer (PBS/WGBH Boston, 2008).

4. Yusef Komunyakaa and Radiclani Clytus, *Blue Notes: Essays, Interviews, and Commentaries* (Ann Arbor: University of Michigan Press, 2000), 31.

5. Kenneth M. Price, *To Walt Whitman, America* (Chapel Hill: University of North Carolina Press, 2004), 4.

6. Yusef Komunyakaa, "Kosmos," in *Massachusetts Review* 33 (Spring 1992): 87.

7. Yusef Komunyakaa, "A Conversation with Yusef Komunyakaa," interview by Jeffrey Dodd and Jessica Moll, *Willow Spring* 56 (2007): 68–79, rpt. in *Conversations with Yusef Komunyakaa,* ed. Shirley A. Hanshaw (Jackson: University Press of Mississippi, 2010), 181.

8. See Studs Terkel's 1961 interview with Baldwin, in which the latter says, "In the South, the white man is continuously bringing up the matter of the Negro; in the North, *never.* So obsessed in one case, so ignored in the other." Fred L. Standley and Louis H. Pratt, *Conversations with James Baldwin* (Jackson: University Press of Mississippi, 1989), 8.

9. Yusef Komunyakaa, *Pleasure Dome: New and Selected Poems* (Hanover, N.H.: Wesleyan University Press, published by University Press of New England, 1998), 13.

10. In Baxandall's words, "'Influence' is a curse of art criticism primarily because of its wrong-headed grammatical prejudice about who is the agent and who is the patient: it seems to reverse the active/passive relation which the historical actor experiences and the inferential beholder will wish to take into account. If one says that X influenced Y it does seem that one is saying that X did something to Y rather than that Y did something to X. But in the consideration of good pictures and painters the second is always the more lively reality. . . . Most of these relations just cannot be stated the other way round—in terms of X acting on Y rather than Y acting on X. To think in terms of influence blunts thought by impoverishing the means of differentiation." Michael Baxandall, *Patterns of Intention: On the Historical Explanation of Pictures* (New Haven: Yale University Press, 1985), 58–59.

11. Walt Whitman, *Leaves of Grass,* 1855, 14. Available on the *Walt Whitman Archive* (www.whitmanarchive.org).

12. Edward Carvalho, "A Branch on the Tree of Whitman: Martín Espada Talks about *Leaves of Grass*," *Walt Whitman Quarterly Review* 26 (Summer 2008): 25.

13. Ralph Waldo Emerson, *Essays: First and Second Series* (New York: Library of America, 1990), 465.

14. "Conversation with Yusef Komunyakaa," 184.

III

Commentaries

Notes from a Lost Notebook

For me, there has to be an absolute flexibility in maintaining a notebook.
My notebooks are really scrapbooks—pieced together with fragments,
phrases, sentences, paragraphs, long and short passages, magazine and
newspaper clippings, postcards, etc. Thus, I attempt to avoid any kind
of note structure. Sometimes the passages are logical and controlled, and
other times they are abbreviated and somewhat improvisational sound-
ing. Later, however, these items seem to dictate their own coherence. Some
are like jump starts for the imagination; others function more like jump
cuts—little bridges that spring up between ideas and feelings. Connec-
tors. Accidental linkages. Surprises. It is often a ledger of emotional pres-
sure points, and I can return to moments in the recent past that link me
to the present and the impending future. I can see and feel the evolution
of an image. As I view the germination of images and poems, I am a
few steps closer to understanding the chemistry of the imagination—how
each word takes on a life of its own. There is that rare poem spun whole
from an image buried in the yellowing pages of a haphazard notebook,
and I call such a poem a gift.

• • •

Lokman (c. 1100 BC). Aesop (c. 560 BC). How could
these two have been the same man? True, they spoke a
similar wit; but maybe this came about only because of the
similarity of background and situation. Both were black
slaves, and they relied on wit and satire to keep sane.
Perhaps so. They were more than stand-up comedians of
antiquity; each was a first-rate fabulist and thinker. There

From *The Poet's Notebook: Excerpts from the Notebooks of 26 Contemporary American Poets*, ed. Stephen Kuusisto, Deborah Tall, and David Weiss (New York: Norton, 1997).

are thousands of African parables with this same caliber of wit. Is there something here beneath this simple deduction?
A basic humanism.
"Prometheus, in making man, did not use water to mix the clay; he used tears."
  —Aesop

"The wise and prudent man will draw a useful lesson even from poison itself, whilst the precepts of the wisest man mean nothing to the thoughtless."
  —Lokman

I call Gold,
Gold is silent.
I call Cloth,
Cloth is silent.
It is people that matter.
  —A saying of the Akan people of Ghana

• • •

(Two corps girls, resplendent in their white tutus for *Etudes*, stand in-front of the stagehands' room, giggling as they read a poster which has been tapped to the wall: "Each one of us is a mixture of qualities, some of which are good and some perhaps not so good. In considering our fellow man we should remember his good qualities and refrain from making harsh judgments just because he happens to be a dirty, rotten no-good son of a bitch.")
  —Franklin Stevens, *Dance as Life*

• • •

Centro Internationale Poesia della Metamorfosi
Comune di Fano
Provincia di Pesaro e Urbino
Regione Marche
Convergno Internazionale
LA POESIA
AMERICANA

I nuovi itinerary
Fano 9, 10, 11 giugno 1988
Palazzo S. Michele—Chiostro delle Benedettine

They want me to talk about jazz and poetry, Vietnam, and contemporary African American poetry. I'm dealing with jet lag, the rich food, and this constant celebration in the air. In fact, at this moment, I'd rather be thinking of Fellini ("Il Mago"); I'm still unable to believe that the Vatican could have branded his *La Dolce Vita* as "obscene" in 1959. Anita Ekberg obscene? War, fascism, hatred, the ability to balance one's heart with gold and pillage—well, now, those are things that I call obscene. Perception has everything to do with the lens we peer through. What we bring to a place or thing. I can almost see James Wright walking the streets of Fano, among these ancient bricks mottled by sea salt. We'll visit Urbino tomorrow. I have no idea what the others are thinking about the infamous ancient city, if they can already see the fields of poppies on the hillsides—*Citta ideale /* Ideal City—I only know that there's an unusual equation in my mind. Urbino: Florence: Africa. After all, it is what we bring to something that curves the equation, right: That "Moor," Alessandro de' Medici, was of course the first Duke of Florence— rumored to be the son of Pope Clement VII himself. After his dramatic demise (the Michaele-Lorenzaccio plot), Alessandro the Moor's body was secretly stashed in the tomb of his nominal father, the Duke of Urbino, under Michelangelo's *Il Penseroso*. But what a huge life this man, whose mother had been a slave, lived in such a short time.

> "I did in fact keep a house-dog—a beautiful, large, shaggy brute that Duke Alessandro had given me. It was a first-rate hunting dog, and when I was out shooting, it used to bring me back any bird or animal that I hit, but it was also a splendid house-guard. As it happened, at that time, as was only fitting at the age of twenty-nine, I had taken a charming and very beautiful young girl as my maid-servant; I used her as a model, and also enjoyed her in bed to satisfy my youthful desires. Because of this, I had my room at quite a distance from where the workmen slept, and also some way from the shop. I kept the young

girl in a tiny ramshackle bedroom adjoining mine. I used
to enjoy her very often, and although I am the lightest
sleeper in the world, after sexual pleasure I sometimes
used to sleep very heavily and deeply."
—Benvenuto Cellini, *Autobiography*

This is how poems happen for me. Bits and pieces, glimpses
and strokes, hints and imagistic nudges, and at some almost-
accidental moment it all flies together—not to make sense but
to induce a feeling. I call these *gifts*. "Florentine Mosaic" is just
such a gift that has been forming itself inside my head.

• • •

"Never again shall the Cock Man come to report sunrise."
—From the story of Yang Kuei-fei, concubine of the emperor
Ming-huang (713–55)

• • •

"Prince Myshkin, the central character in Dostoyevsky's
The Idiot and a victim of epilepsy, is trying to express the
emotions that come over him just before his attacks start.
Dostoyevsky wrote from first-hand experience. He suf-
fered from the disease himself and knew that inspiration
may be a prelude to convulsions as well as to prophesies,
poetry or great novels."
—John Pfeiffer, *The Human Brain*

• • •

I see something or think something that sparks something else,
and then things gel. Germinate. Become. For example: one mo-
ment I'm gazing at Beauford DeLaney's *Portrait of Marian Ander-
son* and the next moment I feel them both here in the room, all
golden and uncompromising. What did Arturo Toscanini say of
her?: "What I heard today, one is privileged to hear only once in
a hundred years." That's right. The Finnish National Opera, the
Salzburg Musical Festival, Carnegie Hall, Paris's Grand Opera,
Buckingham Palace, etc. But do we overlook the fact that the

Daughters of the American Revolution refused to let her appear in Constitution Hall in 1939, when she hadn't been discriminated against even in Nazi Germany? Some of us poets have been challenged to face the beautiful and the ugly—to make art out of what we see, hear, think, and feel.

> "Few artists, I hasten to add, have ever impressed me as being more sane than Beauford Delaney. Beauford's sanity is something to dwell on: it occupies a niche of its own. There are some utterly sane individuals who create the impression that stark lunacy might be a highly desirable state; there are others who make sanity look like a counterfeit check, with God the loser."
> —Henry Miller, *The Amazing and Invariable Beauford Delaney*

In the early 1970s, those years I entertained the idea of becoming a psychiatrist, I believed that racism was a mental illness. Perhaps this idea had a lot to do with a kind of elemental hope. A faith in knowledge and one's capacity to change. If it was illness, it could be cured, right? I remember compiling hundreds of notes on this topic—a treatise. Sex. Environment. Cultural and social indoctrination. Fear. Envy. Nonverbal gestures that pass down racism to the cradle. Language. Literature. I wish I could find those notes.

• • •

Equus is one of my favorite plays. The terror that enters the psyche when passion is denied or undermined. The holiness of passion: an approximation of the Godhead. When opposites merge—the creative act—the myth made flesh. Image. Centaur. Possibility.

• • •

> "When in nineteen-thirty-seven, Etta Moten, sweetheart of our Art Study group, kept her promise, as if clocked, to honor my house at our first annual tea, my pride tipped the sky, but when she, Parisian-poised and as smart as

a chrome-toned page from Harper's Bazaar, gave my
shocked guests this hideous African nude, I could have
cried."
—Margaret Danner, "The Convert"

As I leaned over the *Hen-Shaped Coffin* by sculptor Kane Kwei at
the University Art Museum at Berkeley, almost hurting to pry
open the colorful burial vessel and gaze inside, I realized that
I was envious of such a people who had so intricately woven art
into the social patterns and rituals of their daily lives. Here was
a piece of art defined by an active duality: it's aesthetically chal-
lenging and functional—not merely circumscribed by a glass
case in a museum. Not only is there this decorative coffin, made
of wood and painted with enamels, but also other shapes: an
airplane and onion, also created by Kwei, numerous paintings
and fantastic sculptures of wood and metal. What really brings
this exhibit into focus, creating a necessary tension, is the coex-
istence of the traditional with the contemporary. Herewith also
exists the fuel for controversy. Many of the pieces are skillfully
fashioned with superb technique and care, but is something
missing? The mystery that attracted Picasso and other cubists
to these traditional Iberian masks, has that quality been accul-
turated out of the art through the dynamics of assimilation,
technique, and subject matter? Have the values and principles
shaping the pieces been undermined? Are these still authentic
works of art defined by ancient rituals and customs, or are they
pieces designed for commercial venues? Or are some of us die-
hard idealists who romanticize the past and refuse to celebrate
the changes that these artists have witnessed in their daily lives?
I would like to think that artistic expression is not static, but
organized; that art is defined by time and flexible nuances. It is
this spirit of inclusion that drew me deeper and deeper into the
exhibition. The artists are "doing their thing." They are from
various groups ("approximately 55 paintings, sculptures, photo-
graphs, and mixed-media works by artists from throughout sub-
Saharan Africa—Zaire, Nigeria, Ghana, Senegal, Mali, Sierra
Leone, Mozambique, Gabon, and the Coast") but the underly-
ing matrix of colors and symbolism helps the viewer to see the
chemistry between artists and their imagistic ideas. In the urge

to exhibit the reflections of diversity, what truly arises out of this daring collection of new functional, traditional, international, and urban art, is the unfractured unity of an encompassing artistic tradition. Out of the various themes in "Africa Explores: 20th Century African Art," two that readily surface are the mermaid/merman and twin motifs.

The mermaid images, on the subject of Mami Wata and Papi Wata, are rather narcissistic, depicting figures who gaze into handheld mirrors or recline in self-conscious poses. It isn't just the slight differences in skin tones and physical characteristics that suggest the otherworldliness of these water-bound figures; something deeper and more profound illustrates their separateness from the African terrain and psyche: they are foreigners because the carriage of their bodies betrays them. In other words, they are still seeking pleasure and status through their exaggerated otherness. The figures evolving out of the twin cult, however, seem to celebrate a reverence for the similar. The images evolve out of each other as vivid reflections. It is this same imagistic continuity one finds in pieces such as *Slaves Yoked Together* and *Figures Carrying Water* by Mode Munto: the figures mirror each other, but seem linked or solidified by a silent, unbroken rhythm—a cadence created through subtle colors. One might think that to speak of rhythm as a reference to African artistic expression is to resort to a worn-out phrase. The two moving sculptures, *Festival Boat* and *Decorated Bed for a Christian Wake*, however, are definitely defined by rhythmic complexity. The parts move in a kind of humorous syncopation—a planned and calibrated tonal extension of the structure based on contrapuntal patterns. A surreal humor lives within numerous places in the exhibit. One painting that comes to mind is *The Battle with Mosquitoes* where three characters are using unorthodox methods (slingshot, etc.) for exterminating mosquitoes. The vivid colors and active symmetry of this piece evolve into a dance for the viewer—a ballet of wit. Written text is also incorporated into this painting. Actually, European painters and poets influenced by dadaism easily come to mind. In certain pieces these African artists have incorporated texts excerpted from poetry, parables, folk sayings, and new proclamations. In some pieces it seems natural; in a few others, however, the text is mere extemporaneous embellishment, deflecting the visual energy and continuity of the pieces. This exhibit isn't a marriage of the sacred and the profane. As a whole, with new styles modifying the traditional and the traditional modifying new styles, the exhibit is a pleasurable and surprising success. The politics and rituals are so crystallized by flawless technique and imagination, these artists could venture almost in any direction and still return home honorable.

• • •

At fourteen, I read the Bible through twice, and then abandoned it because there seemed to have been too many contradictions. Six years later I read it through again, and this time came away convinced that Jesus Christ was a socialist and that is what got him nailed to the cross. True, admittedly, I didn't become a model Christian, but I learned a great deal about imagery and metaphor. The Old Testament is pure surrealism.

• • •

The blues has been called The Devil's Music. Maybe it has to do with two words: Possession and obsession. Most artists are obsessed by the creative act, and this is looked upon as negative or abnormal—unless it is linked to money in some way. Then it is viewed as industrious. But possession is a curse, don't care how you turn the key in the lock. Controlled by something (an evil spirit or passion). Mad. Crazed. God forbid if we should lose control. Robert Johnson's music possessed him through passion, and perhaps this is why he said he'd made a pact with the Devil at a crossroad one night in Mississippi. He surrendered himself to folklore and myth so that these black Calvinists didn't question what he was doing. After all, he was possessed and didn't have any control over the blues (at least, that's what they wanted to think). They chose to see him at the mercy of his art; in fact, music was Robert Johnson's only true salvation.

• • •

Lifelines is a limited-edition portfolio of poems and graphics published by San Francisco's Central City Hospitality House—works by the poor and homeless in the Tenderloin. This is raw inspiration doing what art is supposed to do.

• • •

> You may bury my body ooooo down by the highway side
> So my old evil spirit can get a Greyhound Bus and ride
> —Robert Johnson, "Me and the Devil Blues"

• • •

Where Romare Bearden has been rather forthright about the direct influence of quiltmaking on his art, one wonders if quilts—especially the quilts of the poor where pieces of cloth or patches were arranged—haven't influenced the whole concept of modern abstract art. Fine arts. Handicrafts. Low and high cultures. Maybe it is texture and materials that make distinctive differences here. But shouldn't basic concepts matter? Poor black Southern women have always had a tradition of sewing quilts inside quilts as a way of preserving something precious. Don't be surprised if there aren't some bright masterpieces tucked away in semidark rooms in numerous dead-end towns. I believe that Romare Bearden would have known what I'm thinking about.

> "You do something and then you improvise."
> —Romare Bearden

Improvise is an important word/concept to me. I have a habit of underlining it in books; as if I need clues scattered about. *Improvise.*

> "He used to sing, improvising all the time, among the very best voices. His singing was so lovely that Michelangelo Buonarroti, that superb sculptor and painter, used to rush along for the pleasure of hearing him whenever he knew

187

where he was performing. A goldsmith called Piloto who
was a very talented artist, and I myself, used to accompany
him. This, then, was how Luigi Pulci and I came to know
each other."
—Benvenuto Cellini, *Autobiography*

• • •

Since early 1984, the central tone of each of my collections has
been dictated by a "first" poem. In *Dien Cai Dau* it was "Some-
where Near Phu Bai"; of course, in *Magic City*, "Venus's-fly-traps"
embodied the tonal impulse for the collection. The other curi-
ous thing is that I'm usually working on three or four collections
simultaneously—going back and forth between worlds the same
way that I do in my everyday life. I enjoy simplicity and complex-
ity side by side.

• • •

I continue to return to Blake's engravings, particularly this one
called *Negro Hung Alive by the Ribs to a Gallows*. At first, I was an-
gry at the image; now I realize that Blake was a visionary with a
heart—one sees or feels the empathy beneath the ink. Here's an
artist who stepped out of his times. Yes, indeed, some are blessed
to be out of step!
    He also captures Captain Stedman's tyranny and morbid
memory—Europe's imperialism.

• • •

"There are few race-transcending prophets on the current
black intellectual scene. James Baldwin was one. He was
self-taught and self-styled, hence beholden to no white
academic patronage system."
—Cornel West, *Race Matters*

"True black writers speak *as* blacks, *about* blacks, *to* blacks."
—Gwendolyn Brooks, *Jump Bad*

I feel that Gwendolyn Brooks has been undermined by lesser talents who happened to have been popular during the 1960s and 1970s. She was an outsider to them and had to compromise for acceptance (not honor or love). In fact, I think that Gwen had often seen herself as an outsider in her own community. It all has to do with surface appearances—and that's still true. Many of those younger poets around her were stylers in dress and poetry—without any artistic endurance. They were "slam poets" of that era, and Gwen had too much hard-earned discipline for them to cope with. But they knew her one weakness: She desired their love and acceptance. They coerced her into becoming a turncoat against who she really was; thus, her art and creative spirit seem to have suffered greatly. They are the ones who should have been learning from her, but she gave in to their arrogance and bravado. Of course, we are the losers in this literary brouhaha.

• • •

I hope that I can continue to seek out challenges to expand my imagination. Here's something to remember: as the image of Aurora's son, the dark-skinned prince Memnon of Ethiopia, who was killed at Troy fighting for the Trojans (sounds like those street gangs in Boston and L.A. and only God knows where else) takes shape in my imagination, I realize that the classics were often more inclusive and true to history than the work by us present-day poets and writers.

You Made Me

Out of the sanctity of old names,
birth & death cries, the transfigured
future crawls forth on two legs,
like the nine-headed beast
with a question in each eye.
It comes to us, a part of us,
beckoning Old Man River
dragging up earth to the slow mouth
of ragged song & surrender,
in quest, rage & prayer.
Mississippi John Hurt, Johnny
Cash, Big Mama Thornton, B.B.
King, Merle Haggard, the Carter
Family, Son House, Jerry Lee
Lewis, Bessie Smith, Professor Longhair—
roll call & September storm. The past
rises in red bud & bluejay, in blood oath
& ten ways to love a woman
or man. Out of the shapechanger's
lament, my burdened voice unearthed
in mid-sentence—"way down
in Egyptland" lives alongside
the leap-year's makada. The ghosts
at Shiloh Church trade tongues
with sexual lilies beside a millpond,
begging dumb-struck nights & taproot
into the blackest soil this side
of the Mason-Dixon. Out of this
wounded love squinting up
at the Southern Cross

From *Callaloo* 24, no. 4 (2001).

above the Yellow Dog,
singing "Ezekiel saw the wheel"
as someone balled the jack
in a room at least a mile
inside a lonely house. I rise
beyond borrowed blame & the thing
turned inside out—caught
in the hinged jaw of love & hate,
I come forth. Out of good will,
I ride the waves of summertime
till I am back washing the midnight
blue out of work clothes
& Sunday-go-to-meeting suits
& dresses. I am man & woman,
daughter & son, an albino
in thirty-three shades of moonlight
beneath the last chinaberry tree.
Out of would-be kings
among Greek columns & facades
overlooking sharecropper shacks,
singled out & strung up
between tradition & live oak—
worm-hunger at the roots of the
Crosstree. I am a man
who came as a boy
out of Little Rock, Selma,
Mobile & Bogalusa.
Out of a land pregnant
with Indian mounds,
we newcomers stumble
out of English brogans, clod-
hoppers & wooden shoes
shaped like miniature boats.
Out of Sandy Hook,
blood ran into the law
of hands & the fruit
forcing branches to bow
over the graves. The worm
begat the mocking bird,
the mocking bird begat the one-eyed horse,
& the horse begat the idea of man
& woman. Out of frog holler,

love moans, birds of paradise
beside the hand pump
dragging up cool waters
from bedrock, I come
when you call my name
in a Wednesday night
prayer meeting or field
holler at daybreak.
Out of *Birth of a Nation*
& *Gone With the Wind*
a new cry owns the hills
& bank of the Tallahatchie.
I found Shango sitting beneath
a crab apple tree, holding a scorpion
on his palm. The herb man's medicine
had the bossman walking the floor
for seven nights as the two-headed
desire in my body worked
its way out of the blood
in this earth, red leaves
on the edge of an almost forgotten
season. Up from lowlands
to Blue Ridge & Stone Mountain,
our shadows face each other, one
divided into the other: the good
& the bad, this side of the brain
straddling the hex sign drawn
in Louisiana dirt. Out of this—
out of spit & mud, straw
& myth, catgut, love
& doubt, still I sing
till the auctioned-off faces
rise out of the bottomland.
There are no more marks
of ownership on my skin,
no secret kisses & hugs
to pull me under the hush
of white satin & lallygag
of reeds beside the still waters.

More Than a State of Mind

> They who so gravely taught me to split my body from my
> mind and both from my "soul," taught me also to split my
> conscience from my acts and Christianity from southern
> tradition.
> —Lillian Smith, *Killers of the Dream*

I believe that each of us internalizes a landscape composite of
myths and stories, and we carry that psychological terrain within
us as we make our way through the world, whether we are facing
that green divan that Anna Akhmatova slept on in Saint Peters-
burg or gazing out at Stone Mountain in Georgia, an overlay
by which the future is often colored and through which it is of-
ten perceived. However, like Lillian Smith—"Miss Lil"—some of
us attempt to refashion that inherited landscape through con-
sciousness. That is, we attempt to bring ourselves to an aware-
ness of what has shaped us. Since landscape is both regional
and emotional, I learned to meditate on everything around me,
people and nature.

Like the word made flesh, the South has been woven through
my bones. My collection of poetry *Magic City* (1992) is an at-
tempt to capture my early years of growing up in Bogalusa, Loui-
siana. Coming of age there, I was fully aware of both the natural
beauty and the social terror surrounding me. The challenge be-
came to acknowledge and resist this terror. My early emotional
life grew into the kind of questions that lead men to ponder
philosophy and psychology, eventually guiding me to poetry. I
became aware of the troublesome contradictions in my town.

From *Studies in the Literary Imagination* 35, no. 1 (2002).

James Baldwin says a black boy can't survive if he doesn't know the score by fourteen. Of course, this is doubly true in the South I knew in the '50s. This was near the time Emmett Till was murdered in Mississippi.

But the South was also a mecca of language and images. I learned about the naming of things there. The wrong word could get a man killed. The South taught me how to look at things, to see into the shape and design of reality. I began to take things apart. My first ventures alone were into nature, then into my imagination, which allowed me to exit Bogalusa. I saw things when I didn't, when I wasn't supposed to.

I don't view myself primarily as a Southern writer; however, what I depict in my poetry is connected to rural Louisiana. Even in my gazing into a viewfinder as a boy, trying to daydream myself away to Mexico or Japan, into the future, my eyes had been tutored by the green surety and sunlight of that place called home. I continue to pose questions based on my early experiences and observations. While I was briefly in Florida, my mind kept asking, Where is Rosewood? Where are the Seminoles? And, in retrospect, I realize that Bogalusa taught me almost everything I know about writing poetry. It showed me how to get up inside a question and shake it till the insides let go. But home also instructed me in ways to embrace mystery and beauty.

Eros, Words

Words do not have to slide off the tongue like escargot or love to be sensual or erotic. To taste the godliness in language has little to do with nectar and ambrosia, but it seems to suggest that it is made of earth even when it isn't earthy, that it is an emotional apparition of one's feelings—an attempt to make it flesh, temporal. The birth cry is an act of creation; the gods are woven through breath, into words.

I agree with Octavio Paz, in his book *The Double Flame*, when he says:

> The relationship between eroticism and poetry is such that it can be said, without affectation, that the former is a poetry of the body and latter an eroticism. . . . Language—sound that carries meanings, a material trace that denotes nonmaterial things—is able to give a name to what is most fleeting and evanescent: sensation.

Language is erotic because it is conscious. It helps us to penetrate the most fundamental questions, and we cannot divorce the elemental logic from the body. The body is involved in everything we feel, think, and believe. There was eroticism before Eros: sensation was there when humans first attempted to articulate sky and water, when we first tried to *think* our humanness. The music of one word plays against another to create symbolic feelings—context and texture—the same way a musical note embraces another.

Language equals conscious life, or an almost-conscious knowing. Feeling. Meaning. Rhythm. It seems that Anglo-Saxon words—when English embraces poetry—pull the body deeper into language. The small, tender, muscular engine that drives each word makes the most ethereal music corporal—a tiny accordion that pulsates bliss, woe, and wit.

A Letter to *Poetry*

This is the patent age of new inventions
For killing bodies, and for saving souls,
All propagated with the best intentions.
    —*Don Juan*

Dear Editor,

Operation Homecoming[1] reminds me that we had our soldier-poets in Vietnam also; and for the most part, they penned what I call "the boondock doggerel of blood and guts" which was printed by the *Stars and Stripes*. Of course, this was aimed at boosting the morale of the troops. War means to kill or be killed. The more immediate soldiers are to their acts of violence, the less creditable they are as witnesses. (Hell, we have veterans who are now dying, and they are still defending Lt. Calley's actions at My Lai, caught in the freemasonry of violence.) It seems that Homer knew this, and that is why *The Iliad* is a tragedy, as most full-hearted renderings of war are. He shows the blood and guts of war and revenge. After Achilles makes his speech to the soldiers of Achaea, Homer gives us a passage that says almost everything about war, about what occurs after Hector's death:

> The next thing that Achilles did was to subject
> the fallen prince to shameful outrage. He slit
> the tendons at the back of both his feet from heel
> to ankle, inserted leather straps, and made them
> fast to his chariot, leaving the head to drag.

From *Poetry* (November 2004).

The above passage isn't a visual prototype of a chase scene in Hollywood. Indeed, such a graphic description of rage and revenge is the bounty of war, and only an experienced voice can capture its horror and terror through retrospection. We need our young men and women, soldiers and civilians, to read good literature, to come across a voice like Yehuda Amichai's in "What Did I Learn in the War":

> To march in a row and be alone in the middle,
> To dig into pillows, featherbeds, the body of a beloved
>   woman,
> And to yell "Mama," when she cannot hear,
> And to yell "God," when I don't believe in Him,
> And even if I did believe in Him
> I wouldn't have told Him about the war
> As you don't tell a child about grown-ups' horrors.

Writing poetry has hardly anything to do with therapy. If the *need* is there, the would-be poet will find the craft, a way to shape his or her version through honest language.

One doesn't want to grow bull-headed and recalcitrant about Operation Homecoming, but we writers (artists) cannot forget that we are responsible for what we conjure and embrace through language, whether in essays, novels, plays, poems, or songs. I doubt if many people remember Barry Sadler's "The Ballad of the Green Beret." The first verse says:

> Fighting soldiers from the sky,
> Fearless men who jump and die.
> Men who mean just what they say,
> The brave men of the Green Beret.

This song was a commercial success, selling more than seven million copies. It wasn't just RCA that put energy and money behind Sadler's inane words: there were articles in *Life*, *Newsweek*, *Time*, and *Variety*; he appeared on *The Ed Sullivan Show* and *Hollywood Palace*, hosted by Martha Raye. And all this hype supported a song that ends with the following words to a future generation:

Put silver wings on my son's chest,
Make him one of America's best.
He'll be a man they'll test one day.
Have him win the Green Beret.

The song doesn't say anything about winning an early death. Sadler's lyric sounds so similar to the "boondock poems" published by soldiers in Vietnam. And it isn't surprising that the song was embraced by the U.S. Army before its commercial success, as propaganda for war. Poetry cannot serve as an emotional bandage for the blood and guts of warfare; such an industry is doomed to dishonor the dead as well as the living.

At this time, art and music are usually the first programs axed in our elementary and high schools across America. Don't mention poetry! What happened to the Poetry-in-the-Schools Program? Did it disappear in the eighties under President Ronald Reagan, only to be reinvented at the beginning of the twenty-first century as a Poetry-in-the-Military Program? Do we now need to give soldiers ammo to fight the ghosts of those peaceniks from the seventies such as Allen Ginsberg and Denise Levertov?

If anything, the NEA should be leading the vanguard to put poetry back into our schools and the mouths of our citizens who may embrace life over death and destruction.

Yusef Komunyakaa
Trenton, New Jersey

Note

1. Operation Homecoming is a program created by the National Endowment for the Arts "to help U.S. troops and their families write about their wartime experiences in Afghanistan, Iraq, and stateside" (https://www.arts.gov/operation-homecoming/about-operation-homecoming)—ED.

Small Illuminations

Box

You're the prototype escape artist,
    Henry Brown, nailed shut in a box
  tighter than a wooden laughing barrel,

lying in a fetal position dreaming of life
    after death, waiting for someone in Philly
  to pry the lid with a crowbar.

How long to unfold, to stand upright,
    for flight to hold again the shape
  of the clavicle? When the storekeeper

in Richmond was paid to ship you away,
    how many pounds of Virginia cured ham
  or salt peter did he list on the invoice?

When a millwheel turned beneath you
    & every bump in the winding road
  was a mountain, you were a dead man

in his coffin—three feet by two
    & two feet deep—but the whip's crack
  over the horses made you remember

cuts & stings on epic skin. Years later,
    between you & your persona, words
  & deeds, against a backlit panorama,

Box Brown would crawl into his crate
        to show them a free man, saying,
Now you see me, & now you don't.

• • •

Historically, the question of the artist's role in his or her com-
munity has been an ongoing debate. How important is content?
Does a system of aesthetics override all other concerns, and can
such surface matters shape the true character of a work? Should
the artist speak solely to his or her own vision? Is the making
of art really an egotistical, bourgeois endeavor? Perhaps art
wouldn't exist if the questions didn't exist. One only has to look
at Denise Levertov's translation of "The Artist"[1] to understand
how long the critique of the artist has been with us. Of course, a
Toltec artist possessed a rather circumscribed position within his
community, which usually was associated with utilitarian, sacred
rituals. But there's a poignant clarity in "The Artist," in this short
poem-essay:

The artist: disciple, abundant, multiple, restless.
The true artist: capable, practicing, skillful;
maintains dialogue with his heart, meets things with his
    mind.

The true artist: draws out all from his heart,
works with delight, makes things with calm, with sagacity,
works like a true Toltec, composes his objects, works
    dexterously, invents;
arrange materials, adorns them, makes them adjust.

The carrion artist: works at random, sneers at the people,
makes things opaque, brushes across the surface of the face
    of things,
works without care, defrauds people, is a thief.

• • •

Let's face this basic fact: each established writer was also an ama-
teur at one time. It is difficult to guess what works are going to

endure, because talent and time are the final arbitrators. Ideally, a cultivated hierarchy isn't necessarily desirable because the making of art involves a continuous process, an inquiry through observations and questions, and discovery happens in great moments of contemplation and tension. Yes, not the answer, but the question is what often drives the engine into the bloody heart of passion. The making of art changes its creator. When the artist is entangled in the process, he or she cannot have the reader or the receiver staring over his or her shoulder. However, since the poet is condemned and exulted to use language, the very tool that separates human beings from the so-called lower species, that which underlines our commonality, perhaps we are obligated to share meaning. Art is an action. And, of course, we are expected to be responsible for our actions. Early poetry seems to have developed as a way of glancing into mystery, of gaining a semblance of control over the unknown and the unknowable, often addressing spiritual concerns and philosophy; but I refuse to believe, however, that good poetry cannot continue to assist us in confronting that immense existential void, especially for the poet who trusts common language and imagery that surprise. Also, I think that the contemporary poet will find a home in the popular theater that embraces the importance of poetic language on the stage. Collaboration between writers and musicians, actors and dancers, singers and storytellers, all this is important in an era of programmed disconnect and technological hypnosis.

• • •

The popular song lyric cannot replace poetry. The lyric relies so heavily on musical accompaniment and timbre of the human voice for completion. But I do think that an echo of the other can be fruitful. The poet has to remain cognizant that language is our primary music, and that each poem is a composite of images that keeps us connected to the real world. Bridges are crossed in language. Why shouldn't poetry and songs exist in the same frame of reference? There are certain singers—Dylan, Nina Simone, Son House—who place the word *poetry* into my mouth whenever I hear them. After all, we do exist in our time, our own skin-habit, and as artists our work should reflect our memories, observations, dreams, illusions and desires.

• • •

On "Copacetic Mingus"

"Mingus One, Two and Three.
Which is the image you want the world to see?"
—Charles Mingus, *Beneath the Underdog*

Heartstring. Blessed wood
& every moment the thing's made of:
ball of fatback
licked by fingers of fire.
Hard love, it's hard love.
Running big hands down
the upright's wide hips,
rocking his moon-eyed mistress
with gold in her teeth.
Art & life bleed
into each other
as he works the bow.
But tonight we're both a long ways
from the Mile High City,
1973. Here in New Orleans
years below sea level,
I listen to *Pithecanthropus
Erectus*: Up & down, under
& over, every which way—
thump, thump, dada—ah, yes.
Wood heavy with tenderness,
Mingus fingers the loom
gone on Segovia,
dogging the raw strings
unwaxed with rosin.
Hyperbolic bass line. Oh, no!
Hard love, it's hard love.

Everything's copacetic. This means: Yes, everything's fine, okay, all right. For the jazz musician, this phrase underlined the psychological and political template of the music. Though caught in the throes of everyday life, as turmoil and trouble pulsed in the heart of America, somehow the jazz musician was often able to arrive at an existential crossroad where he or she could say, "Yeah, man, everything's cool."

Of course, this belief, this affirmation seems to have been shaped by the musician's attempt to seek perfection on his or her chosen instrument. In seeking the so-called blue note, the musician embraces a concept of devotion. Not that he or she is attempting to touch something godly or holy, but that one's body and soul are being recalibrated by the instrument—horn, piano, bass, drums, et cetera. Through technique and control, the musician surrenders to possibility, and this is the moment when *style* begins to develop.

Copacetic is an attitude; it is a sense of style that underlines a state of being.

• • •

I write everything in longhand. Each poem is sparked by phrases and images that allow us to simultaneously glimpse memory and imagination. No topic is taboo, but a system of aesthetics has to exist. The poet is blessed and condemned to live at the apex of life and death, gazing into and out of, always beckoning to the dark and the light. At times, it seems that we've been tooled and shaped by pathos, but it is also natural to insist that poetry arrives to us from joy and love, dripping with the dew of relentless entanglement. Poetry craves a commitment of the soul, the psyche. We participate in an industry of observation; and what we witness reduces and exults us. In that way, yes, often elements of childhood tyranny defines us. We still run out into the world shouting, "Where, how can that be? I don't believe you." And we trust the language of metaphor and metonymy to deliver us to reality through the pleasures of insinuation. Of course, improvisation is always at the axis of my method of writing poetry. I like how the senses attempt to take in everything at once, but of course music is at the heart of the conjuring and reliving. Finally, the poem is shaped; it is a made thing (pulsing with sensation and revelation). Form and structure comes out of the music of language. The poem challenges me to discover something that is usually a feeling of tangled surprises reaching for clarity. Basic language is important to me because it keeps us honest, true to what we are made of. For me, the poem exists within the time of *now*, and sometimes it even owes something to an echo of history linking us to the past and future. When we consider systems of thinking through the symbolic, poetry is perhaps the most democratic, though it often is a matrix of accidental symbols within natural symbols. In that sense, the making of a poem is an action. Poetry embraces mystery.

• • •

On "Grenade"

There's no rehearsal to turn flesh into dust so quickly. A hair
    trigger,
a cocked hammer in the brain, a split second between a man
    & in-
famy. It lands on the ground—a few soldiers duck & the
    others are
caught in a half-run—& one throws himself down on the
    grenade. All
the watches stop. A flash. Smoke. Silence. The sound fills the
    whole
day. Flesh & earth fall into the eyes & mouths of men. A
    dream
trapped in midair. They touch their legs & arms, their
    groins, ears, &
noses, saying, What happened? Some are crying. Other are
    laugh-
ing. Some are almost dancing. Someone tries to put the
    dead man
back together. "He just dove on the damn thing, sir!" A flash.
    Smoke.
Silence. The day blown apart. For those who can walk away,
    what is
their burden? Shreds of flesh & blood rags gathered up &
    stuffed
into a bag. Each breath belongs to him. Each song. Each
    curse. Every

prayer is his. Your body doesn't belong to your mind & soul. Who are

you? Do you remember the man left in the jungle? The others who

owe their lives to this phantom, do they feel like you? Would his

loved ones remember him if that little park or statue erected in his

name didn't exist, & does it enlarge their lives? You wish he'd lie

down in that closed coffin, & not wander the streets or enter your

bedroom at midnight. The woman you love, she'll never understand.

Who would? You remember what he used to say: "If you give a kite

too much string, it'll break free." That unselfish certainty. But you

can't remember when you began to live his unspoken dreams.

In 2002, I was teaching creative writing for a quarter at Stanford University and had been scheduled to present a noon reading and discussion for the English Department and the Creative Writing Program. I woke that morning of the presentation with "Grenade" in my psyche. I wished to think of other things, but the images wouldn't let go of me. I had recently promised myself not to write about Vietnam anymore, to address aspects of world history instead. I knew "Grenade" was about a protracted question that had been pestering me for years: How could fourteen or fifteen young African American soldiers and marines have thrown themselves on to grenades to shield their squads and platoons, where did that instinctive reaction come from? I knew that it was something one couldn't rehearse, that it came from some deep place within, outside of ideas about justice and democracy. What had shaped these individuals? I had been obsessed with a photograph—a mental picture—of PFC Milton Olive, an eighteen-year-old paratrooper, who had sacrificed himself in the jungles of Vietnam by diving on a grenade and had been awarded the Congressional Medal of Honor posthumously.

"Grenade" is informed by the rhythm of intention rather than the rhythm of insinuation—outside of the short, percussive lines. The longer lines beg for meditation and deliberation. "Grenade" was written in minutes, in a moment of prose that couldn't be reshaped through revision. When such a rare moment happens I call it a gift. I readily accepted "Grenade" for what it is: the poem still seems to me an existential question. For me, "Grenade" can only exist in the tonal shape of prose. It is a meditation on numerous unasked questions. I read the poem that afternoon at Stanford, and I haven't been able to change a word.

• • •

For me, the Black Arts Movement was very important, because it was a psychological foundation and sounding board in which to depart from. It arrived in my psyche after Phillis Wheatley, Paul Laurence Dunbar, James Baldwin, and the Harlem Renaissance, with its necessary thread of contemporaneous urgency, and that alone was more than instructive. It helped to humanize our rage: black anger wasn't merely an outburst, but now it was seen as a thoughtful critique of social injustice through the most ancient art form. Indeed, we human beings seem to live by metaphor.

When I came across a short article in Newsweek on LeRoi Jones (Amiri Baraka), with a few of his poems, in the late 1960s, I was floored. The short selection of poems was mainly from *The Dead Lecturer*; I remember carefully tearing out the two pages from the magazine, folding them up, and sliding them into my wallet. Those poems were different from anything I'd read—up to that point—and they gave me permission to venture into the scary interior of human possibility. The first three lines of "Preface to a Twenty Volume Suicide Note" were a true revelation: "Lately, I've become accustomed to the way / The ground opens up and envelops me / Each time I go out to walk the dog." Those three lines produced a resounding silence that seemed to have echoed from across the centuries; they dredged up the unsaid and unsayable, and that was an illumination. Here was an existential blues that dared to embrace the everyday, mundane rituals of human existence. By this time, I was reading Kierkegaard, Hegel, and Gide, but it was Baraka's *The Dead Lecturer* that truly stunned me with a poetic insight that carried me to the edge of a needful, internal voyage. A poet could be philosophical: he or she could even attempt to bridge the pulsating void. For the black poet and thinker, I thought that this was a different terrain. In many ways, he had been condemned to pursue one path into a singular aspect of human dilemma: this voice could only cry out against the obvious reality of social injustice. He could only unfurl his logbook of grievances and speak as a victim. Of course, the black intellectual had already been castigated by Robert Penn Warren's wrongheaded, reductive statement about blacks and the metaphysical.

Growing up in the South, having closely observed what hatred does to the human spirit, how it corrupts and diminishes, through a gut-level logic I unconsciously disavowed any direct association with the Black Arts Movement. As a graduate student at Colorado State in the mid-1970s, I said to Gwendolyn Brooks, "Ms. Brooks, what is art?" She didn't miss a beat when she said, "Well, art is that which endures." That night, in the midst of silence and loneliness, I thought about how members of the Black Arts Movement had badgered Robert Hayden and Gwendolyn Brooks at Fisk University in 1966. Since that moment of infamous shortsightedness, some of us who followed the visionary Robert Hayden dared to call and respond to a world of extended possibilities—which also resides in the poetry of early Amiri Baraka and Bob Kaufman. We knew the pitfalls of tribal warfare existentially; we were ready to embrace certain commonsense aspects of modernism that allowed at least an illusion of psychological liberation. In many ways, the Civil Rights Movement had intellectually prepared us for this necessary juncture in African American creativity. For the first time, some of us believed we could do anything if a system of aesthetics were at the center of our vision: I think Hayden had conveyed this principle to us through his work and life. An internal dialogue is possible through metaphorical inquiry that is highly political and enduring—an inquiry that continuously reinvent itself. We wanted a poetry that would speak to and for the whole person.

• • •

On "Green"

I've known billy club, tear gas, & cattle prod,
but not Black Sheep killing White Sheep.
Or vice versa. I've known water hoses
& the subterranean cry of a Black Maria
rounding a city corner on two angry wheels,
but couldn't smell cedar taking root in the air.

I've known of secret graves guarded
by the night owl in oak & poplar.
I've known police dogs on choke chains.
I've known how "We Shall Overcome"
feels on a half-broken tongue,
but not how deeply sunsets wounded the Peacock Throne.

Because of what I never dreamt
I know Hafez's litany balanced on Tamerlane's saber,
a gholam's song limping up the Elburz Mountains—
no, let's come back first to now,
to a surge of voices shouting,
Death to the government of potato!

Back to the iron horses of the Basijis
galloping through days whipped bloody
& beaten back into the brain's cave
louder than a swarm of percussion
clobbered in Enghelab Square,
cries bullied into alleyways & cutoffs.

Though each struck bell goes on
mumbling in the executioner's sleep,
there are always two hands holding
on to earth, & I believe their faith
in tomorrow's million green flags waving
could hold back a mile of tanks & turn

the Revolutionary Guard into stone,
that wherever a clue dares to step

a seed is pressed into damp soil.
A shoot, a tendril, the tip of a wing.
One breath at a time, it holds till it is
uprooted, or torn from its own grip.

In writing "Green," I had to first acknowledge that the concept
of freedom in the United States remains a work-in-progress; this
struggle has claimed lives and created strife among citizenry,
and even between fathers and sons, daughters and mothers, all
vying for certain allegiances and blood oaths written in the sand.
This is a simple fact of history. We only have to reflect back to
the abolitionist movement here, how it sought the strength of
voices from afar as well as homegrown ones, seeking an interna-
tional outcry against oppression and repression. For me, keep-
ing this sense of history in mind, in many respects, was the only
way I could imaginatively enter the political terrain of Tehran:
an echo of Selma, Alabama, and Cairo, Illinois, resounded in my
psyche and brought me closer to what those dissenters in Azadi
Square, waving their flags of Mousavi green, must have felt as
the Basij on motorcycles beat them with truncheons. I believe in
the sacredness of human life, that we are connected even when
we attempt to armor ourselves in cultural dogmas handed down
through the ages. I also know the tyranny of protracted social
and political circumscription. I think that Frantz Fanon is right
in *The Wretched of the Earth*, at the end of the charter entitled
"The Pitfalls of National Consciousness," when he declares, "No
leader, however valuable he may be, can substitute himself for
the popular will; and the national government, before concern-
ing itself about international prestige, ought first to give back
their dignity to all citizens, fill their minds and feast their eyes
with human things, and create a prospect that is human because
conscious and sovereign men dwell therein." To update the
rhetoric here, I'd say "sovereign people dwell therein." I believe
that acknowledgment is the primary path that leads to neces-
sary avenues toward change. Human history is a tableau of trans-
gressions and negotiations: we cross rivers and mountains; we
borrow and steal from each other, and then move beyond even
our wildest dreams; we sing each other's songs and dance each
other's dances, only to later engage in obloquy and heartless

battles; we even hold hands and nurse each other back to health and strength—through blood and metaphor.

• • •

Time is different than *time*. At least, this is what I'm thinking as I sit here in Treasure Beach, Jamaica, gazing up at the late-night firmament in springtime, feeling the rhythmic tug and sway of the sea, caught momentarily in its eternal sound. Yes, at this moment, I can't help but think of Time as being uppercase, almost beyond human imagination and illusions of control, that it does not serve us or our inventions, while nature pulsates in her immense, accidental perfection. Of course, as a poet, I'm always aware of the importance of a lowercase time: a human construction, as a musician may regard time. Since I believe that language is our first music, one could say that we speak time; but time as rhythm is neither metaphysical Time nor an approximation of mystery. Time is mystery. It is the alpha and omega of woe and awe. Of course, at times, Time is what we humans have the audacity to dream of measuring ourselves against. In that sense, it is what diminishes us absolutely. Time is always at war with our gods.

• • •

On Inspiration

Sometimes I feel singled out by ideas, images—and compelled to speak. I don't have to search. Perhaps this has to do with when and where I grew up. In the Southern landscape, I was excited by the inherent rituals constructed within such a lively, vivid system of surprises. I learned to see things, but also to see into things. In that sense, I was intrigued by the inner relationships of ordinary things glimpsed often from a scant reference point. Ordinary things collided to create moments of engagement. So in a sense I'm always taking things apart and putting things back together. Nothing gets off the hook. The image is very important to me. But also music, the music embedded in language, is perhaps even more important—I see, hear, and feel the images. This is the point where mind and body merge.

Reading, walking, and, at times, ending up in strange hotel rooms at midnight in cities I would never have dreamt as a boy from rural Louisiana, in such moments, are places of revelation. I arrive at some of those places before my feet even touch the ground. In 2004, it was arranged that I would travel to Africa as a member of the Ghana Education Project to establish a dialogue with the fisherman of Komenda concerning their age-old rituals of sailing to the Ivory Coast and sleeping with the women, then returning to their home village. It seemed they hadn't openly confronted the devastating reality of AIDS. The week before I left for Ghana, I couldn't help but travel to Komenda in my psyche. Images grounded in that troubling reality prompted a voyage that took me to some necessary terrain I hadn't anticipated. This is when I first wrote "Dead Reckoning," which appears in *The Chameleon Couch*. In fact, a second part of the poem is still evolving. Perhaps as I settled into the poem it became more personal and less metaphorical, or imagined. And, as a writer, I think this is how one travels towards or through a matrix of questions. One realizes answers are not the final product of fruitful engagement. Obsession can be a path to passion, which forces us to return to troubling and exhilarating moments in the deep night where one may hear a cry or laughter.

Perhaps the concept of inspiration accentuates the fact that we are indeed complex organisms searching for and responding to the magic of stimuli. One consciously and unconsciously welcomes a psychological climate that is conducive to creativity. I must admit that often because of my allegiance to insinuation and innuendo, I love writing an image that startles me, or makes me laugh.

Note

1. From the Spanish translation of the Toltec *Codice de la Real Academia*, fol. 315v.

How Poetry Helps People
to Live Their Lives

Lately, I feel like I have been cornered by Robert Hayden's infamous Devil's Advocate, the Inquisitor, a shadow figure in the poet's psyche who keeps one edgy and true to each word in his or her personal canon. Maybe this is the same force that prompts us to pick up the pen in the first place: A discourse which leads to discovery. Here, at this moment in our history, as we prepare for millennium parties around the world—big on commerce and short on celebration—perhaps what Plato feared has happened in modern America: The poet has become the philosopher, the composer and caretaker of the most fundamental and urgent questions voiced to the agency of human existence. And, in this sense, it seems that the poet is responsible for questioning and gauging every facet of our system.

The strength of American poetry relies upon a many-sided quest and system of aesthetics. There isn't one taste; it is a reflection of Whitman's democratic vision, embracing a rough grandeur. In any pluralistic system, however, one expects differences and disagreements. We can now envision Ezra Pound beside Amiri Baraka and H. D. flanking Toi Derricotte, Joy Harjo back-to-back with Frank O'Hara and Garrett Hongo alongside William Carlos Williams or Wallace Stevens—a continuum of impulses and possibilities that creates a map that is a challenge. Sometimes the voices are connected through their differences, unable to be cleaved because of this industry of language that defines poetry. We are often a chorus of diversions and chance

From *American Poetry Review* 37, no. 4 (2008).

212

connections, slightly outside of the so-called information revolution, still pulled by the need to create. The poem attempts to objectify mystery; it becomes an artifact.

At this juncture, maybe Hayden's Inquisitor would say: Can poetry save nations? Of course, one's first impulse would be to reply, Hell, No! Even with hundreds of roses tossed on García Lorca's burial ground, with the image of Víctor Jara's hands cut off in a Santiago stadium, and other countless attempts to suppress voices of inquiry, poetry possesses the deep power to summon truths. And I would at this moment ask what has happened to the poets in Kosovo. The answers to this question outwit us. For me, however, I am taken back to Phillis Wheatley as she muses about the sacredness of the human imagination, how she seems to link it to freedom, and this supports the reason poetry is important: It reconnects us to the act of dreaming ourselves into existence. Poetry is an action, and this is a fact I keep in mind.

Picking a Lock to the
Mind-Jail in the City of Asylum

"My poetry is not political," I heard Huang Xiang say to the camera.

It was humbling to sleep two nights in the house at 408 Sampsonia Way, where Xiang's "House Poem" has been painted on the front facade in white calligraphy. I felt psychically safe in this house; it seemed here I had permission to travel dangerously in my head, to plumb a place where the blues come from, to question the covert politics of language. How does one write about grief, about the tender struggles of love, about the unsayable? How would I ever complete this journey into my psyche?

Saturday, September 11, the Year of the White Tiger.

Upstairs, I resumed reading Xiang's book *A Life Is a Promise to Keep*, trying not to overhear the PBS interview being conducted below me, down in the living room / kitchen. This is where Xiang lived for nearly three years after spending five years in prison in China. I was thinking, saying to myself: But even the most simplistic language in certain situations can be political, and in that sense almost every text is elastic, especially since it is a composite of symbols. We live by metaphors. Even silence is political.

I was thinking of our rehearsal the day before with the Oliver Lake Band. At first, with doubt on the faces of some of the musicians, the youngbloods, I was ready for the whole thing to dissolve and fall apart. Our ensemble of voices was international: Khet Mar (Burma), Maryia Martysevich (Belarus), and

From *Sampsonia Way: An Online Magazine for Literature, Free Speech and Social Justice*, September 21, 2010.

Hinemoana Baker (Aotearoa / New Zealand). Each was unique, each conjuring a personal music beckoning interplay with the instruments. How did the Beats during the 50s attempt to bring jazz and poetry together without rehearsals? That is the reason numerous gigs like this failed; this recent history resonated in my head. I chose five poems for the reading: "You Made Me," "When Eyes Are on Me," "Blue Dementia," "Requiem," and "Ode to the Saxophone." Once we were feeling a groove, listening closely to each other, willing to let language and music merge, we were ready to surprise ourselves. A crack appeared in the collective mask. There was something in Lake's compositions, an echo of the blues that embraced my voice. And he had chosen sixteen musicians, each fully connecting to his vision. After three or four attempts, we had reached the nexus. We were running somewhat long, so I cut "Requiem," a piece infused with second-lining riffs that conjured the Crescent City. I could feel a symmetry of intention between all of us.

I heard the cameraman packing up to leave. I heard their voices in the street. I tiptoed to the window and caught a glimpse of Xiang. There was something jaunty in his demeanor, and this surprised me. How could a poet end up behind bars—were we still a few feet inside Plato's cave? Standing there at the window, I realized I was inside a work of art, momentarily residing in someone's necessary vision—The City of Asylum.

The short trek from Sampsonia Way to the New Hazlett Theater was a moment of meditation, as two volunteers escorted me around the Carnegie Free Library, the Bell Tower struck by lightning, the Planetarium renovated into the Children's Museum, buildings that are monuments to the recent past, made to last. The readers and musicians sat in the green room, in the smell of catered food in takeaway containers, trading stories and anticipating riffs. Three young musicians were tossing a blue miniature football, sliding back and forth across the concrete floor.

Actor David Conrad emceed the night; he was at home with the crowd of five hundred. The first set began with readings by Hinemoana Baker, Horacio Castellanos Moya (a terrific magical realist now exiled from El Salvador), Khet Mar, and a surprise poet. These held everyone's attention, especially Baker's amazing voice that seems perfect for the Maori language. And then the night's surprise poet began to chant his poems from the balcony. There was a playful insinuation at the edge of Huang Xiang's presence; many in the crowd knew him. His "Wild Beast" poem ran to the edge of vocalized daring Pandemonium.

The Oliver Lake Band was on the money—cool and hot as the Count and Duke, with a tinge of Mingus. This moment underscores why music travels internationally. Its hard-edged eloquence and authority were crystal clear. Everyone was digging each other—wordsmiths and musicians—listening closely. If any ghosts of the Beats were hanging around the New Hazlett Theater that night, they were finally learning something about how music and words can reach an unbelievable register of bittersweet truth that's unforgettable.

∾

The Procession

Yes, the dust of the Great Migration
is in our dreams & on the soles of our feet,
but we can foxtrot into this bandaged season
limping toward us from the fog. Each question
uncurls a little whip in the air. Can we change
tomorrow? Can we love what's in a deep mirror
& trace fault lines beneath nocturnal streets?
Loneliness & anger always know the road home.
Now the long-lost ones stand at the threshold
& gaze into our eyes. Please don't turn away,
don't retreat into caves of artificial light
& borrowed lowly laughter brimming up.
There's a hard, long road ahead. Nights
& days ahead, one foot in front of the other.

Days ahead, one foot in front of the other
is how we ascend Jacob's tangled ladder.
Bring your lantern & philosopher's stone,
your pick & shovel, ball of twine, hook
& sinker, your slide ruler & plumb bob.
There's some faithful work to be done

on this hill & down in the valley, too.
Bring your running shoes & baseball cap.
I tell you, I'm no one's Benjamin Banneker,
but I know a cul-de-sac is a whiplash
& slipknot. Sometimes you have to bow
to self-given thorns, or weave around a body
of water. Some things you argue against
or for, & then you go straight through bedrock.

You have to go straight through bedrock
to find hope, I said. You can't kill the past
to erase a page. Cut out a tongue singing delta,
& still a windy lamentation crests the hilltop.
Burn odes into ash to smear on the forehead,
but still the laconic cricket calls the night
to sing deeds, blasphemies, & allegories
droning beneath the earth's blueprint.
Yes, even if we parade in secondhand garb
as priestly nobodies, the Daylight Boys,
or other heretical truth-seekers, we know
weeping isn't a fly in a spider's web.
If you can't see hunger on our streets,
at least remember hard songs left behind.

At least remember hard songs left behind
on fields from Concord to the Green Zone.
Our maps go to the edge of a lost frontier,
following every unsolved riddle & tributary,
indigenous souls still in the drizzle & bog
grass, behind hedgerows—beyond imagination.
Now there's one sky, with holes in the ozone.
Limitless steps across snow recast star charts.
All the old gods gaze at us like deathwatch
beetles, waiting to see what we do with this hour.
Let Walt Whitman put his lips to your ear
as he rocks the dead of north & south in his arms.
Words taproot down to what we are made of,
& these hosannas are ours to surrender to.

These hosannas are ours to surrender to
till laurel & olive branch into our footpath,
an eruption of blooms overtaking our heads.

We're here to honor those who came before,
who gladly or sadly gave themselves back
to earth. You know their names. We know
who stood & never lost ground. We know
who knelt beside their contraband drums
& depended on hawthorn to guard them.
Sunlight & water draw roots deep as seed
& oath; their sway & pull can bend an oak
over a grand monument. Evermore pours
from a beggar's tin cup as one thousand
clocks strike inside the stone base.

Clocks strike inside the stone base.
The mainsprings are about to be adjusted
& oiled. For the first time in decades
the blindfold has slipped off her face,
& we are now seeing her true reflection
on the harbor. The shortcuts tell us, no,
the winding road isn't a second guess,
& one could risk one's life getting here.
Where I stand in splendor, at this point
of view, surely, it is already Springtime.
How could it not be? The Sunday-go-to-
meeting clothes, the bright hats cocked
at the true angle that slays blue devils.

How could it not be? This is the hour.
How could it not be? This is the hour
beckoning the North Star & drinking gourd,
waist-deep shadows crossing the Ohio River,
& I hear Fredrick Douglass' voice in a brisk
shiver of dry leaves, saying, "When the dogs
in your streets, when the fowls of the air,
when the cattle on your hills, when the fish
of the sea, & then reptiles that crawl"
The rattle of night pods is the only shaman
at this late hour. Secret markers run
from flatland to river town, pale desert
to mountain, grassland to autumn skyline.
From here I see a lighthouse, love of the planet
bringing a polar bear back to its ice floe.

A Note from
The Best American Erotic Poems

For me, the erotic has to embrace innuendo and insinuation, and it begs the human imagination to participate. Everything isn't spelled out; the erotic is facilitated through suggestion. The sun shining through a thin, pale dress can be more provocative than an airbrushed frontal nude. Magic often resides in the hint, in that which is withheld. If beauty is the cornerstone of erotica, perhaps that explains why *The Arabian Nights* continue to beckon to me across the years.

From *The Best American Erotic Poems: From 1800 to the Present*, ed. David Lehman (New York: Scribner, 2008).

The Mission of American Poets
and Writers Visiting
the 2008 Kolkata Book Fair

The United States is one of the most diverse nations in the world. Likewise, India is similarly diverse, and it is this shared sense of diversity that sparked the idea of selecting a small group of American poets and writers (twelve) to participate in the 2008 Kolkata Book Fair. In a worldwide climate of distrust and violence, we believe that art, especially literature, can still facilitate a peaceful dialogue and fruitful exchange of ideas. The presence of the selected poets and writers will be the physical proof of our attempt to build bridges between Indian and American artists, intellectuals, and publishers. We aim to address questions regarding minority and majority ethnic and linguistic identities in multicultural democracies and the role of the word as bearer of both culture and history. Critical to this project is the effect of poetry on the daily lives and identities of each country's citizenry and its ability to transcend cultural, generational, political, and technological borders.

Rewriting Dante

In a certain sense, America is always attempting to reinvent itself. We have used world literature and culture as elements in that process of reinvention, as the engine through which our myth-making is driven. And, yes, Dante's vision is one of many lenses through which we view aspects of our cultural history. But, of course, like each of us, Dante possessed his own flaws and short-comings. Perhaps that's what draws us to his enchanting vision again and again—his over idealization of earthly matters. We only have to think of the numerous instances where Robert Low-ell's vision intersects with Dante's. At times, it seems that their shared argument concerning the marriage of heaven and hell is almost a single, unbroken song. Each is written with a fluid con-tinuity, and I think, at the center of each vision is that argument with the self. Likewise, the contemporary American poet seems possessed by a similar need for an internal dialogue—a voyage within, to the core. It is that going back and forth, that argument within oneself, within one's heart, that becomes instructive from a contemporary point of view. A clarity of vision is informed by a continuous dialogue, because that is the space from where the spirit of democracy arises. I don't think, however, that I can say that Dante possessed an idea about democracy. Let's face it, Dante was a citizen of his time: his vision is based on a class structure that is primarily feudalistic. Matter of fact, Dante prob-ably sees class distinction as a necessary mechanism for elevat-ing his central character, Beatrice, beyond this human world. That is, Beatrice couldn't exist as Beatrice if she didn't possess (in Dante's mind) certain attributes that would transport her beyond reason. She's depicted as a soul beyond flesh. Such an

From *Semicerchio-Rivista di poesia comparata* 36 (2007).

abstraction is based on illusions embedded in class and its various stratification. Robert Pinsky addressed the problem of the United States sending young men off to war, of those inducted into a military machine which is definitely class-based. Indeed, perhaps we are drawn to Dante because he does wrestle with doubt and mystery. That need to inquire into the depth of one's spirit as an artist—as a country—is what ties the contemporary poet to that medieval seer.